THE LANGUAGE OF ARGUMENT

Professor Durant Demonstrates Psychokinesis

Dr. James Durant, Professor of Psychology at Millburn University, demonstrates to a companion his celebrated powers of psychokinesis. The photograph was taken at the Faculty Club before a dozen professors. The event was supervised by Dr. Xavier Crosert, dean of the College of Arts and Sciences. (Redstone Wire Service photo)

THE LANGUAGE OF ARGUMENT

THIRD EDITION

Daniel McDonald
University of South Alabama

HARPER & ROW, PUBLISHERS

NEW YORK

Cambridge   London
Hagerstown   Mexico City
Philadelphia   Sao Paolo
San Francisco   *1817*   Sydney

For IRENE

Sponsoring Editor: Phillip Leininger
Project Editor: Pamela Landau
Production Manager: Marion Palen
Compositor: American Book–Stratford Press
Printer and Binder: Halliday
Art: Vantage Art Studio

The Language of Argument, Third Edition

Library of Congress Cataloging in Publication Data

McDonald, Daniel Lamont, comp.
 The language of argument.
 Incudes bibliographical references.
 1. College readers. 2. English language—
Rhetoric. 3. Debates and debating. I. Title.
PE1431.M28 1980   808'.04275   79–19840
ISBN 0-06-044358-8

Contents

DEDUCTION 69

ARGUMENT BY AUTHORITY 98

Subjects Discussed in this Book

THERAPY
> "You Feel the Way You Think"
> *Robert A. Harper*

TOBACCO
> "The Case for Tobacco"
> *James Council*

KING TUT
> "Deadly King Tut Curse Strikes Again"
> *Ron Caylor and Gordon Gregor*

UNIDENTIFIED FLYING OBJECTS
> "Intelligent Life Elsewhere'
> *Edward U. Condon*

> "Easter Island: Land of the Bird Men"
> *Erich von Däniken*

VITAMINS
> "Vitamin E in the Hands of Creative Physicians"
> *Ruth Adams and Frank Murray*

WOMEN
> "It's a Man's Universe"
> *Esther Vilar*

Preface

The purpose of this text is to teach students how to read argument and to provide materials around which they can write argumentative essays of their own. As in the previous editions, the selections cover a range of provocative issues. Some of these are notably persuasive; some are not.

The book has a new section, "Eight Rules for Good Writing," which offers considerably more material on composition than was given in the preceding edition. Further, to promote student writing, it adds a long essay, "Was Alger Hiss Guilty?" together with a selected bibliography and a number of topics for short themes.

I must acknowledge the contribution of my students in English 388 (Expository Writing) and the continuing contribution of my wife, Irene.

The editor who selects and annotates controversial essays must work to keep his own opinion out of his textbook. I *have* tried.

DMc

PART I
The Forms
of Argument

Logic and Composition

Good English is not merely correct English.
—Robertson and Cassidy, *The Development of
Modern English*

Good writing is that which gets the result you want. And a knowledge of the techniques of persuasion will help you win whatever you're after.

A study of logic will make you concerned about your audience and about writing patterns that have a good or bad effect on them. It will keep you from speculating vaguely on some topic that is not subject to evidence and will help you know when you are making sense.

WIN YOUR AUDIENCE

To make a persuasive case, you must know the character of your audience. This knowledge will help you to choose your words and shape your style.

One body of readers—say, a group of fraternity men—will respond to a direct appeal in strong language; another group—say, members of the DAR—will reject your whole argument if you use a word like "crap." One group will respond to wit, another to biblical quotation, and still another to a spread of statistics. There are particular readers who will be offended if you write "Ms.," "ain't," "Negro," "symbiotic," "de jour," or "and/or." Most audiences will be bored if you write vaguely about "Responsibility" or "Tomorrow's Promise," but there are groups who favor high-flown rhetorical generalities. To make your case effectively, you have to know your audience.

A central feature in argument is creating a personal voice to express your views to your audience. Too often a spokesperson with an im-

3

pressive case fails to be persuasive because of an inadequate writing style, which makes the person sound like a computer, a demanding top-sergeant, a condescending aristocrat, or a stubborn child.

Most readers respond favorably to a concerned and courteous spokesperson. Whatever your personal character, let your writing reflect a warm, human personality. When addressing a committee, refer to the committee members in your presentation. ("I'm sure you ladies and gentlemen recognize how complex this question is.") When writing a business letter, try to use a direct, personal voice. ("I'm sorry about your problem, Mr. Majors, and hope we can do more for you next time.") Routinely, work to avoid a brittle or hostile tone. Don't say, "You must do this," when you can say, "We would like to have you do this promptly." Don't write, "I will not do this," when you can write, "For these reasons I cannot do this now." Don't say, "You seem incapable of understanding my argument"; say, "I am sorry I did not make myself understood."

This tone can be difficult to maintain. At times you will want to express righteous indignation or ego-gratifying scorn. Although the outburst may be personally satisfying, remember that anger never persuaded anyone. In argument, nice guys finish first.

DEFINE THE ISSUE

A study of logic shows the importance of defining your issue. Some topics you may want to discuss are in flatly unarguable form. They would produce vague and incoherent essays.

Some issues rely more on definition of terms than on evidence. When two people argue whether Senator Ted Kennedy is handsome, for example, they are not disagreeing about his hair, teeth, or clothes, but about a definition of "handsomeness." If they can agree on a definition, they will probably agree about Senator Kennedy as well. Similarly, the question of whether capital punishment is wrong hinges not so much on the character of the act (the pain, the possibility of error, the protection afforded society) as on the definition of "wrongness."

Aesthetic and moral questions are often not susceptible to evidence because individuals cannot agree about the terms of argument. The meaning of any word is what people agree it is. (A telephone is called a *telephone* because English speakers regularly use that word to denote it.) And in these areas, people do not agree. What is handsomeness? What is beauty? Theoreticians have sought objective standards, but the quest seems fruitless. Is a Greek temple more beautiful than a Gothic cathedral? Is Whistler's "Mother" handsomer than da Vinci's *Mona Lisa* or Andy Warhol's *Marilyn Monroe*? Who can say? The decision rests on a subjective judgment, which does not lend itself to argument. Taste is indisputable.

Like beauty, the idea of goodness is not subject to easy definition. Seeking an objective basis for calling actions right and wrong, authorities have cited Scriptural precedents; they have based systems on the inalienable rights of each human being; they have insisted that nature provides a moral example. But such definitions have won no universal acceptance. If two disputants could agree that morality resides, say, in a natural law, they might then *begin* to argue about capital punishment. But in general usage, moral terms remain so ill defined that such issues often cannot be argued meaningfully at all. (If you have to write on a moral or aesthetic topic, focus it on some concrete example—say, arson or pop art or Elton John—and work in as many "for example" and "for instance" references as you can.)

Moral and aesthetic questions are further removed from argument because they often elicit emotional responses. Two individuals who agree in defining "handsomeness" might, for example, still disagree about Senator Kennedy because one objects to his liberal politics or to the Chappaquiddick incident. It is, of course, unreasonable to let emotions color such a judgment, but the attitude is not uncommon. You might be completely persuaded that capital punishment is cruel and barbaric yet, at a given moment, argue that hanging is too good for a child murderer or a political assassin.

Vagueness of definition precludes argument in other areas as well. Pontiac has been advertised as "America's No. 1 *road* car"; Kent as America's "largest-selling *premium* cigarette"; and Schenley Reserve as the "whiskey *of elegance.*" Are these claims true? Until the key words are defined, the claims are no more subject to evidence than is "Razzle dagons popple stix." Nonsense is neither true nor false.

It is only when terms are defined and mutually accepted that you can begin marshalling evidence to prove something. You can, for example, argue whether Jim Brown or Bronko Nagurski was the better football player, because their records, the merits of their supporting and opposing teams, and the qualities of a good running back are generally agreed on. Is it true that cigarette smoking causes lung cancer, that Vice President Agnew took bribes, that Toyota is an economical car to own? The questions can at least be argued.

MAKE YOUR CASE

Finally, the study of argument will let you know when you are making sense. It will tell you if your sample is sufficient to support an inductive conclusion, if the expert you want to quote is a reliable authority, if your words express the meanings you want, and if your statistics are relevant.

A survey of logic will make you a more perceptive reader. You will be better able to recognize strengths and weaknesses in particular arguments. It will show you patterns to imitate and those to avoid.

You cannot become a good writer simply by knowing how words are spelled and where commas go. You need a clearly defined subject, a personal voice, and an effective presentation of your information. *What you have to say is of the essence of good writing.* And the study of logic should make what you have to say more persuasive and meaningful.

EXERCISES

Can you argue the truth of these assertions?

1. Blessed are the pure in heart; for they shall see God.
2. In the whole Watergate affair, President Nixon did not break one single law.
3. It is wrong to say "between you and I."
4. Babe Ruth was a better baseball player than Dizzy Dean.
5. There are no pianos in Japan.
6. The child is father to the man.
7. Abortion is a sin.
8. Not all cigarettes are True.
9. The purest and most thoughtful minds are those which love color the most.
10. This $20 bill is counterfeit.
11. Dogs are better pets than cats.
12. Olympia Spalanzani is a doll.
13. Nothing does it like 7-Up!

Hal Higdon

IS RUNNING A RELIGIOUS EXPERIENCE?

It is almost as though it has become a religion. Each Sunday the faithful gather. Sometimes they do so in a church-like structure where they listen to words of advice from one who would make them better individuals. Sometimes they carry their public worship into the outdoors, setting off on a mass pilgrimmage which eventually becomes each individual's quest for immortality, for spiritual pleasure through flagellation of the body, for that certain beatific moment when body becomes one with spirit.

The act is not worship of God, although some insist that the act of running is a form of worship. One young female runner states: "Communing with nature, watching the changing of the seasons, this makes me feel closer to God. Running makes me feel good. When I feel good, I'm happy to be alive and glad God gave me life."

Is running a new religion? Even to consider the question might be considered by some as sacrilegious, a form of heresy. But for an increas-

Reprinted with permission *Runner's World Magazine*, P.O. Box 366, Mountain View, CA 94042.

ing number of people today, running has become if not an organized religion, at least *the* most important activity of their life. In fact, it has become a *way* of life and all hope. Running is something that now consumes their previously idle hours, or previously wasted hours: a purifying activity that often dominates their weekends with races and preparations for future races, becoming their Sabbath, taking over their Sunday mornings, the traditional time when at least the Christian majority in the United States attends church. Even the stretching that runners do before starting their activity might be considered a form of genuflection.

There is also the phenomenon of the born-again runner, akin to the born-again Christian, the individual, often middleaged, who might have been active athletically in youth, but then lapsed into sinful ways: eating too much, drinking too much, cavorting with wicked women (or scandalous men), allowing the body, described by the scriptures as the "temple of the spirit" to degenerate to the point where the temple appeared threatened by destruction (i.e., occluded coronary arteries).

When that person decides to run, it is in the form of a spiritual as well as physical reawakening, a conversion to a new discipline which will result in a rebirth of the spirit. "And for many people," states one new runner, born-again, after nearly a decade away from the sport, "running is spoken of in very religious terms: 'I saw God when running up the side of Pike's Peak,' or something like that. Maybe running is one of the religions of tomorrow. It certainly isn't any worse a religion than a few of the others making the rounds."

In considering the question of whether or not running has become a religion, we first need to consider a definition for religion. Strictly speaking, religion means a belief in a divine or superhuman power, or powers, to be worshipped as the creator and ruler (or creators and rulers) of the universe. In other words, there is "something out there," and more than the space creatures we saw in the final reel of *Close Encounters of the Third Kind.*

Central to most religions is a belief in God. Whether or not God exists, a significant percentage of Americans believe that He (or She) does exist. Religion might further be defined as an expression of this Godly belief in conduct and ritual.

Religion, in this respect, takes on a further meaning beyond its most basic belief in God, since it also serves as a specific *system* of worship and conduct, often involving a code of ethics and a philosophy, for instance, the Christian "religion," the Jewish "religion," or the Moslem "religion." But in its broadest sense, religion must be considered *any* system of beliefs, practices, or ethical values likened to such a system. To some people, work becomes a religion. Or collecting stamps. Or sports, as in: "He follows the New York Giants religiously." Atheists deny the existence of God and reject all religious belief, but semantically speaking, you can practice atheism religiously—although some people probably would prefer substitution of the term "zealously."

Thus, in the *broadest* sense of religion being a system of beliefs and practices, running might be considered a form of religion.

Running also might provide a form by which certain individuals practice their religion. "I exhort you therefore, brethren," writes St. Paul in his "Letter to the Romans" (12:1), "by the mercy of God to present your bodies as a sacrifice, living, holy, pleasing to God—your spiritual service." A body capable of carrying its owner through the 26 miles, 385 yards of a marathon might be considered more "pleasing" to God than a body which, through its owner's indolence, has been allowed to deteriorate into a blob of flesh that quivers from the strain of moving from couch to kitchen for another beer. Running is one way of serving God's will.

If running has a Messiah, it may be Kenneth H. Cooper, M.D., whose best-selling series of books on *Aerobics* served as the starting point for the early wave of joggers that began to crest in the late 1960s. Dr. Cooper professes a deep Christian commitment and has shared podiums with Billy Graham. On one of Graham's evangelistic crusades, Dr. Cooper gave a 10-minute testimony on the interrelationship between spiritual and physical fitness before 240,000 people in a Brazil stadium. He has a photo of that event on the wall of his office in the Cooper Clinic in Dallas. Perhaps *the* most active traveler on the fitness lecture circuit, Dr. Cooper refuses to make appearances on Sundays for religious reasons and says he plans some day to collaborate with a theologian on another book that would link aerobics and religion.

Anyone who has ever heard Dr. Cooper lecture on the benefits of good health through running recognizes the evangelical roots implicit in his style, which though soft-spoken, also is electric, fast-paced and so compelling that it makes you want to move from your chair and shout, "I do believe!"

In fact, a large percentage of those swelling the fields of long-distance races throughout the country, if not a majority, are born-again runners; people who have had no (or little) base as competitive track athletes, but who have taken up running after years of wicked living.

Like born-again Christians, these individuals are often the most active proselytizers of others, attempting to convert the non-believers into practitioners of their new-found sport/faith under the theory that if it feels this good to me, everybody else should be doing it too. "Now I know what it feels like to be a born-again Baptist," comments one 35-year-old female runner of the Jewish faith. "I try to convert my non-running friends."

New-born runners often dramatically change their life-styles, shedding cigarette-smoking friends, sometimes divorcing their wives (or in the case of running wives, divorcing their husbands), because their new evangelism no longer is compatible with their old selves. "I have abandoned the non-running world," states Jim Cavindess, a Masters runner from Noblesville, Ind., whose entire family runs. "Runners are my reference now."

A 29-year-old runner adds: "Friends, or should I say acquaintances, I had before running, are sort of turned off by my enthusiasm and I don't see many of them as often as I used to. My new running friends seem more important to me." He adds wistfully, "My wife tolerates my running—sometimes barely."

Running, while having a positive effect on a person's physical well-being, thus may have a negative effect on the spiritual being if it causes weakening of the family structure, whose strength often is at the core of many religions, particularly Roman Catholicism, for which divorce is a no-no punishable by excommunication.

One female runner, who was baptized a Catholic, turned off to organized religion because of what she describes as "the structuralized institution of the church. Money becomes the issue rather than true improvement of oneself." A finisher in the Boston and New York City Marathons, she recently has also turned away from racing though she continues to run noncompetitively eight miles a day. She said she abandoned competition because of being repelled by the commercialization of many races. She speculates: "Your everyday jogger and runners are the ones who are more spiritually enlightened and closer to God. The personal accomplishment is stronger than the publicity. Joggers are less concerned with victory over their fellow runners and more involved with peace among their fellow man."

The purity of the jogger as compared to the performance-oriented racer, however, might be contradicted by a reading of the Bible, particularly the parable of the talents (Matthew:25:14–30), where two servants who cause their talents to multiply are praised while a third servant who hid his talent in the earth is reviled: "As for the unprofitable servant, cast him forth into the darkness outside, where there will be the weeping, and the gnashing of teeth." The master had given each of his servants different talents (five to one, two to another, one to a third) and they were judged not by how much they profited, but by their ability to use what they had.

Others see no contradiction between running to win and religious experiences. The 29-year-old runner previously mentioned began running six years ago and trained for his first marathon last summer. Feeling he needed additional strength, he began reading the Bible for the first time since taking Bible study classes in grade school. He found what he considered a personal message in St. Paul's "Letter to the Corinthians" (9:24): "Do you know that those who run in a race, all indeed run, but one receives the prize? So run as to obtain it. And everyone in a contest abstains from all things—and they indeed do receive a perishable crown, but we an imperishable. I, therefore, so run as not without a purpose; I so fight as not beating the air; but I chastise my body and bring it into subjection, lest perhaps after preaching to others I myself should be rejected."

The runner comments about the marathon he ran: "I didn't finish first, but I did win my marathon and I found great strength through this passage and others. As a result, I have a greater closeness to God than I ever have had before."

The Bible, of course, can serve as an instant Rorschach Test for those who read it and want to interpret it to their own needs, which is one of the Bible's strengths as well as its greatest weakness. Depending on how you interpret St. Paul's message, you can run for victory (*so run as to obtain it*) and for a crown that is merely perishable (*such as an Olympic medal*) as opposed to one that is imperishable (*a body that through chastisement is brought into subjection and thus becomes eligible for rewards beyond this world*).

The book of Isaiah (40:31) from the Old Testament also speaks of running: "But they that hope in the Lord shall renew their strength; they shall take wings as eagles; they shall run and not be weary; they shall walk and not faint."

Rev. Tony Ahlstrom, an ordained minister who works with the Plymouth Foundation in Chicago, ran across the United States with his brother Joel on two occasions, in 1971 and again in 1976. On the latter trip they covered 51 miles a day, going the 2957-mile distance from San Francisco to Washington, D.C. in 58 days, carrying with them a Bible which they presented to President Gerald Ford. Tony recalls meditating on that passage from Isaiah while limping through the mountains of Colorado on the 1971 journey when his one foot became so troubled with tendonitis that he could hardly run.

At the end of their leg into Glenwood Springs, Colo., Joel had to help Tony into the camper and it seemed he would be unable to continue the next day. "I lay awake all night wrestling with the Lord," Tony recalls, "asking him to let me continue. Most people think of the Bible as a book of rules, because it contains the Ten Commandments, but actually it is a book of promises. If you believe in God's words, he will supply your needs."

The next morning Tony, Joel and three others accompanying them held their regular prayer meeting before beginning what was scheduled as a 32-mile leg up steep grades. They prepared to leave the camper and Tony put on his running shoes, being unable to lace the shoe on his injured foot because it was so swollen. An aura of doom hung over the group since one of their party seemed to be on the verge of failure. Tony recalls that there was an almost eerie silence as they began to run. He began by limping badly, then started to move somewhat faster, finally he was able to run. Joel looked at his brother and said: "The ankle's all right, isn't it?"

"Yeah," Tony said, "let me stop and tie this shoe." They finished their cross-continent run without Tony having any further major injuries.

Some people speak in religious terms even if they do not consider themselves religious. For example, one female runner says she attends synagogue only once a year. Having started running two years ago, she runs from 3–11 miles daily. "One of the reasons I most love running is that it is the first time in my life I have ever believed in something unambivalently. The satisfaction that I get, the 'highs,' the time to think and problem-solve, the energy, are all proofs that running works. Therefore 'devotion' to running makes me happier, makes life better. This is what religion does for many people. It gives meaning to their lives. I don't completely understand why, but running has given my life a certain sense of purpose that I never had before.

"There is a difference between a traditional religion and running," she continues to explain. "When one believes in a religion and in God, it is a belief in something outside one-self, in a way an abandoning of power to something outside. On the contrary, a belief in running, 'the new religion,' is a belief in oneself, in one's power, in one's ability to improve, discipline and take charge of one's own life. In the past, I've often been a little envious of people who had faith, which got them through difficult times. Now I have a faith of my own. In this sense, running has strengthened my own religious, or maybe irreligious beliefs."

One runner feels that if running may seem like a religion, it may only be that Sunday morning, with light traffic on the roads, is a good time to run. Being Catholic, he can get to noon Mass following his morning run of five miles. He sees no connection between running and faith, but between running and living—yes.

"Religion to me has a direct reference to God, or a reasonable substitute," he says. "Running makes me feel good, but that's another thing entirely. Religion, especially the legitimate kind, might not make you feel good at all. In fact, it might make you feel bad. If some people think they have religion because they feel good while running, they just don't know what religion is all about. Thomas Aquinas said it's the sum total of man's duties toward God and that's not something you achieve marthoning."

Is running a new religion? "Absolutely not," said one young female runner who has been running a few miles a day for about a year. "If you see running as the newest fad (as many marketers of sneakers and sports clothes do) then you are looking, perhaps, at the replacement for Transcendental Meditation. For those of us, however, who are building foundations to run on for the rest of our lives, worshipping God is one thing and conditioning our bodies is something else."

As to whether running brings people closer to God, causing them on certain occasions to have, while running, what they might consider a spiritual experience, that may more often be in the eye of the beholder. It is possible to see God in any activity, or even lack of activity.

Many people say that getting out into nature allowed them to contemplate the creativity of God, in effect, confront his works. The New Testament describes Jesus Christ going up into the mountains to fast for 40 days to achieve an awareness of his own being. Physiologists likewise suggest 40 days as about the length of time it takes an untrained runner to revitalize his body, that being the period of time required for capillarization, the improvement of the oxygen transport system that causes running to suddenly become easier after earlier days of strain. Once a runner achieves this first level of training and perhaps also achieves a level of fitness that permits jogging for an hour, it is possible to experience what might be called "the 40-minute effect," the point at which certain psychologists (Thaddeus Kostrubala, for example) believe that runners experience the so-called runner's high, that sense of euphoria, the breaking free of the mind from the body which allows persons to reach a meditative state similar to that attained by Eastern mystics who place themselves into a trance by saying, over and over: "Ommmmmm."

But is this runner's high a spiritual experience? It probably is if you want to identify it.

"Running has promoted religious thought," says Donald Higdon* of Ridgewood, N.J., an Episcopalian who attends church only a few times a year but considers himself religious. "I see the world less in terms of *me* and more as a marvel in which I am fortunate to fit."

Donald Higdon, who began jogging five years ago at the age of 36, feels that he is a better person because of his running. "I am healthier, rarely ill. I feel good. In spite of old habits, I find myself desiring things that are 'good for me.' I am less tense. I accept things more willingly. I am more patient. I've discovered abilities I did not know I had. Feeling better about myself, I think better of others. I am more tolerant of the weaknesses of others, if they are beyond the person's control. However, I am less tolerant of sloth, obesity, excessive drinking, smoking and habits which are clearly controllable. I have had occasional surges of wonderment or good feeling about the world. However, the same thing has happened when I was alone in a sailboat or preparing to launch a hang

(*No relation to the author, Hal Higdon.*)

glider." As to whether running had become a substitute for religion, Donald Higdon feels that it merely offers another perspective toward life and the world.

A female runner in her late 20's, who began running eight months ago and now runs five miles each morning, answers the question about whether running is becoming a substitute for religion by saying, "It probably isn't if one defines religion in terms of God and spiritual experiences. However, using a broader definition of 'religion,' running does give one a sense of order in life, a 'plan,' a chance to belong to a group and share the values and beliefs of that group and a whole new world view. Even the beginning runner like myself has to make major changes in his life to find the time to run and to put up with minor discomfort. So I'm forcing myself to develop a *commitment* to the endeavor—or else to quit. I prefer *not* to call this a substitute for religion as defined in the traditional sense of belonging to a church and believing in God."

One of the individuals we spoke with was Dan Cloeter, winner of the Mayor Daley Marathon and a theology student at Concordia Seminary in Fort Wayne, Ind. Dan said, "I've heard people say that they don't need 'church' anymore, now that they've found running. It's my opinion that those people probably only had 'church' and not a faith and trust relationship with God."

Cloeter feels that running and his faith and trust in God complement each other. "I enjoy running and experiencing things in my surroundings which reflect God's glory."

Father Kevin O'Rourke, a priest who works with the Catholic Hospital Assoc. in St. Louis, says he often prays when he runs his regular four or six miles early in the morning: "If one knows how to pray, then running will dispose for prayer, but running is not prayer, nor does it cause prayer. While I run, I feel that I can put the coming events of the day in spiritual perspective. Getting out of the daily sedentary routine helps me appreciate more simple things in life, thus freeing me to pursue values and objectives that have spiritual meaning. Personality integration should be stressed as an important potential for running. Thus, all aspects of person—spiritual, psychological and physical—benefit and are able to work more cooperatively together."

The 29-year-old previously quoted stated: "Running does make me more aware of the world around me and the beauty that truly exists. It's made me feel a very common bond with hundreds and thousands of people who aren't phony and maybe this isn't a religious experience as such, but if all mankind would start running maybe the world would be a better place."

Perhaps, perhaps not, but individuals would at least make better temples of their bodies. Rev. Tony Ahlstrom, the cross-continent runner, sometimes uses time spent on his daily runs to memorize parts of the

Bible. He quotes St. Paul's "Letters to the Romans" (12:1): "I exhort you therefore, brethren, by the Mercy of God to present your bodies as a sacrifice, living, holy, pleasing to God—your spiritual service."

Rev. Ahlstrom believes that Jesus Christ is a spirit and in this world he needs hands, legs, eyes, and ears: "If I present my body to the Lord," Ahlstrom insists, "I think it does make a difference what shape that body is in. The Old Testament law said that if you made a sacrifice it couldn't merely be something you no longer wanted. The law called for a spotless lamb. So if your body is going to be the temple of God, the better shape my body is in, the more the Lord can do with it."

As for whether one can meet God while running, the answer is both yes and no. He can be met in this manner, as He can be met almost anywhere, but there is no guarantee.

DISCUSSION QUESTIONS

1. The essay quotes several individuals who claim that running is a religious act. Categorize the several effects of running that they feel are religious.
2. The essay quotes individuals who deny that running is religious. What religious quality (or qualities) do they say it lacks?
3. Do those who think running is religious admit it lacks what the skeptics say it lacks? Resolve the contradiction if you find one.
4. Do the quotations from Paul and from Isaiah support or oppose the claim that running is religious?
5. The author presents a fairly balanced essay. Is there any evidence suggesting his view on the question?
6. Does the point in dispute here really have much to do with running?

Esther Vilar

IT'S A MAN'S UNIVERSE

Man, unlike woman, is beautiful, because man, unlike woman, is a thinking creature.

This means:

Man has a thirst for knowledge (he wants to know what the world around him looks like and how it functions).

Man thinks (he draws conclusions from the data he encounters).

Man is creative (he makes something new out of the information achieved by the above processes).

Man is sensitive (as a result of his exceptionally wide, multidimensional emotional scale, he not only registers the commonplace in fine gradations but he creates and discovers new emotional values and makes them accessible to others through sensible descriptions, or re-creates them as an artist).

Of all the qualities of man, his curiosity is certainly the most impressive. This curiosity differs basically from that of woman.

A woman takes interest only in subjects that have an immediate personal usefulness to her. For example, if she reads a political article in the newspaper, it is highly likely that she wants to cast a spell on some political-science student, not that she cares about the fate of the Chinese, Israelis, or South Africans. If she looks up the names of some Greek philosophers in the dictionary, it does not mean she has suddenly taken an interest in Greek philosophy. It means she is trying to solve a crossword puzzle. If she is studying the ads for a new car, she is not doing it with a platonic interest in its technical features, but because she wants to own it.

It is a fact that most women—mothers included—generally have no idea how the human fetus is formed, how it develops in the womb, what stages it passes through before birth. Of course it is entirely unnecessary for her to know about these things, since they cannot influence the development of the embryo anyway. It is only important to know that a pregnancy lasts nine months and that for the duration one must take care of oneself and, in case of complications, immediately consult one's doctor, who will, of course, restore everything to order.

Man's curiosity is something quite different. His desire for knowledge has no personal implications, is purely objective, and, in the long run, is much more practical than a woman's attitude.

One has only to watch a man go past a building site where a newly developed machine is being used, for example a new kind of dredger. There is hardly a man—regardless of social status—who will pass by without a glance. Many will stop to have a good look and to discuss the characteristics of the new machine, its advantages and disadvantages, and its differences from previous models.

A woman would never think of stopping at a building site unless, of course, the crowd was so big that she thought she might miss something exciting ("Construction Worker Crushed by Bulldozer"). In that case she would demand to know all the details and then look the other way.

Man's curiosity is universal. There is almost nothing that does not interest him, whether it is politics, botany, nuclear physics, or God knows what. Even subjects out of his province hold his interest, such as bottling fruit, preparing a cake mix or caring for a baby. And a man could not be pregnant for nine months without knowing all the functions of the placenta and ovaries.

Men not only observe the world around them, it is in their nature to make comparisons and to apply the knowledge they have gained elsewhere with the ultimate aim to transform this newfound knowledge into something else, something new.

One need not emphasize the fact that practically all the inventions and discoveries in this world have been made by men, and not only in the fields of electricity, aerodynamics, gynecology, cybernetics, mathematics, quantum mechanics, hydraulics, and the origin of the species. In addition, men have devised the principles of child psychology and infant nutrition, as well as pasteurization and other means of preserving food. Even the changes in women's fashions or other such trivial matters as the creation of new menus and palatal nuances are traditionally the province of men. If one wishes to have an unusual culinary treat, generally one will not find it at home but at a restaurant, where, of course, the chef is male. A woman's sense of taste is so blunted and deadened by the repetitive preparation of unimaginative, run-of-the-mill, tasteless, everyday cooking that, even if she wanted to try out new foods, she would not be capable of it. There is no female gourmet; women are good for almost nothing.

With his many gifts man would appear to be ideally suited, both mentally and physically, to lead a life both fulfilled and free. Instead he chooses to become a slave, placing his many discoveries at the service of those who are incapable of creation themselves—at the service of "mankind," man's own synonym for women, and of the children of these women.

How paradoxical that this very sex, which is capable of leading a life as nearly perfect as possible, is prepared to give it up, to offer it all to the female sex, which is not interested in such perfection. We have grown so accustomed to the blunted mechanism of onesided exploitation of one group of human beings by a parasitic clique that all our moral values have become completely perverted.

Without really giving the matter any thought, we consider the male sex as a kind of Sisyphus: he has come into the world to learn, to work, and to father children: his sons, in their turn, will learn to work and produce children, and so it will continue forever; it has become almost impossible to think why else men should be here.

If a young man gets married, starts a family, and spends the rest of his life working at a soul-destroying job, he is held up as an example of virtue and responsibility. The other type of man, living only for himself, working only for himself, doing first one thing and then another simply because he enjoys it and because he has to keep only himself, sleeping where and when he wants, and facing woman when he meets her, on equal terms and not as one of a million slaves, is rejected by society. The free, unshackled man has no place in its midst.

How depressing it is to see men, year after year, betraying all that they were born to. New worlds could be discovered, worlds one hardly dares even to dream of could be opened by the minds, strength, and intelligence of men. Things to make life fuller and richer—their own life, that is, of which women are ignorant—and more worthwhile could be developed: all these things could be done by men. Instead, they forsake all these tremendous potentials and permit their minds and their bodies to be shunted onto sidings to serve the repulsively primitive needs of women. Man has the key to every mystery of the universe in his hand, but he ignores it, he lowers himself to the level of woman and insinuates himself into her favor.

With his mind, his strength, and his imagination, all intended for the creation of *new* worlds, he opts instead for the preservation and improvement of the *old*. And if he happens to invent something new, he needs to prefix it with the excuse that it will one day be useful to "all mankind," i.e., to women. He apologizes for his achievements, for making space flights instead of providing more comforts for his wife and children. The most tiresome aspect of technological advances is having to translate them for television ads into female language composed of children's prattle and sweet lovetalk. Man is begging woman to be patient with him and his discoveries, or at least to buy them. Women's proven lack of imagination makes clear that they have no *a priori* need for new inventions. If they did, they would invent things more often themselves.

We are so accustomed to men doing everything with women in view that anything else seems unthinkable. For example, couldn't composers create something apart from *love* (dependency) songs? Couldn't writers give up their romantic novels and *love* (dependency) poems and try to write literature? Can painters only produce nudes and profiles of women, abstract or realistic? Why can't we have something *new* after all this time, something we have never seen before?

It should really be possible for scientists to forget dedicating their works for their wives; anyhow, they will never, never be able to understand them. When will the time come when experimental films have no longer to be weighted down by sexy female bodies, when news reports on space travel do not need to be encumbered with interviews of peroxided astronauts' wives? Even the astronauts themselves might stop having schmaltzy *love* (dependency) songs played to them during their interplanetary travels.

We have absolutely no idea what the world would be like if men really used their intelligence and imagination instead of wasting it. Inventing pressure cookers that cook faster, wall-to-wall carpeting that is more stain-resistant, detergents that wash whiter, and lipsticks that are more water-resistant *is* a waste of time. Instead of producing children who will in turn produce children, thus pushing the enjoyment of life still further out of their own reach, they should try living *themselves*. Instead of probing the depth of woman's "mysterious" psyche—"mysterious" only because there is nothing behind it—they should study their own psyche, perhaps even that of creatures possibly inhabiting other planets, and think out new ways and means of establishing contact with *them*. Instead of inventing ever more deadly weapons to fight wars destined only to defend private property, i.e., women's, they should be developing ever more efficient methods of space travel—travel which would tell us more about worlds we never dreamed of.

Unfortunately, men who are capable and willing to work and think in every other field of research have declared everything concerning woman taboo. What is worse is that this taboo has always been so effective that it is no longer recognized as such. *Women's* wars, *women's* children, *women's* towns—all these are made by men. Women just sit back getting lazier, dumber and more demanding—and, at the same time, richer. A primitive but effective system of insurance policies—policies for marriage, divorce, inheritance, widowhood, old age, and life—ensures this increasing wealth. For example, in the U.S.A. half of the total private capital is in the hands of women. Yet the number of working women has constantly decreased over the last decades. The situation is not much different in industrial Europe. At this time women already have complete psychological control over men. It won't be long before they have material control as well.

Men seem to be quite unaware of these facts and go on finding happiness in their own subjugation. There could be justification for their attitude only if women really were the charming, gracious creatures men believe them to be: fairy princesses, angels from another world, too good both for men themselves and for this earthly existence.

It is quite incredible that men, whose desire for knowledge is unbounded in every other field, are really totally blind to these facts, that they are incapable of seeing women as they really are: with nothing else to offer but a vagina, two breasts, and some punch cards programmed with idle, stereotyped chatter; that they are nothing more than conglomerations of matter, lumps of stuffed human skin pretending to be thinking human beings.

If men would only stop for a moment in their headlong creativity and think, they could easily tear the masks off these creatures with their tinkling bracelets, frilly blouses, and gold-leather sandals. Surely it would take them only a couple of days, considering their own intelligence, imagination, and determination, to construct a machine, a kind of human female robot to take the place of woman. For there is nothing original in her—neither inside nor out—which could not be replaced. Why are men so afraid to face the truth?

DISCUSSION QUESTIONS

1. "A woman takes interest only in subjects that have an immediate personal usefulness to her." They are "incapable of creation." They have "complete psychological control over men." What evidence is offered to support these (and similar) claims?
2. The author does offer some evidence that is (or seems to be) factual. Men

made most of the world's inventions and discoveries. Most chefs are male. Men would probably be more likely to look on at a building site. The astronauts were men. What conclusion can you draw from this?

3. Define the stereotype. Accepting the view of the author, spell out what women are, what they do, what they want. What evidence do you have that this is a false stereotype?

4. Again, acceping the author's stereotype, describe how a free man, unencumbered by woman, would spend his time during a particular day. Does this seem a realistic conception?

5. Were men not enslaved by women, "New worlds could be discovered, worlds one hardly dares even to dream of." Dream of them. What does the author say or suggest that men might do?

6. Is it something of a paradox that man with "his mind, his strength, and his imagination" allows himself to be enslaved? Doesn't the essay—despite the author's extreme view—suggest that women are the superior sex?

7. Do you think that "Esther Vilar" is really a woman? Don't answer too soon.

Edward U. Condon

INTELLIGENT LIFE ELSEWHERE

Whether there is intelligent life elsewhere (ILE) in the Universe is a question that has received a great deal of serious speculative attention in recent years. A good popular review of thinking on the subject is *We Are Not Alone* by Walter Sullivan (1964). More advanced discussions are *Interstellar Communication,* a collection of papers edited by A. G. W. Cameron (1963), and *Intelligent Life in the Universe* (Shklovskii and Sagan, 1966). Thus far we have no observational evidence whatever on the question, so therefore it remains open. An early unpublished discussion is a letter of 13 December 1948 of J. E. Lipp to Gen. Donald Putt (Appendix D). This letter is Appendix D of the Project Sign report dated February 1949 form Air Materiel Command Headquarters No. F-TR-2274-IA.

The ILE question has some relation to the ETH [Extra-terrestrial Hypothesis] or ETA [Extra-terrestrial Actuality] for UFOs as discussed in the preceding section. Clearly, if ETH is true, then ILE must also be true because some UFOs have then to come from some unearthly civilization. Conversely, if we could know conclusively that ILE does not exist, then ETH could not be true. But even if ILE exists, it does not follow that the ETH is true.

For it could be that the ILE, though existent, might not have reached a stage of development in which the beings have the technical capacity or the desire to visit the Earth's surface. Much speculative writing assumes implicitly that intelligent life progresses steadily both in intellectual and in its technological development. Life began on Earth more than a billion years ago, whereas the known geological age of the Earth is some five billion years, so that life in any form has only existed for the most recent one-fifth of the Earth's life as a solid ball orbiting the Sun. Man as an intelligent being has only lived on Earth for some 5000 years, or about one-millionth of the Earth's age. Technological development is even more recent. Moreover the greater part of what we think of as advanced technology has only been developed in the last 100 years. Even today we do not yet have a technology capable of putting men on other planets of the solar system. Travel of men over interstellar distances in the foreseeable future seems now to be quite out of the question. (Purcell, 1960; Markowitz, 1967.)

The dimensions of the universe are hard for the mind of man to conceive. A light-year is the distance light travels in one year of 31.56 million seconds, at the rate of 186,000 miles per second, that is, a distance of 5.88 million million miles. The nearest known star is at a distance of 4.2 light-years.

Fifteen stars are known to be within 11.5 light-years of the Sun. Our own galaxy, the Milky Way, is a vast flattened distribution of some 10^{11} stars about 80,000 light-years in diameter, with the Sun located about 26,000 light-years from the center. To gain a little perspective on the meaning of such distances relative to human affairs, we may observe that the news of Christ's life on Earth could not yet have reached as much as a tenth of the distance from the Earth to the center of our galaxy.

Other galaxies are inconceivably remote. The faintest observable galaxies are at a distance of some two billion light-years. There are some 100 million such galaxies within that distance, the average distance between galaxies being some eight million light-years.

Authors of UFO fantasy literature casually set all of the laws of physics aside in order to try to evade this conclusion, but serious consideration of their ideas hardly belongs in a report on the scientific study of UFOs.

Even assuming that difficulties of this sort could be overcome, we have no right to assume that in life communities everywhere there is a steady evolution in the directions of both greater intelligence and greater technological competence. Human beings now know enough to destroy all life on Earth, and they may lack the intelligence to work out social controls to keep themselves from doing so. If other civilizations have the same limitation then it might be that they develop to the point where they destroy themselves utterly before they have developed the technology needed to enable them to make long space voyages.

Another possibility is that the growth of intelligence precedes the growth of technology in such a way that by the time a society would be technically capable of interstellar space travel, it would have reached a level of intelligence at which it had not the slightest interest in interstellar travel. We must not assume that we are capable of imagining now the scope and extent of future technological development of our own or any other civilization, and so we must guard against assuming that we have any capacity to imagine what a more advanced society would regard as intelligent conduct.

In addition to the great distances involved, and the difficulties which they present to interstellar space travel, there is still another problem: If we assume that civilizations annihilate themselves in such a way that their effective intelligent life span is less than, say, 100,000 years, then such a short time span also works against the likelihood of successful interstellar communication. The different civilizations would probably reach the culmination of their development at different epochs in cosmic history. Moreover, according to present views, stars are being formed constantly by the condensation of interstellar dust and gases. They exist for perhaps 10 billion years, of which a civilization lasting 100,000 years is only 1/100,000 of the life span of the star. It follows that there is an extremely small likelihood that two nearby civilizations would be in a state of high development at the same epoch.

Astronomers now generally agree that a fairly large number of all main-sequence stars are probably accompanied by planets at the right distance from their Sun to provide for habitable conditions for life as we know it. That is, where stars are, there are probably habitable planets. This belief favors the possibility of interstellar communication, but it must be remembered that even this view is entirely speculation: we are quite unable directly to observe any planets associated with stars other than the Sun.

In view of the foregoing, we consider that it is safe to assume that no ILE outside of our solar system has any possibility of visiting Earth in the next 10,000 years.

This conclusion does not rule out the possibility of the existence of ILE, as contrasted with the ability of such civilizations to visit Earth. It is estimated that 10^{21} stars can be seen using the 200-inch Hale telescope on Mount Palomar. Astronomers surmise that possibly as few as one in a million or as many as one in ten of these have a planet in which physical and chemical conditions are such as to make them habitable by life based on the same kind of biochemistry as the life we know on Earth. Even if the lower figure is taken, this would mean there are 10^{15} stars in the visible universe which have planets suitable for an abode of life. In our own galaxy there are 10^{11} stars, so perhaps as many as 10^8 have habitable planets in orbit around them.

Biologists feel confident that wherever physical and chemical conditions are right, life will actually emerge. In short, astronomers tell us that there are a vast number of stars in the universe accompanied by planets where the physical and chemical conditions are suitable, and biologists tell us that habitable places are sure to become inhabited. (Rush, 1957.)

An important advance was made when Stanley L. Miller (1955) showed experimentally that electrical discharges such as those in natural lightning when passed through a mixture of methane and ammonia, such as may have been present in the Earth's primitive atmosphere, will initiate chemical reactions which yield various amino acids. These are the raw materials from which are constructed the proteins that are essential to life. Miller's work has been followed up and extended by many others, particularly P. H. Abelson of the Carnegie Institution of Washington.

The story is by no means fully worked out. The evidence in hand seems to convince biochemists that natural processes, such as lightning, or the absorption of solar ultraviolet light, could generate the necessary starting materials from which life could evolve. On this basis they generally hold the belief that where conditions make it possible that life could appear, there life actually will appear.

It is regarded by scientists today as essentially certain the ILE exists, but with essentially no possibility of contact between the communities on planets associated with different stars. We therefore conclude that there is no relation between ILE at other solar systems and the UFO phenomenon as observed on Earth.

There remains the question of ILE within our solar system. Here only the planets Venus and Mars need be given consideration as possible abodes of life.

Mercury, the planet nearest the Sun, is certainly too hot to support life. The side of Mercury that is turned toward the Sun has an average temperature of 660° F. Since the orbit is rather eccentric this temperature becomes as high as 770° F, hot enough to melt lead, when Mercury is closest to the Sun. The opposite side is extremely cold, its temperature not being known.[1] Gravity on Mercury is about one-fourth that on Earth. This fact combined with the high temperature makes it certain that Mercury has no atmosphere, which is consistent with observational data

---

[1] Mercury rotates in 59 days and the orbital period is 88 days, so there is a slow relative rotation.

on this point. It is quite impossible that life as found on Earth could exist on Mercury.

Jupiter, Saturn, Uranus, Neptune and Pluto are so far from the Sun that they are too cold for life to exist there.

Although it has long been thought that Venus might provide a suitable abode for life, it is now known that the surface of Venus is also too hot for advanced forms of life, although it is possible that some primitive forms may exist. Some uncertainty and controversy exists about the interpretation of observations of Venus because the planet is always enveloped in dense clouds so that the solid surface is never seen. The absorption spectrum of sunlight coming from Venus indicates that the principal constituent of the atmosphere is carbon dioxide. There is no evidence of oxygen or water vapor. With so little oxygen in the atmosphere there could not be animal life there resembling that on Earth.

Although it is safe to conclude that there is no intelligent life on Venus, the contrary idea is held quite tenaciously by certain groups in America. There are small religious groups who maintain that Jesus Christ now sojourns on Venus, and that some of their members have travelled there by flying saucers supplied by the Venusians and have been greatly refreshed spiritually by visiting Him. There is no observational evidence in support of this teaching.

In the fantasy literature of believers in ETH, some attention is given to a purely hypothetical planet named Clarion. Not only is there no direct evidence for its existence, but there is conclusive indirect evidence for its nonexistence. Those UFO viewers who try not to be totally inconsistent with scientific findings, recognizing that Venus and Mars are unsuitable as abodes of life, have invented Clarion to meet the need for a home for the visitors who they believe come on some UFOs.

They postulate that Clarion moves in an orbit exactly like that of the Earth around the Sun, but with the orbit rotated through half a revolution in its plane so that the two orbits have the same line of apsides, but with Clarion's perihelion in the same direction from the Sun as the Earth's aphelion. The two planets, Earth and Clarion, are postulated to move in their orbits in such a way that they are always opposite each other, so that the line Earth-Sun-Clarion is a straight line. Thus persons on Earth would never see Clarion because it is permanently eclipsed by the Sun.

If the two orbits were exactly circular, the two planets would move along their common orbit at the same speed and so would remain exactly opposite each other. But even if the orbits are elliptical, so that the speed in the orbit is variable, the two planets would vary in speed during the year in just such a way as always to remain opposite each other and thus continue to be permanently eclipsed.

However, this tidy arrangement would not occur in actuality because the motion of each of these two planets would be perturbed by the gravitational attractions between them and the other planets of the solar system, principally Venus and Mars. It is a quite complicated and difficult problem to calculate the way in which these perturbations would affect the motion of Earth and Clarion.

At the request of the Colorado project, Dr. R. L. Duncombe, director of the Nautical Almanac office at U.S. Naval Observatory in Washington, D.C., kindly arranged to calculate the effect of the introduction of the hypothetical planet Clarion into the solar system. The exact result depends to some extent on the location of the Earth-Sun-Clarion line relative to the line of apsides and the computations were carried out merely for one case.

These calculations show that the effect of the perturbations would be to make Clarion become visible from Earth beyond the Sun's limb after about thirty years. In other words, Clarion would long since have become visible from Earth if many years ago it were started out in such a special way as has been postulated.

The computations revealed further that if Clarion were there it would reveal its presence indirectly in a much shorter time. Its attraction on Venus would cause Venus to move in a different way than if Clarion were not there. Calculation shows that Venus would pull away from its otherwise correct motion by about 1″ of arc in about three months time. Venus is routinely kept under observation to this accuracy, and therefore if Clarion were there it would reveal its presence by its effect on the motion of Venus. No such effect is observed, that is, the motion of Venus as actually observed is accurately in accord with the absence of Clarion, so therefore we may safely conclude that Clarion is nonexistent.[2]

In his letter of transmittal Dr. Duncombe comments "I feel this is definite proof that the presence of such a body could not remain undetected for long. However, I am afraid it will not change the minds of those people who believe in the existence of Clarion."

We first heard about Clarion from a lady who is prominent in American political life who was intrigued with the idea that this is where UFOs come from. When the results of the Naval Observatory computations were told to her she exclaimed, "That's what I don't like about computers! They are always dealing death blows to our fondest notions!"

Mars has long been considered as a possible abode of life in the solar system. There is still no direct evidence that life exists there, but the question is being actively studied in the space research programs of both the United States and Soviet Russia, so it may well be clarified within the coming decade.

At present all indications are that Mars could not be the habitation

---

[2] These calculations assume Clarion's mass roughly equal to that of the Earth.

of an advanced civilization capable of sending spacecraft to visit the Earth. Conditions for life there are so harsh that it is generally believed that at best Mars could only support the simpler forms of plant life.

An excellent recent survey of the rapidly increasing knowledge of Mars is *Handbook of the Physical Properties of the Planet Mars* compiled by C. M. Michaux (NASA publication SP-3030, 1967). A brief discussion of American research programs for study of life on Mars is given in *Biology and Exploration of Mars*, a 19-page pamphlet prepared by the Space Science Board of the National Academy of Sciences, published in April 1965.

The orbit of Mars is considerably more eccentric than that of the Earth. Consequently the distance of Mars from the Sun varies from 128 to 155 million miles during the year of 687 days. The synodic period, or mean time between successive oppositions, is 800 days.

The most favorable time for observation of Mars is at opposition, when Mars is opposite the Sun from Earth. These distances of closest approach of Mars and Earth vary from 35 to 60 million miles. The most recent favorable time of closest approach was the opposition of 10 September 1956, and the next favorable opposition will be that of 10 August 1971. At that time undoubtedly great efforts will be made to study Mars in the space programs of the U.S.S.R. and the United States.

Some of the UFO literature has contended that a larger than usual number of UFO reports occur at the times of Martian oppositions. The contention is that this indicates that some UFOs come from Mars at these particularly favorable times. The claimed correlation is quite unfounded; the idea is not supported by observational data. (Vallee and Vallee, 1966, p. 138.)

Mars is much smaller than Earth, having a diameter of 4200 miles, in comparison with 8000 miles. Mars' mass is about one-tenth the Earth's, and gravity at Mars' surface is about 0.38 that of Earth. The Martian escape velocity is 3.1 mile/sec.

At the favorable opposition of 1877, G. V. Schiaparelli, an Italian astronomer, observed and mapped some surface marking on Mars which he called "canali," meaning "channels" in Italian. The word was mistranslated as "canals" in English and the idea was put forward, particularly vigorously by Percival Lowell, founder of the Lowell Observatory of Flagstaff, Arizona, that the canals on Mars were evidence of a gigantic planetary irrigation scheme, developed by the supposed inhabitants of Mars (Lowell, 1908). These markings have been the subject of a great deal of study since their discovery. Astronomers generally now reject the idea that they afford any kind of indication that Mars in inhabited by intelligent beings.

Mars has two moons named Phobos and Deimos. These are exceedingly small, Phobos being estimated at ten miles in diameter and Deimos at five miles, based on their brightness, assuming the reflecting power of their material to be the same as that of the planet. The periods are $7^h 39^m$ for Phobos and $30^h 18^m$ for Deimos. They were discovered in August 1877 by Asaph Hall using the then new 26-inch refractor of the U.S. Naval Observatory in Washington. An unsuccessful search for moons of Mars was made with a 48-inch mirror during the opposition of 1862.

I. S. Shklovskii (1959) published a sensational suggestion in a Moscow newspaper that these moons were really artificial satellites which had been put up by supposed inhabitants of Mars as a place of refuge when the supposed oceans of several million years ago began to dry up (Sullivan, 1966, p. 169). There is no observational evidence to support this idea. Continuing the same line of speculation Salisbury (1962), after pointing out that the satellites were looked for in 1862 but not found until 1877, then asks, "Should we attribute the failure of 1862 to imperfections in existing telescopes, or may we imagine that the satellites were launched between 1862 and 1877?" This is a slender reed indeed with which to prop up so sensational an inference, and we reject it.

DISCUSSION QUESTIONS

1. Discuss the tone of this essay. How is it different from Esther Vilar's in "It's a Man's Universe"?
2. Does the author specifically say that he does not believe UFOs are space ships?
3. Note how the author supports his conclusions. Consider the evidence contributing to these sentences:

   "In view of the foregoing, we consider that it is safe to assume that no ILE outside of our solar system has any possibility of visiting the Earth in the next 10,000 years."

   "It is regarded by scientists today as essentially certain that ILE exists."

   ". . . it is safe to conclude that there is no intelligent life on Venus."

   ". . . so therefore we may safely conclude that Clarion is nonexistent."

   "At present all indications are that Mars could not be the habitation of an advanced civilization capable of sending spacecraft to visit the Earth."

4. Did the author have to mention the groups who believe that Jesus now lives on Venus, the lady who introduced the subject of Clarion, and Shklovskii's and Salisbury's sensational thesis concerning the satellites of Mars? Why did he introduce these?

S. L. Varnado

SOME THOUGHTS
ON PROFESSOR SHOCKLEY

I don't know anything about Science but I know what I like. And what I like is for Science to leave me alone. My attitude toward Science is the same as my attitude toward Rock Music, and might best be described as benign neglect. Let Science (and Rock Music, for that matter) go its way; I will go mine.

I know nothing, for instance, of DNA. I don't know what Boyle's Law is all about and I don't much care. I am not curious about Black Holes—in fact, I am not sure that I believe in them. Dr. B. F. Skinner grew old and famous before I even knew who he was. And when I found out, I labored for some time under the impression that *Beyond Freedom and Dignity* was some sort of study of marriage.

Enough, you say. The man is obviously an untutored lunatic, or at best an amateur obscurantist whose views need scarcely detain a denizen of the twentieth century. I admit this. There are scientists and pseudo-scientists enow, and to them I leave the field. Once in a while, however, a

Abridged from *National Review*, August 30, 1974, pp. 975, 993–994. Reprinted with permission of *National Review*, 150 East 35th Street, New York NY 10016 (Subscription: $19).

scientist comes along with a theory that sets my ganglia on edge, and one such man is the eminent Professor William Shockley. I take a keen—even an unhealthy—interest in him. I see his theories as jeopardizing not only The Races of Man (a problem The Races of Man can worry about) but my own hitherto happy marriage. Of course, when something like this happens, I drop all pose of amateur obscurantist. Gathering my charts, my graphs, my proliferating data, and my Gatorade about me, I attack without quarter.

Professor William Shockley, as I suppose everybody knew before I did, is the genius who helped invent the conjunction transistor, for which feat he was awarded part of the Nobel Prize (and for which feat he must bear part of the guilt for Rock Music). Then, having no new solid states to conquer, and not content to rest upon his components, he turned a roving eye upon the science of genetics. This, I take it, is a dangerous thing to do, especially when you are approaching middle age, as Shockley was. It is the scientific equivalent of philandering, and if Shockley wasn't aware of the signs, his wife should have been. She should have put him to beating rugs and working crossword puzzles. But she didn't. The wife is always the last to know.

From Shockley's affair with Genes and Permutations came a number of conclusions (all of them disputable), which I shall attempt to summarize. First, Shockley has collected statistics which tend to show that the median IQ scores of the Black Race are 10 to 20 points lower than the median IQ scores of members of the White Race. Shockley, I have noticed, always says "10 to 20 points"—never "10 points" or "20 points." This gives his statistics a casual air that offends even such an obscurantist as I. (It is the way my wife talks.) Second, he has statistics indicating that the poorer members of both the Black and White Races—and especially those with low IQ scores—are outbreeding the rest of the population. This, he feels, is lowering the general IQ score of the nation, a condition that causes him great pain.

All this sort of thing (racial IQ disparity, overpopulation by low IQ scorers, etc.) Shockley calls by the name Dysgenics. Now *Dysgenics* is an interesting word. It means "the retrogressive evolution through the disproportionate reproduction of the genetically disadvantaged." Shockley apparently loves both the word and its fantastic definition. It has the sort of sesquipedalian hue that colors most of his statements. One imagines him going around the house muttering this sort of thing.

At any rate, having analyzed the evils of Dysgenics, Shockley goes on to propose solutions. (By "evil," I mean evil to Shockley. To me, Dysgenics is an appealing process. Imagine people "evolving" backwards! I know several ladies I would much prefer as horses.) Shockley's solutions to this problem all turn, in one way or another, on sterilization. He wants to sterilize Poor Blacks and Poor Whites. He proposes to sterilize those who pay no income tax. And especially he hopes to offer monetary inducements to people below 80 IQ to get themselves voluntarily sterilized. That's his program.

It is solutions of this kind that have me stirred up. I am worried about the effects of this sort of thing on my marriage. Let me explain briefly.

I am married to a woman whose IQ score is 10 to 20 points higher than mine. (Count 'em: 10 to 20.) We have established this unhappy condition many times by taking *Reader's Digest* IQ tests. No matter how vigorously I concentrate, no matter how much extra time my wife allows me, the results are always the same. She comes out 10 to 20 points ahead. (Needless to say, my wife revels in this condition. She goes around the house complaining "I wish they would establish a chapter of Mensa in this hick town.")

Now in addition to my low IQ score, our marriage shows a tendency toward what Shockley calls "disproportionate reproduction." We have six children. Finally, while we are not statistically "poor" we are rapidly becoming so. My salary rises a bit every year but not so fast as to outpace that constantly rising mark which the government sets each year as its "poverty level." Some day it will undoubtedly overtake it, and when it does our marriage will have all the notes of classic Dysgenicism: a questionable IQ gradient (in at least one partner), a mass of progeny, and some degree of statistical destitution. My bitterness toward the Shockley theories should now be understandable. I am threatened.

But this is not the whole story.

Dysgenics is a two way street, and there is another side to the matter which Shockley ought to hear. There are factors in my marriage which work to ameliorate this seemingly hopeless situation, and I am going to tell them not only to refute Shockley, but to console other Dysgenics.

Despite her superior IQ score, my wife is the victim of a hereditary flaw. She has had from childhood what can only be described as a Bad Driveway Gene. She must have got it from her mother, since her father did not know how to drive. The Gene in question is, I am inclined to think, Recessive.

(I suppose I should stop, right about now, and explain for the lay reader the meaning of the terms *Recessive* and *Dominant.* Briefly, there are two kinds of Genes: Dominant and Recessive. A Dominant Gene is simply a gregarious, extroverted Gene—the sort that tries to "Take over." This Gene is much like the person who, when he goes to a party, drinks and talks too much and ends up forcing everybody to play charades. On the other hand, a Recessive Gene is an introvert—shy, sensitive, refined. It prefers a book or a quiet chat with a friend, it is easily exploited by a Dominant Gene, and its life is probably not too happy.)

My wife's Bad Driveway Gene, as I said, is of this Recessive type. It belongs to a group known as the Automobile Driving Complex, and the other Genes in this group (evidently Dominant) keep it under control on freeways and streets. But when it gets in a driveway—on home ground, so to speak—it feels more relaxed and begins to assert itself. It is this Bad Driveway Gene that causes my wife to run into things in driveways: garbage cans, mail boxes, you name it.

I discovered this particular Gene in my wife before we were married. After some sad experiences, she confessed she had driven through the garage doors twice. She had struck her mother's Lincoln several times. She had raked a visitor's Mercury, parted a caladium bed, and so forth. I married her anyway. I was not one to let Genetics impede the marriage of true minds. Besides, I knew my Driveway Gene was good, and being a male chauvinist, I figured it was Dominant. My children, I reasoned, would inherit from me—and as a matter of fact, they have. It is reassuring to watch the careful way in which they wheel their bicycles and velocipedes in and out of the driveway. (Our girl shows a tendency to follow in her mother's tire tracks, but I imagine it's psychological imitation.)

Now here is the point of my argument.

Suppose my wife, knowing my weak IQ score, had sacrificed herself to the Higher Genetics and married somebody more intelligent. She might have gotten some stuffy little prodigy who, unknown to her, had a Driveway Gene as bad as her own. They would have then proceeded to unleash upon society a whole brood of Bad Driveway Factors. But as things stand now, we have bred out the bad strain.

A small victory, perhaps, but I often think of it when I read of Shockley, or observe the dents in our station wagon.

DISCUSSION QUESTIONS

1. What is Dr. Shockley's proposal that disturbs the author? Does the proposal seem unreasonable to you?
2. Does the author specifically deny the correctness of Shockley's premises and conclusions?
3. How does he criticize Shockley as a person? What evidence is there that this criticism is just?
4. Judging from the essay, what kind of person does the author seem to be? What effect does his personality have on his argument?
5. Is it fair to say that the author is arguing more with style than with substance?
6. Would this essay be less effective with a general audience than a more factual point-by-point refutation of Dr. Shockley?

Induction

What I tell you three times is true.
—Lewis Carroll, *The Hunting of the Snark*

Induction is the process of arriving at a general conclusion on the basis of incomplete evidence. Almost everything you know, you know by induction.

You believe, for example, that polar bears are white. But because you have not seen all polar bears, your judgment is based on limited evidence. The two or three polar bears you have seen were white. Those shown in *National Geographic* and on *Wild Kingdom* were white. Everyone you know agrees they are white. From this information you reasonably decide that all polar bears are white.

This process is induction. You consider evidence you have seen or heard to draw a conclusion about things you have not seen or heard. The intellectual movement from limited facts—called a *sample*—to a general conviction is called an inductive leap. Most conclusions regarding past, present, and future events are based on this kind of leap. You believe that Balboa discovered the Pacific Ocean, that taking Anacin eases a headache, that the Republicans will win the next Presidential election. Because you can never secure all the evidence relating to these questions, you reasonably make judgments from the evidence you have.

It is equally reasonable, on hearing induced conclusions, to inquire about the number and kinds of facts that went into them. For a claim to be creditable, its sample must be (1) known, (2) sufficient, and (3) representative. If you are told simply that the CIA is directed by Jewish conspirators, you can withhold belief on the ground that the sample is not known. No evidence is given to support the accusation. If you hear a famous athlete's low IQ cited to demonstrate that all athletes (or all members of the athlete's race or nationality) are intellectually weak, you can respond that the sample is not sufficient. One example proves nothing about a large group. And if you hear the cruelties of the Spanish Inquisition used as evidence of the repressive views of Catholics in general, you can insist that the sample is not representative. Spanish practice in the fifteenth century is hardly typical of worldwide Catholicism today.

You should recognize such unsubstantiated claims when you see them, and you should work to keep them out of your own writing.

IS THE SAMPLE KNOWN?

You frequently hear statements that lack evidence. Advertisements announce that, "Ban is preferred by seven out of ten American women," and that, "four out of five top movie stars use Lustre-Creme Shampoo." It is rumored that Viceroy filters are made of harmful fiberglass and that fluoridated drinking water can cause brain damage. Such claims can be dismissed if no evidence is ever offered to support them.

A variation popular with sensational writers is to make an extravagant claim and point to conclusive evidence—which happens to be unavailable. They charge that Warren Harding was murdered by his wife and that Franklin Roosevelt was poisoned by the Russians at Teheran; then they regret that evidence is lost in the past. They affirm the existence of abominable snowmen, Atlantis, and the Loch Ness Monster; then they lament that proof remains out of reach. They know that UFOs are extraterrestrial spaceships and that a massive conspiracy led to the assassinations of John and Robert Kennedy; then they protest that the U.S. Air Force, FBI, CIA, and Dallas police are all withholding crucial evidence. These too are inductions with an absent sample.

IS THE SAMPLE SUFFICIENT?

Induction with an insufficient sample is common. You regularly hear charges like these:

> Most labor leaders are crooks. Look at Tony Boyle, Frank Brewster, and Jimmy Hoffa.
> The Social Security system is unfair. Let me tell you what happened to my father-in-law.
> Don't talk to me about Puerto Ricans. I lived next to a Puerto Rican family for two years.

Clearly, the indicated samples—*three* labor leaders, *one* relative, and *one* family—are inadequate evidence on which to base any broad conclusion.

Advocates of a particular view commonly try to broaden the effect of limited examples by declaring them "typical" or "average." They remain limited examples. *In argument, the words "typical" and "average" deserve immediate suspicion.*

IS THE SAMPLE REPRESENTATIVE?

A sample is said to be unrepresentative when it in not typical of the whole class of things being studied. It is easy to see that you cannot gauge your town's attitude toward a proposed liquor tax by polling only the citizens at a corner tavern or only members of the local Baptist church.

Nevertheless, conclusions based on an unrepresentative sample can be quite deceptive on first hearing: for example, "Women are better drivers than men; they have fewer accidents." Here the sample is large enough—a substantial body of accident statistics—but it is not broad enough to be meaningful. Then conclusion concerns *all drivers*, but the sample group includes only *drivers who have had accidents.* To be representative (that is, typical of the whole area under discussion), the sample must include all four groups involved:

1. men
2. women
3. drivers who had accidents
4. drivers who had no accidents

With this broad sample you could see that there are fewer women in automobile accidents because there are fewer women driving. The isolated accident statistics are meaningless if not compared to those for all drivers.

Similarly, if you hear that 60 percent of all lung-cancer victims were moderate-to-heavy smokers or that 80 percent of all San Quentin convicts came from homes that served liquor, you can draw no significant conclusion. The implied judgments describe *everyone*, but the samples include only *cancer victims* and *convicts;* there are no general statistics with which to make comparison. Perhaps 60 percent of all adults are moderate smokers and 80 percent of all homes serve liquor. Then, of course, the narrower statistics become meaningless.

Any induced conclusion is open to question, then, if its sample is too small or is unduly weighted in some way. The Nielsen rating service claims to know the audience size for American television programs. But because its information comes from 1100 audiometers (one for every 50,-000 homes), the sufficiency of the sample is doubtful. The Kinsey report was said to reveal the sexual habits of American women. But because the information came from 5940 women—most of whom were well educated, white, non-Catholic, and Gentile, and all of whom were willing to describe their sex lives to interviewers—the representativeness of the sample is open to question.

Any poll with a selective sample—that is, where some individuals choose to respond to it and others do not—is unrepresentative.

POLLING

A person can misuse a poll to make it express a desired opinion. He can announce the results of surveys that were never taken. (Politicians have for years made good use of "private polls" to enhance the prestige of a lagging condidate.) He can phrase a poll question to draw the response he seeks. ("Should America surrender its rights in Panama to a corrupt Communist dictator?") Or he can inflate someone else's poll. (In 1972, Washington television station WTTG asked viewers to write in their opinion of President Nixon's decision to mine North Vietnamese harbors: the final count showed 5157 supporting the president and a much smaller number opposing him. Later investigation showed that some 4000 of the votes favorable to Mr. Nixon came directly from the Committee to Re-elect the President.)

What is an adequate sample on which to base a reliable judgment? There is no easy answer. Size varies with the character of the question and with the degree of probability one seeks.

You should remember, however, that a small sample—if genuinely representative—can sustain a broad conclusion. George Gallup assesses the opinions of the American public by polling 1500 individuals. But because his sample is chosen so that every adult American has an equal chance of being interviewed, the Gallup Poll (like similar polls) is a reliable source of information. The mathematical probability is that, 95 times out of 100, a selection of 1500 anonymous people will give results no more than 3 percentage points off the figures that would be obtained by interviewing the whole population.

Modern polling can be disturbingly accurate. Just before the 1972 Presidential election, the Gallup Poll reported that Nixon would receive 62 percent of the vote, and McGovern 38 percent; the Harris Poll predicted 61 percent and 39 percent. And after 77,734,195 individual citizens made their personal choice, the count showed 1 percent for minor candidates, 61 percent for Nixon, and 38 percent for McGovern. (The polls did not pinpoint the 1976 Carter–Ford contest with the same degree of accuracy, but results were well within the 3 percent margin of error.)

OCCAM'S RAZOR

Even in everyday experience, you commonly use very limited information to draw a tentative conclusion. This is not unreasonable. If you see a girl not wearing her engagement ring and behaving despondently, you may speculate that she has broken her engagement. The evidence is not sufficient for you to offer condolences, but it will keep you from making jokes about marriage. If you hear from a friend that a new movie is disappointing, you will probably choose not to see it—at least until you hear a contrary report. Your conclusion is based on a tiny sample, but it is all the sample you have. As your sample grows, so will your degree of conviction.

With induction, you should remember *Occam's razor*, the maxim that when a body of evidence exists, the simplest conclusion that expresses all of it is probably the best. A perfect illustration occurred in 1967, when New Orleans District Attorney James Garrison sought to prove that Clay Shaw, a local businessman, was involved in the assassination of President Kennedy. He submitted that Shaw's address book carried the entry "Lee Odom, P.O. Box 19106, Dallas, Texas"; and that the number "PO 19106," when properly decoded, became "WH 15601," the unlisted phone number of Jack Ruby, slayer of Kennedy's assassin Lee Oswald. (The process involved "unscrambling" the numerals and—since P and O equal 7 and 6 on a telephone dial—subtracting 1300.) Thus Garrison used the entry in Shaw's address book as inductive evidence leading to a sensational conclusion. But Occam's razor suggests a simpler explanation, one that proved to be a fact: Shaw was acquainted with a businessman named Lee Odom, whose Dallas address was P.O. Box 19106.

You should remember Occam's razor when you read the many books and articles that "reexamine" famous crimes. Routinely they conclude that people like Lee Harvey Oswald, Alger Hiss, Lizzy Borden, Bruno Hauptmann, James Earl Ray, the Rosenbergs, and Sacco and Vanzetti were really innocent. The true criminal was either a shadowy figure whom nobody saw or members of some complex and incredible conspiracy. Occam's razor submits that the person with the motive and the opportunity and the weapon is probably guilty.

As you read, examine carefully the facts underlying conclusions. Are they given? Are they sufficient and representative? As you write, support your generalizations as much as you can.

EXERCISES

How reliable are these inductive arguments?

1. In a study of a possible relationship between pornography and antisocial behavior, questionnaires went out to 7500 psychiatrists and psychoanalysts, whose listing in the directory of the American Psychological Association indicated clinical experience. Over 3400 of these professionals responded. The result: 7.4 percent of the psychiatrists and psychologists

had cases in which they were convinced that pornography was a causal factor in antisocial behavior; an additional 9.4 percent were suspicious; 3.2 percent did not commit themselves; and 80 percent stated they had no cases in which a causal connection was suspected.

2. "Proven most effective against colds."—Listerine Antiseptic advertisement

3. *The Hite Report* is based on results of a questionnaire disturbed by the New York chapter of the National Organization for Women "to women all over the country, from every age and economic group and from all walks of life." The result: "Here—for the first time—women themselves speak out about their own sexuality."

4. I'm not going to sign up for Professor Vitulli's class. Several of my friends had the course and disliked it.

5. How can you argue that large families frustrate the individual child? Benjamin Franklin was the eighth child of his parents. There were six in the Washington family, and Abraham Lincoln had seven brothers and sisters. The Jeffersons numbered ten, the Madisons, twelve, the Longfellows, eight; and the Beethovens, twelve.

6. I don't care what you say about stereotypes. Most of the blondes I know *are* dumb.

7. Cola drinkers were asked to compare glasses of Coke and Pepsi for better taste. The Coke was in a glass marked *Q*, and the Pepsi in a glass marked *M*. A majority of those tested said they preferred the taste of Pepsi.

8. Certainly it's obvious from the newspaper reports that rich and famous people have a higher proportion of divorces than the general public.

9. A study of 3400 New York citizens who had had recent heart attacks showed that 70 percent of them were 10–50 pounds overweight. Clearly, obesity is a cause of heart disease.

10. Arguing that eighteenth-century English poetry was essentially prosaic, Matthew Arnold offered a passage from "Pope's verse, take it almost where you will":
    To Hounslow Heath I point and Banstead Down;
    Thence comes your mutton, and these chicks my own.

11. Don't tell me that homosexuals aren't sick. I'm a psychiatrist with a large number of homosexual patients, and all are deeply disturbed. Every one of them.

12. Four out of five dentists surveyed recommended Trident sugarless gum for their patients who chew gum.

13. Poll question for Alabama parents: "I (We) prefer that my (our) child be taught by a teacher of the following race: White. Negro. Other."

ESSAY ASSIGNMENTS

Write an essay either affirming or opposing one of these statements. The arguments you encounter in your background reading will probably be inductive, and so will your essay.

1. Prisoners should be brainwashed.
2. ESP has been proved to exist.

3. Absurd drama is a waste of time.
4. Rock music is a national danger.
5. Jogging is a perfect exercise.
6. American Catholicism is approaching heresy.
7. X is worth saving. (Fill in the X.)

Susy Smith

WHY DOES ESP HAPPEN?

Ever since the earliest days of psychical investigation, researchers have been trying to find out why ESP happens, and hoping to understand all of its characteristics. Yet through all experimentation, then and subsequently, *psi* (as the psychic power is often called) has remained so elusive and unfathomable that no exact explanation of it has ever been formulated.

Because of this, research has tended to take the direction of trying primarily to indicate ESP's existence and to prove that it is repeatable. Tests have been made over and over again for almost a century with the object of identifying various forms of extrasensory perception and very little more. One wonders why it seems necessary for researchers to repeat this so endlessly, until it is realized that because of psi's very intangibility, proving its existence on acceptable scientific grounds becomes an enormous challenge.

The importance of tests which would utilize chance probabilities

Reprinted from *Esp for the Millions* (Los Angeles: Sherbourne Press, Inc., 1965), pp. 46–61. Reprinted by permission of Charter House Publishers, Inc.

was remarked by Gurney: "Of course the first question for science is not whether the phenomena can be produced to order, but whether in a sufficient number of series the proportion of successes to failure is markedly above the probable result of chance." This basic statement has been repeated incessantly by others.

Although Gurney spoke so wisely of chance, it is Professor Charles Richet of France who gets credit for the initial use of the mathematics of chance in evaluating results of telepathy tests. And in 1885, Sir Oliver Lodge, another great physicist who interested himself in psychical research, proposed that conclusive evidence for telepathy might be produced by card-guessing in quantities. He worked out a mathematical formula for estimating the number of hits above those to be expected by chance. When the probability of naming the right card on the basis of chance was known it was easier to compute how much evidence of telepathy the results showed. While an experimenter in chemistry might be content to achieve a result in which the odds were 20-to-1 against chance, in a subject as offbeat as psychical research it seemed imperative to devise a system in which results could be estimated which were 200-, 2,000- or 20,000-to-1 against chance. With card tests repeated endlessly (known as quantitative testing) such results could be achieved.

Although some of these first tests were surprisingly well done, they are not now considered to have been as carefully executed as are those which have been conducted in recent years. With the new techniques he devised, Dr. J. B. Rhine can take the credit for having made quantitative testing for ESP acceptable and successful. Before he started in this field, Dr. Rhine had previously worked for many years with plant physiology and botany, in which he took three degrees at the University of Chicago. His wife, Louisa, was also a graduate in that field. When they encountered some impressive reports of paranormal events, the Rhines became interested in psychical research. After a year in which they both studied psychology at Harvard under Professor William McDougall, they were more than ever taken with parapsychology, in which McDougall had a keen interest.

When McDougall was called to the chair of psychology at Duke University he soon made a professional opportunity in parapsychology available to the Rhines. From 1930 to 1934 they carried forward pioneer experimental investigations in telepathy and clairvoyance, using students as laboratory subjects.

Dr. Rhine knew that in order to break down the persistent opposition to paranormal phenomena it would be necessary to find a method of examination which paralleled the laboratory techniques of other scientific research. He also knew that in order to rule out the argument that ESP was nothing but pure chance or coincidence, he would have to repeat his experiments in even greater numbers, and that he would have to perform each test under such rigid control that there could be no question of sensory cues. Helped by advances in the science of statistics, Rhine was able to devise techniques which made a very large number of experiments possible. First acting as agent (or conductor of the test) himself, Dr. Rhine found the students responding to his stimulating personality with cooperative enthusiasm. He soon had a few star performers who were able to produce outstanding ESP.

The tests were made with what were at first called the Zener cards (now usually referred to as ESP cards). In a pack of twenty-five playing-size cards there are five each of five different symbols: circle, square, cross, star, and wave. When the cards are run face down, by the mathematics of probability the subject would expect to guess one symbol correctly out of five trials. Running the entire twenty-five cards, the subject may be expected to average five chance hits. Repeatedly getting more than five hits is an indication of extrasensory perception, but it is only when hundreds of runs have been made and the score is still higher than chance that the test can be considered significant.

Since the time that these cards were first used at Duke there have been millions of runs made, under conditions varying to indicate whether the ESP is to be identified as telepathy, clairvoyance, general ESP, or precognition.

In 1934 a book entitled *Extrasensory Perception* by Dr. Rhine appeared. In it were accounts of the tests which had been run at Duke; and with its publication a new era in psychical research began. The Pearce-Pratt experiment, the book's most startling feature, introduced Dr. Rhine's research assistant, J. Gaither Pratt, and Hubert E. Pearce Jr., a ministerial student since deceased. Pearce was such an outstanding subject that he would average from six to eleven hits per run at any experimental session. Once, in an informal but nonetheless impressive set of circumstances, he scored a perfect run of 25 hits.

In this experiment which Rhine and Pratt carried out with Pearce in August and September, 1933, the aim was to set up conditions which would exclude all the factors that could reproduce extrachance scores except ESP. Dr. Pratt handled the pack of cards (known as the target pack) whose symbols were to be guessed by Pearce. He was in the Social Science Building at Duke. Pearce was seated 100 yards away in a reading cubicle in the stacks at the back of the Duke Library.

At the start of each session the two men synchronized their watches. After Pearce left for his cubicle, Pratt shuffled the cards and placed the pack at a left-hand corner of his table. At the agreed-upon starting time Pratt removed the top card and, without looking at it, placed it face down on a book in the middle of the table and left it there for a minute. He then removed the card, still face down, to the right-hand corner of the table and immediately picked up the next card and put it on the book. This routine was continued until all the cards were transferred, one at a time, to the other corner. Thus twenty-five minutes were taken for each run of twenty-five trials. Pratt then looked at the faces of the cards and recorded in duplicate the order in which they had fallen and, as a safeguard, before he met with Pearce, sealed one copy in an envelope for delivery to Dr. Rhine.

In the meantime, Pearce had put down on his record sheet during each minute the symbol which he thought was on the card Pratt had in position at the time. At the end of the run he, too, made a duplicate of his record of the twenty-five calls and sealed one copy in an envelope for Rhine's records before checking his duplicate with Pratt. Thus each one of the men had individual records which they could check independently of the others. In this way, also, any question of the individual good faith of any one of the three was disposed of.

Two runs through the pack were made per day and the total series consisted of 12 runs of 300 trials. The number of hits expected on a theory of pure chance was 20 percent of 300 or 60 hits. Pearce obtained a total of 119 hits or just one short of double the number expected from chance. His average run score was 9.9 hits per 25 or 39.7 percent of the total trials made. A score as large as 119 hits in 300 trials would be expected to occur by chance only once in approximately a quadrillion (1,-000,000,000,000,000) of such experiments. The experimenters were sure, therefore, that every reasonable man would, without further argument, join them in dismissing the chance explanation. Their optimism was magnificent!

There are no known sensory processes that could be supposed to operate under these conditions. No type of rational inference could apply to a case of this kind. They, therefore, could hardly help but decide that, whatever clairvoyance or the extrasensory perception of objects *is*, this was a case of it. It was a case in which results were obtained under the strictest control ever until that time observed.

The report of this Pearce-Pratt experiment initiated what Dr. Rhine calls "what was doubtless the most heated controversy American psychology has ever experienced." The results of the experiment were attacked on the grounds of poor observation, mathematical inadequacy, and even fraud.

But some of the criticism, or hypercriticism, while it might not have applied directly to the Pearce-Pratt experiments, could still be helpful in a general way to all ESP testing. So it was taken very seriously by Drs. Rhine and Pratt and their associates. They made efforts to correct anything to which these complaints might intelligently apply.

For instance, it was pointed out that if the Zener cards were too thin, some persons might be able to read through their backs the symbols on their faces. Against the contingency that this might possibly have been the case, Dr. Rhine immediately saw to it that new decks were made of thicker material.

Another criticism: there was always a possibility that the sender, unknown to himself, might give certain unconscious cues which made the receiver's accurate guessing possible. Involuntary whispering might occur or the sender's facial muscles might contract with the potential that anyone familiar with muscle reading could known which was the key symbol. Though certain sounds emitted by the agent might be far too faint for a guesser in the next room to be consciously aware of, yet they might be of sufficient intensity to register at a subconscious level, it was suggested. It was also insisted that checks be made to see if the sender was unconsciously reacting to a particular symbol by coughing, or tapping his feet.

The problem of inadequate shuffling of the cards was a more intelligent point. It was suggested that during repeated shufflings by hand it might be possible for several cards to stick together. So hand shuffling was discontinued altogether and shuffling machines were substituted. Special cuts were also concocted to eliminate any possibility of interference from the mind of the subject, in case such might be occurring. In many tests now performed a table of random numbers is used to prepare the deck so that each symbol is bound to be in a scientifically haphazard position.

There were also accusations that errors in recording must have been made in order to account for the greater-than-chance results. To check this, numerous re-evaluations were made of a great many previously scored tests. In one exhaustive recheck of 500,000 card matchings, only 90 mistakes were found. Seventy-six of those turned out to be hits which had not been recorded! It is now accepted from many rechecks of both successful and unsuccessful data, that no errors in checking were sufficient to affect results significantly.

To counteract the assumption that his mathematics might be wrong, Dr. Rhine called in the American Institute of Mathematical Statistics for an appraisal of his conclusions. Their reply, after a thorough checking of the procedures used at Duke, was: "On the statistical side recent mathematical work has established the fact that, assuming that the experiments have been properly performed, the statistical analysis is essentially valid. If the Rhine investigation is to be fairly attacked, it must be on other than mathematical grounds."

While spending years giving careful consideration to all the criticism of their previous work, Drs. Rhine and Pratt were at the same time conducting numerous experiments to see if results above chance could still be obtained when safeguards were set up against all counter-hypotheses that had been suggested. They could.

One of the most striking of these new tests was the Pratt-Woodruff series carried out in 1939. This experiment was designed to meet all the criticisms that had flourished during the years of controversy. It was carried out with more controls against all possible error than any other experiment which had ever been devised. I won't go into detail about how this was conducted, but the results were that in 2,400 runs through the pack of cards there were 489 hits above the number to be expected by chance. The likelihood that this could occur by chance is around one in a million.

Right after the publication of Rhine's book in 1934, psychical researchers had all been exuberant. But it was then found that others could not duplicate the amazing achievements of Rhine and Pratt. The English parapsychologists, particularly, became very discouraged after running numerous series of tests and always coming out with chance results. Eventually however, G. N. M. Tyrrell, a former radio engineer who had deserted electronics for the challenge of this new field of interest, was able to produce the same kind of well-founded results that distinguished Rhine's work. And his personality and techniques threw light on Rhine's accomplishments as well as his own, for Tyrrell had the same rare combination of qualities needed for dealing with so elusive a trait as ESP, hidden as it is in the subconscious. Tyrrell possessed not only scientific training but also a sympathetic approach which never impeded a subject who might be hesitant and doubtful of his extrasensory powers. In addition he had the ability to make a general conception from apparently unrelated particulars. After the report of Tyrrell's test was published, parapsychologists realized that it was also these qualities in Rhine that were largely responsible for his achievements.

Tyrrell was keenly aware of a fact that most researchers, intent on making their experimental conditions as like as possible to those of the physical sciences, had tended to forget; physical conditions are not the only ones operative in ESP. Psychological conditions, he told his fellow experimenters with some emphasis, were equally important. The reason they were surprised at being unable to duplicate Rhine's successes was their own *a priori* conception of ESP. They assumed it to be a fixed characteristic possessed by A, but not by B, and one which could always be revealed by a simple test with a pack of cards. But they were wrong. That so many percent of Dr. Rhine's subjects scored high did not imply that the same percentage would so anywhere, in any conditions. The experimenter's task, said Tyrrell, is to remove the subject's inhibitions—to induce the faculty to work—to get the extrasensory material externalized. This needs personal influence.

Tyrrell's first successor to achieve fruitful results was W. Whately Carington, who devised a system of testing for ESP which used statistical methods of assessment with pictures of objects instead of the monotonous ESP cards.

His procedure was simple enough. At 7:00 on ten successive evenings, he would hang up one of a series of ten drawings in his study. Each drawing depicted a single target object which had been chosen at random. They remained there with the door locked until 9:30 the next morning. Between those hours his subjects—he had 251 of them, all living at a distance—were asked to draw what they imagined the target object to be. This series of ten constituted one experiment. After a gap in time the procedure was repeated. When a group of experiments was over, the shuffled drawings from the whole group were sent to an outside judge for matching up with the shuffled originals.

These experiments with drawings were a marked success, for the hits were significantly more than one would expect from chance. But in addition the experiments gave some clues about ESP which had not previously been suspected. Carington found, for instance, that percipients seemed to pick up ideas more often than visual forms, also that it did not seem to matter whether the target was actually drawn, so long as the agent had thought of it. But the most unexpected relevation was of the existence of "displacement."

Hits on a particular target were naturally most frequent on the night it was drawn. If the target on Monday was a pyramid, most percipients who drew pyramids drew them on Monday. But some people also drew pyramids on Sunday or Tuesday, even sometimes two days before or two days after Monday. This really started Carington to thinking. If hits on a target drawing could occur both before and after that drawing was made, what about card-naming experiments? Maybe similar displacement had occurred in them.

At Carington's urging, Dr. S. G. Soal, who had previously done many unsuccessful tests with the Zener cards, now re-evaluated his results with respect to displacement. He discovered that two of his subjects, Basil Shackleton and Gloria Stewart, had been scoring hits on either the card before or the card following the target. This seemed to have occurred with such regularity that Dr. Soal was encouraged to attempt new tests with these subjects. He took even more extreme precautions than before, but he had remarkable success this time.

In a grand total of 37,100 trials for telepathy, Miss Stewart hit the target card 9,410 times. Chance expectancy for this number of trials was 7,420 hits. Her results showed odds against chance in the neighborhood of 10^{70}-to-1.

Basil Shackleton was also successful in telepathy tests, especially when checked for displacement. He struck the plus-1 card (the one immediately following the target card) 1,101 times in 3,789 trials, which represents odds against chance of 10^{35}-to-1.

Dr. Soal, like Carington, became bored to death with ESP cards. Abandoning the impassive Zener symbols, he substituted cards on which were vividly colored pictures of an elephant, a giraffe, a lion, a pelican, and a zebra. The more photogenic fauna were gratefully received by his subjects. For a long series of tests, the subject's interest declines and ESP declines with it. Then what is known as "psi missing" occurs. At some point along the seemingly interminable runs, the percipient will suddenly start hitting consistently lower than chance expectancy because he is utterly fatigued and bored. This is another indication that ESP exists, and is an unconscious power; for if he consciously tried to miss he couldn't succeed at it any better than he could make successful *hits* by consciously trying to do so.

Other characteristics of ESP have been established by laboratory experiments, such as the fact that time and space have been found to affect psi not at all. In the Pearce-Pratt tests, the two protagonists were 100 yards apart. Further tests were performed in England with subjects as distant as Scotland, Holland, and the United States, and in the United States with subjects in India. The far-away guessers did just as well as those close at hand. Illness was no obstacle to extrasensory perception, and although mental state affected it, physical conditions apparently did not.

Despite all the brilliant, if sporadic, achievements of the laboratory in demonstrating ESP by quantitative experiments, in spite of exhaustive and successful efforts by dedicated workers, the returns have been all too meager. Nevertheless, it can be truthfully said that for all its shortcomings, quantitative testing served its purpose well and thoroughly in establishing investigation of the paranormal as a legitimate scientific pursuit.

However, as has been noted, testing endlessly with cards is a highly boring procedure, because conclusions can be reached only by the assembling of overwhelmingly repetitious numerical data. There are, fortunately, other means which can be used for testing. These are called "Qualitative," and involve the drawing of pictures and other more spontaneous and interesting techniques. As Whately Carington showed in the tests he devised, they can also be controlled and evaluated statistically. And so at the present time the trend in formal experimentation is away from quantitative testing and toward the qualitative.

A simple example of a qualitative test is for me to think very firmly of a picture—say of a hat. You, in another room, trying to capture my thoughts, draw a picture of a hat and so identify it. If we could do anything so successful as this repeatedly, it would seem fairly evident to anyone, wouldn't it, that telepathy on your part is indicated?

A series of tests which gave this kind of interesting evidence was undertaken by the well-known American author, Upton Sinclair, and his wife, Mary Craig Sinclair. After watching a young man's feats of apparent telepathy, Sinclair and his wife had become curious, although they were doubtful of the genuineness of the performance. Mrs. Sinclair decided to resolve her doubts by learning "to do these things myself." In the experiments she attempted, Mrs. Sinclair was the percipient and her husband the agent. On a few occasions her brother-in-law, R. L. Irwin, who lived forty miles away, acted as agent.

The experiments usually followed this uninvolved procedure: The agent would make a set of drawings of fairly simple things—a bird's nest with eggs, a helmet, a tree, a flower—and enclose each one in its own opaque envelope. Then, or later, Mrs. Sinclair would relax on a couch, take the envelopes in hand one at a time, and after she believed that she knew its contents, she would draw them. She spent three years at this kind of testing. Out of 290 drawings, 65 were hits, 155 partial hits, and 70 failures. This is an extremely good rate of success. Upton Sinclair was convinced by it of the existence of telepathy. In his book, *Mental Radio,* he wrote:

> For the past three years I have been watching this work, day by day and night by night, in our home. So at last I can say that I am no longer guessing. . . . Regardless of what anybody can say, there will never again be a doubt in my mind. I KNOW!

DISCUSSION QUESTIONS

1. The author describes the educational background and experience of Dr. and Mrs. Rhine, as well as their relationship to Professor McDougall. Is this a preface to her argument or part of it?
2. The author reports that Hubert Pearce once scored a perfect run of twenty-five hits, then calls that "impressive." Why does she use such a weak adjective to describe a seeming miraculous event?
3. One aim of the Pearce-Pratt experiment was "to set up conditions which would exclude all the factors that could reproduce extrachance scores except ESP." Were all such factors excluded? Can anything other than ESP explain the 1 in 1,000,000,000,000,000 results?
4. What is implicit in the criticism that some of the ESP results could have derived from see-through cards or from muscular cues?
5. The Pratt-Woodruff experiments were designed to answer all early test criticisms, and they produced a 1 in 1,000,000 result. Describe the controls that assured the tests' scientific character?
6. What advantages do these features give to individuals seeking to prove the existence of ESP?

   psychological conditions
   displacement
   psi missing
   qualitative experiments

7. The Upton Sinclair experiments produced 65 hits, 155 partial hits, and 70 failures. Describe a partial hit.
8. Describe a test that you believe would prove the existence of ESP. Would it frustrate the efforts of a clever magician?

Lewis Regenstein
Gene Lyons

WILDLIFE HUNTING:
PRO AND CON

[LETTER FROM LEWIS REGENSTEIN]

Gene Lyons's defense of "sport" hunting ["Politics in the Woods," July] repeats the propaganda of the Hunting Establishment that tells us that hunting is good—even essential—for conservation. Hunters vigorously deny that hunting is, or has been, a threat to endangered species, but the facts are there for anyone willing to examine them. It is thoroughly documented that over the years hunters have been reposnsible for helping wipe out numerous species of American wildlife, such as the heath hen, the Eastern elk, the passenger pigeon, the Merriam elk, the Carolina parakeet, the ivory-billed woodpecker, the Eskimo curlew, and the Badlands bighorn. Hunting by man—for sport or profit—has been a major factor in the decline of many of the birds and mammals that are today considered endangered or threatened, such as the grizzly bear, the whooping crane, the leopard, the jaguar, the Key deer, and the Mexican

Reprinted from *Harper's*, September 1978, pp. 184–186. Regenstein letter reprinted by permission of author. Lyons' letter copyright © 1978 by *Harper's Magazine*. All rights reserved. Reprinted by special permission.

duck. After two years of extensive hearings the Senate Commerce Committee in mid-1973 issued a report recommending new legislation to protect endangered species. It stated that "the two major causes of extinction are hunting and destruction of habitat."

Countless other animals are threatened by legal, "legitimate" sport hunting. Today, hunting is threatening the future existence of such animals as the grizzly bear, the bobcat, the bighorn sheep, the leopard, the jaguar, and the mountain lion.

Hunters consistently claim that deer herds must be "culled" to prevent overpopulation and starvation. But these winter die-off situations arise to some extent every year *whether or not there is hunting;* it is nature's way of eliminating the sick, the weak, and the very old animals. In any event, winter die-offs are often brought about and made worse by hunter-run state fish and game departments propagating and "managing for" deer in so-called wildlife restoration programs.

The main reason some areas temporarily end up with more deer than the habitat can support is that wildlife management officials deliberately try to create a "surplus" of deer—through stocking programs and manipulation of habitat—in order to stimulate a demand for, and sell, a maximum number of hunting licenses, their main source of revenue. It is simply untrue that deer, when left alone, always overpopulate and starve to death.

The argument that animals *need* to be culled for their own good is a central tenet of wildlife management and *the* primary justification of, and rationale for, hunting. But this theory has, over the years, been shown to be invalid. Moreover, it in no way justifies the hunting of predators, such as wolves and cougars, that *do* help keep deer herds from overpopulating.

Such specious propaganda was clearly debunked in the widely publicized 1971 controversy over whether or not to allow a deer hunt at the Great Swamp (New Jersey) National Wildlife Refuge. Hunters, wildlife "management" officials, and "game bioloists" all claimed that if the hunt were not held, the long-protected and "overly large" deer population would suffer a massive die-off from starvation. This specious argument is repeated by Mr. Lyons in his misleading account of the Great Swamp situation. But when a lawsuit by conservationists halted the hunt, the deer made it through the winter just fine, and in fact got along well for the next several years. When the hunt was finally held years later, there had been no massive die-off as predicted, *none* of the deer "taken" was starving, and observers at the scene described them as looking fat and healthy. (Despite all this, the U.S. Department of the Interior has now made the hunt an annual event.) Moreover, animals in national parks—where there is no hunting or trapping—generally get along just fine without being subjected to periodic slaughter. Sometimes it appears that the greatest threat to the hunting ethic is an unhunted, unmanaged, healthy deer herd.

What is not in dispute about deer hunting is that few if any hunters seek out the starving deer, the one that won't make it through the winter. Most want to kill the largest and strongest member of the herd, the 12-point buck whose antlers will look best on his wall, the one the species needs most to survive and evolve. By repeatedly removing the best of the breeding population, be it a bear, an elephant, or a bighorn sheep, the hunter upsets nature's law of natural selection and survival of the fittest. It is possible that killing off the bravest, most aggressive animals—the ones the hunter is most likely to encounter or be challenged by—while leaving the timid, secretive ones, can, over time, change the very nature of a species.

Is waterfowl hunting any better than shooting mammals? The U.S. Department of the Interior estimates that some 2.5 million ducks are crippled each year by hunters, not counting the millions more hit but less seriously wounded by buckshot. Nor does the carnage end when the hunter leaves the field. Each season, according to Interior, an estimated 2–3 million waterfowl die a slow and painful death from poisoning by lead buckshot, which builds up in marsh bottoms and is ingested by feeding ducks.

Does hunting finance conservation? It is true that hunting has raised substantial revenues for conservation and wildlife-management programs. But far too much of this money goes to pay for such things as propagating deer and manipulating habitat, salaries for hunting-dominated fish and game bureaucrats and such nonconservation-related activities as hunting-safety programs.

And we hear so often of the "success" of such "conservation programs" as reintroducing pheasant and wild turkey to an area, but we seldom hear that such programs often involve killing off the local predators—foxes, coyotes, raccoons, and any pet dogs or cats that happen along—by poisoning, trapping, and shooting, in order to guarantee the propagation of the introduced "game"species.

Further, consider the remarks of Sandra Oddo of Hurley, New York, published in the July, 1975, issue of *Smithsonian* magazine; this is more or less typical of what happens to many inhabitants of rural and suburban areas during the deer season:

> We live in a house surrounded by woods, our property bounded on one side by a hunt club and within a mile of state land where organized hunting is permitted. We have bullet holes in our windows. Our children are not allowed to play outside during hunting season. When they visit friends, they are taken by car. Ours is red.
>
> The toll from six families along a mile-long stretch of road has been twelve cats, five dogs, and a pony during the last five hunting seasons.

The gun lobby is constantly talking about the "rights" of hunters. But what about the rights of farmers, homeowners, and ordinary people who would just like to take a walk in the woods or take their family on a picnic without outfitting them in helmets and bulletproof vests? If there are some 16 million Americans who hunt, then there are some 200 million who do not—and these people, representing 90 percent of the population, are demanding a greater voice in what happens to our wildlife heritage.

LEWIS REGENSTEIN
Executive Vice-President
The Fund for Animals
Washington, D.C.

[RESPONSE BY GENE LYONS]

My apologies to Cleveland Amory, who, as several readers have pointed out, is president not of Friends of Animals, but of The Fund for Animals. The mistake was due to a simple error in copying from my notes.

Had I ghostwritten it myself, I could not have produced a document more supportive of the central point of my article than Mr. Regenstein's letter. That point was the antihunting zealots and the Bolinas ideologues of "zero growth" are joined in a puritanical wish to rid themselves of the ambiguities of an imperfect world.

Mr. Regenstein, for example, reverses as "nature's way" the starvation of deer, but cannot abide death or pain inflicted upon the same animals by individual human action. He contrives to avoid the fact that *all* food comes from living tissue and requires the "slaughter" of same. Old MacDonald, after all, retired some time ago. In his place are production-line techniques in which animals are not only killed and butchered in very much the same way automobiles are assembled, but are raised in conditions not far removed. A friend of mine regularly challenges his more strident acquaintances to accompany him on a hunting trip and to a slaughterhouse. He has never had any takers.

Regenstein's melodramatic view of benign nature and wicked man forces him to reject facts as nonexistent and scientific findings as corrupt when they do not accord with his preconceived positions. Note that he neither produces nor even alludes to a shred of scientific evidence supporting his assertion that deer do not overpopulate. The matter of the Great Swamp deer is a case in point: starvation and disease infestation caused by weakness and overcrowding were documented by wildlife biologists and pathologists (from the New York Department of Environmental Conservation's Wildlife Research Lab in cooperation with the New Jersey Division of Fish, Game, and Shell Fisheries) on the scene. For their findings, which are readily available,* Regenstein would substitue the impressions of "observers," most of whom arrived carrying signs. Neither does he consider that the hunt was conducted in the fall, when deer are as fat as they are ever going to be. The University of Connecticut study was conducted in late winter. There are no large predators in the Great Swamp save the suburban dog; nor do any exist in North America that could survive on just 6,000 acres surrounded by suburbs. The Point Reyes situation, involving, as it does, exotics, is in many ways unique. But both cases are noteworthy not because they are unusual, but because they are examples of exactly what would happen were sport hunting to be widely abolished. Virtually all of North America south of the Arctic Circle is what the Sierra Club calls a "degraded ecosystem," i.e., one in which human activity has altered habitat sufficiently to render nature's mythic "balance" a sentimental memory. Unlike their natural "enemies" among predators, deer thrive upon agriculture and logging.

I am almost embarrassed at having to make so elementary a point, but "nature's way" in not always the best way. One of nature's ways of coping with human overcrowding, after all, was the bubonic plague. This is not to beg the question of human reponsibility to animals we find useful or aesthetically pleasing (I assume Regenstein has no objection to the slaughter of rats), but rather to insist upon it. According to the National Wildlife Federation, the Eastern elk, passenger pigeon, Merriam elk, Carolina parakeet, and Badlands bighorn—species Regenstein lists as having been made extinct by hunters—were extinguished by the first decade of this century, most of them by a combination of market hunting and the destruction of habitat. All quite before wildlife conservation or hunter licensing were even thought of. Both hunter organizations and groups such as the National Wildlife Federation, the Audubon Society, and the Sierra Club (my criticism of which was directed only at the San Francisco Bay Area Chapter) keep a close and informed watch on matters involving the well-being of both game and nongame species, and debate the relative ethics of aspects of the hunt such as the seeking of trophy heads and the killing of predators. Even so, there is no cause for moral absolutism or undue alarm. Men have been seeking trophy stags since the dawn of history without real effect upon truly wild populations. Twelve-point bucks get so big not by being bold and aggressive, but by being cunning and wary. By the time big bucks are taken they are near the end of their natual lives in any case, and will have fathered hundreds of descendants. One of the problems facing wildlife managers, in fact, is perusading hunters to take does in order to keep herds at supportable levels. The problem of lead pollution in areas of heavy duck hunting has

* See the article by Douglas Roscoe et al. in the *Journal of Wildlife Diseases*, January, 1975.

been addressed, as I suspect Regenstein knows, by the Fish and Wildlife Service of the Department of the Interior, which requires steel shot.

Nobody, as I wrote to begin with, defends brutality, piggishness, poaching, and the reckless shooting indulged in by an oafish minority of fools. That is why I am bewildered at Regenstein's hostility to spending money generated by license fees on hunter education and regulation. Finally, if 90 percent of the population does not hunt, organizations opposed to hunting should have no difficulty at all in having their point of view written into law.

DISCUSSION QUESTIONS

1. Mr. Regenstein protests that hunters have contributed to the extinction or the near extinction of the heath hen, the Eastern elk, the passenger pigeon, the Merriam elk, the Carolina parakeet, the ivory-billed woodpecker, the Eskimo curlew, the Badlands bighorn, the grizzly bear, the whooping crane, the leopard, the jaguar, the Key deer, the Mexican duck, the bobcat, and the mountain lion. How does Mr. Lyons answer this charge?

2. Mr. Regenstein denies that deer need to be hunted to avoid overcrowding and starvation, and cites the canceled Great Swamp hunt as evidence that unhunted deer survived "looking fat and healthy." How does Mr. Lyons answer this claim?

3. Mr. Regenstein deplores the kind of indiscriminate shooting that "is more or less typical of what happens to many inhabitants of rural and suburban areas during the deer season." He champions the "rights of farmers, homeowners, and ordinary people who would just like to take a walk in the woods or take their family on a picnic." Is Mr. Lyons concerned about the rights of these people?

4. Mr. Regenstein speaks of "slaughter" and "carnage"; Mr. Lyons, of "antihunting zealots" and their "puritanical" and "melodramatic" views. Is such language necessary to their arguments? Which is more given to this kind of emotional language?

5. Mr. Lyons asserts that shooting in the woods is more humane than the butchering that regularly goes on in slaughterhouses. Is this an effective argument for hunting?

6. Mr. Lyons concludes: "Finally, if 90 percent of the population does not hunt, organizations opposed to hunting should have no difficulty at all in having their point of view written into law." Is he suggesting that 90 percent of the population does not oppose hunting? Or is he boasting that it would do them no good if they did?

David Abrahamsen, M.D.

NIXON:

Childhood and Formative Years

When Frank Nixon moved his family from Yorba Linda in 1922 after his lemon ranch failed, he settled in East Whittier with Hannah and their children. Times were hard. To make a living Frank started a gasoline station at Whittier Boulevard and Santa Gertrudes Avenue, and, in addition, Hannah began a small grocery store in the same place.[*][1] To start the family business he had to choose between two pieces of property, and settled for the smaller one. Ironically, oil was discovered soon afterward on the other property in Santa Fe Springs. Suspecting that there might be oil on Frank Nixon's property too, a speculator offered a considerable price for it; but Frank, who also thought that his land might contain oil, refused to sell. Characteristically, he never found oil. He followed the pattern of failure that had predominated in his family.

[*] Other versions have it that at first Frank sold bread and milk from his refrigerator as well as gasoline. As the demand for other foods rose, he added to his supplies, and thus began the grocery store.

Reprinted from *Nixon vs. Nixon: An Emotional Tragedy* by David Abrahamsen, M.D. Copyright © 1976, 1977, 1978 by David Abrahamsen. Reprinted with the permission of Hill & Wang (now a division of Farrar, Straus & Giroux, Inc.).

The whole family had to work hard to survive, particularly Hannah, who "repaired and pressed the clothes for the whole family, worked in the store during the day, and at night thriftily emptied the shelves of fruit that might spoil in another day and baked it into pies, which she put on sale in the morning."[2] Nixon family life was spartan, but not uncommonly so.

> They [the children] were reared to frugality and hard work. There was little time for play. They walked a half mile to school every day. When the children were not busy with school work, there always were jobs to be done about the store and filling station.
>
> "I sold gas and delivered groceries and met a lot of people," Mr. Nixon recalls. "I think this was invaluable as a start on a public career."
>
> Old neighbors remember the boy who was to be President as bookish and withdrawn. He found science and mathematics difficult, so he worked especially hard at these subjects. He practiced the piano dutifully, if unenthusiastically, and later learned the violin too. . . .
>
> Religious training was emphasized. . . . Card playing and dancing were forbidden. Church attendance three times on Sunday and once at midweek were compulsory. Richard once taught a Sunday-school class.[3]

In a household where money was scarce and every member had to make a contribution, Richard was his mother's "best helper." His brothers noted that his most outstanding distinction was as a potato masher. "He never left any lumps," Hannah said. "He used the whipping motion to make them smooth instead of going up and down the way the other boys did."[4]

While this activity is perhaps trivial, it does reveal a significant trait. Even as a child, Richard loved to excel and be recognized. His mother said, "He was the best potato masher one could wish for. . . . Even in these days, when I am visiting Richard and Pat in Washington, or when they visit me, he will take over the potato mashing. My feeling is that he actually enjoys it."* [5]

Richard helped his mother in the store and in the kitchen; he also washed the dishes. Before he would stoop to perform this latter task, however, which he must have thought was girlish, he would draw the blinds very tight so that no one would see him.†

That a boy wouldn't want anyone to see him washing dishes would

---

* Nixon's fascination with potato mashing had psychoanalytic implication. Most children his age release aggression through play, athletics, and peer-group activities. What is unusual in Richard is that he chose to release his energy through potato mashing, which was one way to be close to his mother, to win her love, to be her favorite. The extent and intensity of this activity might suggest that this potato mashing was a form of aggression against an inanimate object which was a substitute for people. Potato mashing allowed this apparently tense and moody child to express his unconscious anger.

† This is known from Earl Mazo, who talked with Richard's mother. James David Barber also refers to it.[6] I have also discussed this point with Mrs. Rose Olive Marshburn.

not be considered unusual. But that his mother noticed his shame would indicate that his discomfort was uncommonly severe. To Richard, washing dishes seemed degrading; "only girls did it." It is possible, but unlikely, that he regarded having to wash dishes as a humiliating proof of their poverty. Richard's status as mother's best helper was one cause for his brothers to tease him. They may have resented him because they felt he was Hannah's favorite. Nixon in turn resented them. As his younger brother Donald said with a great deal of vehemence:

> Dick used his tongue more than his fists. One time he lit into me and gave me a dressing-down I'll never forget. I've forgotten what his beef was, but I had it coming. He didn't just talk about the problem at the moment; he aired all his gripes of the past two or three years.[7]

Nixon used his tongue as a weapon, and he seemed to bear grudges for a long time. He held in his feelings, and he was not to change as he grew older.

Certainly his later relationships with his surviving brothers were distant. Richard's closeness to his mother was deep, and was in all probability heightened by his own daydreams and fantasies. Although some thought him to be her favorite—and he may indeed have been—Nixon's relationship with his mother was at times pathetic. A letter that he wrote to his mother on November 23, 1923, when he was almost eleven, illustrates both their relationship and his fantasy world.

> My dear Master:
>   The two boys that you left with me are very bad to me. Their dog, Jim, is very old and he will never talk or play with me.
>   One Saturday the boys went hunting, Jim and myself went with them. While going through the woods one of the boys triped and fell on me. I lost my temper and bit him. He kiked me in the side and we started on. While we were walking I saw a black round thing in a tree. I hit it with my paw. A swarm of black thing came out of it. I felt pain all over. I started to run and as both my eyes were swelled shut I fell into a pond. When I got home I was very sore. I wish you would come home right now.
>
> *Your good dog*
RICHARD[8]

Nixon's letter is succinct, but his account and his imagery suggest a high level of confusion and despair. Although we do not know whether the incident actually occurred or whether it is a purely imaginary story, the fact that he assumes the role of a dog, not a human being, is highly significant; it shows a strong sense of fantasy. The action he describes is significant: "I lost my temper and bit him." Not only does biting indicate emotional instability; it also expresses an oral drive—his mouth is a weapon to inflict punishment.

From a psychoanalytic point of view, this letter is highly revealing.

Biting at the age of ten or eleven is rare; usually it occurs during the first, the oral, period, which lasts until a child is about one year old (and may in certain abnormal circumstances continue until perhaps the age of four or five).

Biting is one of the most primitive responses we have. It is an animal reaction and belongs to the earliest stage of human development. In young Richard's mind, it was the only recourse for dealing with an adversary. During the latency period of childhood (from seven to twelve years) the practice of biting will normally disappear, though it may appear again in puberty or adolescence as an expression of oral hostility and aggression. That Richard wrote that he bit one of the boys at an age when a child would normally have passed through this stage long before, reinforces our impression that the oral hostile aggression Richard harbored as an infant had been prolonged beyond the norm and had become fixated. The degree to which he regressed into a fantasy is abnormal.

We can surmise therefore that the details were not incidental: they reflect an instinctive response which stayed with him long after he had learned that biting was not socially acceptable. Expressions of this kind of response appear in his adult behavior. In his political life, Nixon was often vindictive and revengeful. He was sarcastic, cutting, and caustic. His mother, too, had a "dreaded tongue," and Richard had learned how to use his mouth to express his biting power.*

Returning to his curious letter, we are struck by the final sentence—"I wish you would come home right now." It is a cry for help—a pitiful and despairing wish that his mother would come to console him and soothe his hurt feelings. He feels alone, rejected, surrounded by a threatening world, with someone described as "very old" who "will never talk or play with me." Clearly, this pathetic letter, filled with self-pity and hurt, pictures a hostile world against which he feels vulnerable.

The "very old" Jim he mentions may be his father, who never talks or plays with him and whose name he is obviously afraid to use. If it is, he felt threatened and wanted another father.

We must also note his description of "a black round thing in a tree" which "I hit . . . with my paw." Then "a swarm of black thing came out of it." They stung, and he was blinded and ran and fell into a pond. We suspect he is referring to wasps or bees, which are not black, although they may seem so to a frightened child. Richard became so surprised and shocked when the insects flew toward him that they appeared to be black. Black connotes a sense of evil or, more fundamentally, danger,

---

* The bite impressed itself deeply upon Richard. We can say that he took the bite in, incorporated it into himself. To take in (or be taken in) gives a feeling of cheating, capturing by trickery or by surprise—a behavior which Richard later on repeatedly exhibited. This is a psychological defense mechanism which we often enounter in psychoanalysis.

death. Not only did he run away, but his emotions—his fears and anxieties—also ran away with him.

The story he relates must be taken seriously because it mirrors his state of mind as a child. His account reveals fantasies of depression and loneliness, which draw us closer to the inner Nixon.

Although we don't know, of course, whether Hannah was actually away at this time, we do know that in 1923 Arthur was five years old and may already have been ill and needed the full-time attention of his mother. Richard felt her absence acutely.

He subserviently addresses the letter to "My Dear Master," indicating that he regarded her as his master and guide, the person who controlled him and to whom he owed his loyalty. Without her, he seems to be lost and vulnerable to attack from a hostile world. The person who was closest to him had "left" him. It was an early feeling of betrayal, a feeling which later grew in him as he became more prominent.

The fact that Richard closes his letter with "Your good dog" shows a sense of fidelity and subservience and a lack of self-esteem. But it also suggests an indictment. Why had he, who had worked hard and had obeyed his mother, been deserted? Richard looked upon himself as a victim in a cruel and heartless world. He had always believed in his mother, and had always thought she was right, but how could she desert him when he was being attacked by other boys and by a swarm of bees? When he sat down to write this letter, he was filled with anger and dejection. His letter, which may reflect a real or imaginary fight with his brothers, may also have been a way Richard released his anger against his mother (and father), who had forsaken him.

Young Richard Nixon not only thought of himself as a victim; he was also concerned that he would become seriously ill. Frank surely had told him years before about the death of his mother, Sarah Ann. His illnesses and accidents may have had a psychosomatic root, suggesting an unconscious need to attract his mother's attention.

Notes

1. *Los Angeles Times*, October 1, 1967.
2. *Time*, August 25, 1952, p. 13.
3. "The New President: Richard M. Nixon," *U.S. NEWS & World Report* (article prepared but not printed, July 4, 1958), p. 2.
4. Earl Mazo, *Richard Nixon: A Political and Personal Portrait* (New York: Harper & Brothers, 1959), p. 16.
5. James David Barber, *The Presidential Character: Predicting Performance in the White House* (Englewood Cliffs, N.J.: Prentice-Hall, 1972), p. 400.
6. *Ibid.*, p. 402.
7. Bela Kornitzer, *The Real Nixon: An Intimate Biography* (Chicago: Rand McNally & Company, 1960), p. 50.

8. Barber, *The Presidential Character*, p. 401; originally cited by Kornitzer, *The Real Nixon*, p. 57.

DISCUSSION QUESTIONS

1. What insights does the author draw from the fact that Nixon was an outstanding potato masher? From the fact that he closed the blinds very tight before washing dishes? (How does one close blinds "very tight"?)
2. Mashing potatoes well and fearing that washing dishes would appear unmanly—are these abnormal acts? Are they even unusual acts?
3. "Dick used his tongue more than his fists. One time he lit into me and gave me a dressing-down I'll never forget. I've forgotten what his beef was, but I had it coming." Donald Nixon, according to the author, said this "with a great deal of vehemence." Do the lines sound vehement to you?
4. Most of the essay analyzes the eleven-year-old Nixon's letter to his mother, in which he pretended to be a dog. If you didn't know it came from ex-President Richard Nixon, would you say the letter revealed "confusion and despair" or "hostility and aggression"?
5. What psychological conclusions does the author draw from these features of the letter:

   the boy pretends to be a dog

   he bit a boy who fell on him

   he does not mention his father's name

   he was stung by black bees

   he misses "his master"

   Are these conclusions inescapable?
6. How would Occam's razor interpret the letter?
7. What inevitable weaknesses attend psychohistory?

Robert A. Harper, Ph.D.

YOU FEEL THE WAY YOU THINK

"What you say, Dr. Harper, seems on the surface plausible and sensible. And it would delight me if people actually worked as simply as you indicate they do! But, frankly, what you and Dr. Ellis call your theory of rational therapy sounds to me, when you probe a little into it, very superficial, antipsychoanalytic, and like a few pages out of the how-to-lift-yourself-by-your-bootstraps school of slick magazine psychology."

The speaker, Dr. B., attended my lecture to a group of educators to whom I had set out to describe the tenets of rational-emotive therapy. And his views had some truth. Some of our ideas of RET *do* sound superficial. And they definitely oppose the views of orthodox psychoanalysis—though they overlap with the teachings of Alfred Adler, Karen Horney, Harry Stack Sullivan, Erich Fromm, Eric Berne, and the psychoanalysts who stress "ego psychology."

Still, I couldn't help taking my heckler somewhat to task—not be-

Reprinted from *A New Guide to Rational Living* by Albert Ellis and Robert A. Harper (North Hollywood, Calif.: Wilshire Book Company, 1978), pp. 8–12.

cause I thought I could change his mind, for who can unfreeze the preju-dices of a trained psychotherapist?—and not because I itched to put him in his place (for the luxury of venting one's spleen on others holds, as we shall show later in this book, little reward for the rationally inclined per-son), but because I thought that his objections might demonstrate one of the main principles of RET for the rest of my audience.

"You presumably object," I said, "to our view that human feelings significantly overlap with thoughts, and you believe that they cannot get changed, as I have just said they could, mainly by changing one's think-ing. Do I grasp your main point?"

"Yes. We have fifty or a hundred years' history of experimental and clinical findings that prove otherwise."

"Perhaps so. But suppose we forget this hundred years of history for a moment and concentrate on the history of the last few moments. Just a short while ago, as I gave my talk on RET, you experienced some intense feelings, did you not?"

"I certainly did! I felt that you acted idiotically and should not go on spouting such nonsense."

"Fine," I said, as the rest of my audience gleefully howled. "But you also," I persisted, "had another emotion, just before you stood up to speak against me, did you not?"

"I did? What kind of an emotion do you mean?"

"Well, I would say that judging from the high and uneven pitch of your voice as you just spoke, you had at least a little bit of anxiety about getting up among your peers here and voicing your anti-Harperian opin-ion. Do I judge incorrectly about this?"

"Uh . . ." My antagonist hesitated for several long seconds (while the knowing smiles of the members of the audience changed in my favor). "No—. I guess you don't judge totally incorrectly. I did have some anxiety just before speaking and during the first part of my words; though I don't have it now."

"All right. Just as I imagined, then. You had two emotions while I spoke: anger and anxiety. And now, at this present moment, you seem to have neither? Correct?"

"Definitely. I no longer feel anxious or angry—though perhaps I feel a little pity for you for still holding to an untenable position." Touché! Again the smiles backed him.

"Good. Maybe we'll examine the feeling of pity for me a little later. But let's, for a moment, get back to the anxiety and anger. Do I wrongly assume that behind your anger lay some chain of sentences such as: 'That idiot, Harper—along with that other nincompoop colleague of his, Ellis—mouths utter hogwash! They ought to outlaw his boring us to tears with this kind of stuff at an otherwise high scientific meeting?'"

"Precisely! How did you guess?" Again the chorus of snickers pretty solidly supported him. I continued:

"My clinical intuition! Anyway, you did have such a thought, and by it you made yourself angry. Our thesis in rational therapy holds just that: From your thought—'Dr. Harper not only mouths hogwash but he *shouldn't* do so'—comes the real source of your anger. Moreover, we believe that you do not, at this present moment, still feel angry, because you have replaced the original thought with quite a different one, namely: 'Oh, well, if Dr. Harper wrongly believes this nonsense, and if the poor fellow wants to keep believing it, let him have this problem.' And this new thought, Dr. Ellis and I would contend, lies at the heart of your present state of feeling, which you accurately describe, I think, as 'pity.' "

Before my opponent could say anything further, another member of the audience interjected: "Suppose you rightly see the origins of Dr. B.'s feelings of anger and now pity. What about his anxiety?"

"According, again, to the theories of rational-emotive psychology," I replied, " his anxiety occurred as follows. As I spoke, and as he incited himself to anger by telling himself how badly I behaved—and *should* not behave—Dr. B. also said to himself something along these lines: 'Just wait till Harper stops talking! Boy, have I something to say that will show everyone how idiotically he acts (and how cleverly I come across for showing him up before everyone!). Let me see, now, how shall I squelch him, when I get the chance?'

"And then, I further suggest, Dr. B. tested several opening sentences in his mind, rejected some of them quickly, thought others might do, and kept looking for still better ones with which to annihilate my views. Not only, however, did he try to discover the best set of phrases and sentences he could use against me, but he also kept saying to himself: 'What will the other members of the group think? Will they think I act just as foolishly as Harper? Will he sway them by his charm? Will they think I feel jealous of his and Ellis's success with clients and with their writings? Will it *really* do me any good to open my big mouth against him?' "

"These self-created sentences of Dr. B's, I hypothesize, caused him to feel anxious. True, Dr. B.?"

"Not entirely wrong," my opponent acquiesced, with more than a shade of embarrassed redness of his face and nearly bald pate. "But doesn't everyone, do not all of us, say things to ourselves like this before we get up to talk about almost anything in public?"

"We most certainly do," I heartily agreed. "And, believe me, I use your internalized beliefs as an example here only because they illustrate what virtually all of us do. But that precisely covers my main point: that exactly because we keep telling ourselves these kinds of sentences, we feel anxious before speaking in public. Because we tell ourselves (a) 'I might make a mistake and fall on my face before this group of my peers' and, much more importantly, tell ourselves (b) 'And I have to think it *awful* if I do make a mistake and fall on my face in public.'

"Precisely because we tell ourselves these catastrophizing sentences, we almost immediately begin to *feel* anxious. Otherwise, if we told ourselves only sentence (a) and instead of (b), said to ourselves quite a different sentence, which we might call (b̄), namely, 'Too bad! If I make a mistake and fall on my face, I won't think it great, but I still don't have to view it as *awful*'—if we told ourselves *this* at (b̄), we would practically never feel anxious."

"But suppose," asked the same educator who had asked about Dr. B.'s anxiety, "you correctly see, Dr. Harper, how B. created his anxiety. How do you explain its later disappearance, in terms of your theory of RET?"

"Very simply again. Having screwed up sufficient courage to speak in spite of his self-created anxiety, Dr. B. found that even though he did partly fall on his face, the world did *not* come to an end, and no actual horror occurred. At worst, he found that I kept standing up to his assault and that some of the members of the audience remained on my side, although perhaps some also sided with him. So he changed his internalized beliefs to something like:

" 'Oh, well. Harper still doesn't really get my point and see his errors. And several others still side with him. Too damned bad! You can always fool some of the people, and I just can't expect anything different. I'll just bide my time, continue to present my view, and even if I don't win everyone over, I can still hold it myself.'

"With these new, anti-awfulizing beliefs, Dr. B. has dispelled the anxiety he previously caused himself and now feels, as he again has probably accurately reported, more pitying than angry. Correct?"

My opponent again hesitated a moment; then replied, "I can only repeat that you may prove partially right. But I still don't feel entirely convinced."

"Nor did I expect that you would. I just wanted to use your own example to induce you to give this matter some additional thought, and to encourage the members of this audience to do likewise. Maybe rational psychotherapy has, as you say, superficiality and slickness. I only ask that you professionals give it an honest try to see for yourself whether it really works."

As far as I know, I have not yet convinced my heckler of the soundness of my position. But several other members of my audience now enthusiastically see that human emotions do *not* magically exist in their own right, and do *not* mysteriously flow from unconscious needs and desires. Rather, they almost always directly stem from ideas, thought, attitudes, or beliefs, and can usually get radically changed by modifying our thinking processes.

When we first began thinking and writing about rational-emotive therapy, in the latter half of the 1950's, we could cite little research material to back up the idea that humans do not *get* upset, but that they *upset themselves* by devoutly convincing themselves, at point B, of irrational beliefs about what happens to them (the Activating Events or Activating Experiences of their lives) at point A. The field of cognitive psychology, then in its formative stages, only included rare psychologists, such as Magda Arnold, who viewed emotions as linked with thinking. Since that time, hundreds of experiments have clearly demonstrated that if an experimenter induces, by fair means or foul, individuals to change their thoughts, they also profoundly change their emoting and behaving. Evidence that we feel the way we think keeps accumulating, steadily reaffirmed by the work of many experimenters, including Rudolf Arnheim, Richard S. Lazarus, Donald Meichenbaum, Stanley Schachter, and numerous others.

All of which brings us back to the paramount thesis of this book: namely, that people can live the most self-fulfilling, creative, and emotionally satisfying lives by disciplining their thinking. All the pages that follow will, in one way or another, bear testimony to this central rational-emotive view.

DISCUSSION QUESTIONS

1. The author writes of a dispute that occurred between him and a Dr. B. What advantages exist for the spokesman who writes both sides of an argument?
2. RET concepts "definitely oppose the views of orthodox psychoanalysis." What are these views? What does orthodox psychoanalysis say causes individuals to experience unpleasant and counterproductive emotions?
3. The author argues that negative emotions derive from wrong thinking. Show the a→b sequence he uses to illustrate this.
4. The author demonstrates his thesis by showing the process that produced Dr. B's distress.

    What wrong thoughts led to Dr. B's anger?

    What wrong thoughts led to his anxiety?

    What right thoughts eventually relieved him of these negative emotions?

5. What might a trained psychoanalyst believe led to Dr. B's anger and anxiety?
6. Why do people continue to have counterproductive feelings and activities when all they need to improve themselves is to discipline their thinking?
7. Why does the author mention that RET ideas overlap with the teachings of Alfred Adler, Karen Horney, Harry Stack Sullivan, Erich Fromm,

Erich Berne, and the psychoanalysts who stress "ego psychology."
Why does he mention the experimental work affirming his position
done by Rudolf Arnheim, Richard S. Lazarus, Donald Meichenbaum,
Stanley Schacter, and "numerous others"?

Deduction

All men are Socrates
—Woody Allen

Deduction is the opposite of induction. While induction moves from specific facts to a general conclusion, deduction moves from a general statement to a specific application. Because there are many kinds of deduction—some quite complicated—this discussion aims to be little more than a useful oversimplification.

The vehicle of deduction is the syllogism. This is an argument that takes two existing truths and puts them together to produce a new truth. Here is the classical example:

MAJOR PREMISE: All men are mortal.
MINOR PREMISE: Socrates is a man.
CONCLUSION: Socrates is mortal.

In everyday affairs, you meet many examples of deductive thinking. The syllogism is often abbreviated, however, with one of the parts implied rather than stated:

You haven't registered, so you can't vote. (IMPLICIT MAJOR PREMISE: Anyone who does not register cannot vote.)
No man lives forever. Even old Bob Peterson will die someday. (IMPLICIT MINOR PREMISE: Bob Peterson is a man.)
Anyone can make a mistake. After all, Roger is only human. (IMPLICIT CONCLUSION: Roger can make a mistake.)

Many informal arguments can easily be resolved into syllogistic form. You do this so that you can judge their reliability more systematically.

A deductive argument is considered reliable if it fulfills three conditions: (1) the premises must be true, (2) the terms must be unambiguous, and (3) the syllogistic form must be valid. These requirements will be considered in turn.

ARE THE PREMISES TRUE?

First, the premises must be true. Because the major premise of a syllogism is usually derived by induction (that is, it is a general statement drawn from specific facts), you can judge its reliability by asking whether the facts that produced it are known to be sufficient and representative. Here is a vulnerable example:

> Gentlemen prefer blondes.
> Walter Mondale is a gentleman.
> Walter Mondale prefers blondes.

This syllogism reaches an unreliable conclusion because the major premise is doubtful. The generalization about blondes exists only as a cliché (and as a title by Anita Loos); it is induced from no known sample. Political spokesmen regularly use dubious major premises (a war hero would make a good President; a divorced man would make a poor one; etc.) to produce desired conclusions.

IS THE LANGUAGE UNAMBIGUOUS?

The terms of deductive argument must be clear and consistent. If definitions change within a syllogism, arguments can be amusingly fallacious:

> All cats chase mice.
> My wife is a cat.
> Therefore . . .

> All men are created equal.
> Women are not men.
> Therefore . . .

But sometimes they can be genuinely misleading. The advertisement "See *King Kong*—the Academy Award Winner" is based on this syllogism:

> The Academy Award winning movie is worth seeing.
> *King Kong* is this year's Academy Award winning movie.
> *King Kong* is worth seeing.

Here the term "Academy Award winning movie" is ambiguous. In the major premise it refers to the movie chosen the best of the year; in the minor premise, to a movie winning one of the many minor awards given annually. *King Kong* won its award for "Special Effects."

Ambiguous syllogisms are not always frivolous. A major argument of our time is based on this deduction:

Killing an innocent human being is murder.
Abortion kills an innocent human being.
Abortion is murder.

Not all ambiguities are easily resolved.

IS THE SYLLOGISM VALID?

A reliable syllogism must have a valid form. This requirement introduces a complex area because there are many types of syllogisms, each with its own test for validity. Commonly, "valid form" means that the general subject or condition of the major premise must appear in the minor premise as well. It is easy to see that this argument is false:

All murderers have ears.
All Baptists have ears.
All Baptists are murderers.

But what makes the argument reliable syllogistically is that the term "murderers" does not recur in the minor premise. A major premise about "all murderers" can only lead to a conclusion about murderers. Similarly, the premises "If Taylor loses his job, his wife will leave him" and "Taylor does not lose his job" produce no necessary conclusion. The condition "lose his job" does not appear in the minor premise.

When an invalid syllogism appears as argument, it usually maintains that features with one quality in common have a kind of identity. Such argument is not uncommon:

The father of Miss Smith's baby has blood type O.
Charles Harwell has blood type O.
Therefore . . .

The American Communist Party opposes loyalty oaths.
Gene Knepprath opposes loyalty oaths.
Therefore . . .

Abraham Lincoln was a much-attacked President.
Richard Nixon was a much-attacked President.
Therefore . . .

Because the crucial term does not appear in both premises of these syllogisms, any conclusions would be no more valid than the claim that all Baptists are murderers.

These three tests, then, permit you to judge the reliability of a deductive argument.

INDUCTION OR DEDUCTION?

Because most syllogisms begin with an induced major premise, certain arguments can be analyzed as either induction or deduction. Here is an example: "Mike Hiers doesn't drink; he'll make some girl a fine husband." You can read this as a syllogism and attack the implicit major premise "Anyone who doesn't drink will make a fine husband." Or you can treat it as induction and argue that the sample (the fact that Mike Hiers doesn't drink) is insufficient to sustain a conclusion about his prospects as a husband. With such arguments, it is best not to quibble over terms; either approach is satisfactory.

Having weighed a syllogism, it is best to judge it not as true or false, but as reliable or unreliable. An unreliable conclusion, it must be remembered, may nevertheless be true. From the doubtful major premise ("Anyone who does not drink . . ."), you cannot reasonably deduce that Mike Hiers will make a fine husband. But he might, in fact, make a very fine husband. In rejecting the syllogism as unreliable, you simply say that the fact is not proved by this argument.

You can recognize the distinction between truth and a reasonable conclusion by recalling a passage from Ionesco's *Rhinoceros*. In it the Logician argues, "All cats die. Socrates is dead. Therefore Socrates is a cat." And his student responds, "That's true. I've got a cat named Socrates."

Recognizing the syllogistic form of an argument will help you analyze its reliability.

It will also help you to structure an argumentative essay. Commonly, in deductive writing the first paragraph offers the major premise and the last paragraph the conclusion. The body of the theme tries to demonstrate the minor premise. (This is, for example, the structure of the Declaration of Independence.)

EXERCISES

How reliable are these deductive arguments?

1. Of course Sylvia is a poor driver. She's a woman, isn't she.
2. How can you say you don't believe in miracles? The sunrise that occurs every day is a miracle.
3. Professor Costello's new book on marriage should be pretty informed. After all, he's been married four times.
4. Genuinely oppressed people (like the blacks) have lower academic scores and shorter life spans. Women do not have these. Women are not oppressed.

5. All lemons are yellow. My girl friend's brother is a lemon. My girl friend's brother is yellow.
6. Some years ago, *Human Events* attacked the physical fitness program proposed by President Kennedy by warning that both Hitler and Mussolini fostered comparable programs.
7. A medical procedure that preserves life and health is good. Legal abortion preserves life and health that would be endangered in an illegal clandestine operation. Legal abortion is good.
8. I'm from Milwaukee and I ought to know. Blatz is Milwaukee's finest beer.
9. My condition is beyond the help of medical science. Fortunately, Dr. Harris is a quack.
10. Both Catholics and Protestants are Christians. No one can be both Catholic and Protestant. Therefore no one can be a Christian.
11. I love you; therefore I am a lover. All the world loves a lover. You are all the world to me. Therefore you love me.

ESSAY ASSIGNMENTS

Write an essay either affirming or opposing one of these statements. The arguments you encounter in your background reading will probably be deductive, and so will your essay.

1. Evolution is a foolish theory.
2. Marriage has a bleak future.
3. The Easter Island statues must have been erected by beings from outer space.
4. America needs stronger libel laws.
5. U.S. schools should not teach standard English exclusively.
6. The miracles of Jesus prove he was God.
7. X is a disease; it should not be punished but cured. (Fill in the X.)

Justice Harry Blackmun

THE BAKKE DECISION

I participate fully, of course, in the opinion, *ante*, p. ——, that bears the names of my Brothers BRENNAN, WHITE, MARSHALL, and myself. I add only some general observations that hold particular significance for me, and then a few comments on equal protection.

I

At least until the early 1970's, apparently only a very small number, less than 2%, of the physicians, attorneys, and medical and law students in the United States were members of what we now refer to as minority groups. In addition, approximately three-fourths of our Negro physicians were trained at only two medical schools. If ways are not found to remedy that situation, the country can never achieve its professed goal of a society that is not race conscious.

I yield to no one in my earnest hope that the time will come when

Reprinted from Supreme Court document: Regents of the University of California, *Petitioner* v. *Allan Bakke*, June 28, 1978.

an "affirmative action" program is unnecessary and is, in truth, only a relic of the past. I would hope that we could reach this stage within a decade at the most. But the story of *Brown* v. *Board of Education*, 347 U.S. 483 (1954), decided almost a quarter of a century ago, suggests that that hope is a slim one. At some time, beyond any period of what some would claim is only transitional inequality, the United States must and will reach a stage of maturity where action along this line is no longer necessary. Then persons will be regarded as persons, and discrimination of the type we address today will be an ugly feature of history that is instructive but that is behind us.

The number of qualified, indeed highly qualified, applicants for admission to existing medical schools in the United States far exceeds the number of places available. Wholly apart from racial and ethnic considerations, therefore, the selection process inevitably results in the denial of admission to many *qualified* persons, indeed, to far more than the number of those who are granted admission. Obviously, it is a denial to the deserving. This inescapable fact is brought into sharp focus here because Allan Bakke is not himself charged with discrimination and yet is the one who is disadvantaged, and because the Medical School of the University of California at Davis itself is not charged with historical discrimination.

One theoretical solution to the need for more minority members in higher education would be to enlarge our graduate schools. Then all who desired and were qualified could enter, and talk of discrimination would vanish. Unfortunately, this is neither feasible nor realistic. The vast resources that apparently would be required simply are not available. And the need for more professional graduates, in the strict numerical sense, perhaps has not been demonstrated at all.

There is no particular or real significance in the 84–16 division at Davis. The same theoretical, philosophical, social, legal, and constitutional considerations would necessarily apply to the case if Davis' special admissions program had focused on any lesser number, that is, on 12 or 8 or 4 places or, indeed, on only 1.

It is somewhat ironic to have us so deeply disturbed over a program where race is an element of consciousness, and yet to be aware of the fact, as we are, that institutions of higher learning, albeit more on the undergraduate than the graduate level, have given conceded preferences up to a point to those possessed of athletic skills, to the children of alumni, to the affluent who may bestow their largess on the institutions, and to those having connections with celebrities, the famous, and the powerful.

Programs of admission to institutions of higher learning are basically a responsibility for academicians and for administrators and the specialists they employ. The judiciary, in contrast, is ill-equipped and poorly trained for this. The administration and management of educational institutions are beyond the competence of judges and are within the special competence of educators, provided always that the educators perform within legal and constitutional bounds. For me, therefore, interference by the judiciary must be the rare exception and not the rule.

II

I, of course, accept the propositions that (a) Fourteenth Amendment rights are personal; (b) racial and ethnic distinctions where they are stereotypes are inherently suspect and call for exacting judicial scrutiny; (c) academic freedom is a special concern of the First Amendment; and (d) the Fourteenth Amendment has expanded beyond its original 1868 conception and now is recognized to have reached a point where, as MR. JUSTICE POWELL states, *ante*, p. 24, quoting from the Court's opinion in *McDonald* v. *Santa Fe Trail Transp. Co.*, 427 U.S. 273, 296 (1976), it embraces a "broader principle."

This enlargement does not mean for me, however, that the Fourteenth Amendment has broken away from its moorings and its original intended purposes. Those original aims persist. And that, in a distinct sense, is what "affirmative action," in the face of proper facts, is all about. If this conflicts with idealistic equality, that tension is original Fourteenth Amendment tension, constitutionally conceived and constitutionally imposed, and it is part of the Amendment's very nature until complete equality is achieved in the area. In this sense, constitutional equal protection is a shield.

I emphasize in particular that the decided cases are not easily to be brushed aside. Many, of course, are not precisely on point, but neither are they off point. Racial factors have been given consideration in the school desegregation cases, in the employment cases, in *Lau* v. *Nichols*, 414 U.S. 563 (1974), and in *United Jewish Organizations* v. *Carey*, 430 U.S. 144 (1977). To be sure, some of these may be "distinguished" on the ground that victimization was directly present. But who is to say that victimization is not present for some members of today's minority groups, although it is of a lesser and perhaps different degree. The petitioners in *United Jewish Organizations* certainly complained bitterly of their reapportionment treatment, and I rather doubt that they regard the "remedy" there imposed as one that was "to improve" the group's ability to participate, as MR. JUSTICE POWELL describes it, *ante*, p. 35. And surely in *Lau* v. *Nichols* we looked to ethnicity.

I am not convinced, as MR. JUSTICE POWELL seems to be, that the difference between the Davis program and the one employed by Harvard is very profound or constitutionally significant. The line between the two is a thin and indistinct one. In each, subjective application is at work. Because of my conviction that admission programs are primarily for the educators, I am willing to accept the representation that the Harvard program is one where good faith in its administration is practiced as well as professed. I agree that such a program, where race or ethnic background is only one of many factors, is a program better formulated than Davis' two-track system. The cynical, of course, may say that under a program such as Harvard's one may accomplish covertly what Davis concedes it does openly. I need not go that far, for despite its two-track aspect, the Davis program, for me, is within constitutional bounds, though perhaps barely so. It is surely free of stigma, and, as in *United Jewish Organizations*, I am not willing to infer a constitutional violation.

It is worth noting, perhaps, that governmental preference has not been a stranger to our legal life. We see it in veterans' preferences. We see it in the aid-to-the-handicapped programs. We see it in the progressive income tax. We see it in the Indian programs. We may excuse some of these on the ground that they have specific constitutional protection or, as with Indians, that those benefited are wards of the Government. Nevertheless, these preferences exist and may not be ignored. And in the admissions field, as I have indicated, educational institutions have always used geography, athletic ability, anticipated financial largess, alumni pressure, and other factors of that kind.

I add these only as additional components on the edges of the central question as to which I join my Brothers BRENNAN, WHITE, and MARSHALL in our more general approach. It is gratifying to know that the Court at least finds it constitutional for an academic institution to take race and ethnic background into consideration as one factor, among many, in the administration of its admissions program. I presume that that factor always has been there, though perhaps not conceded or even admitted. It is a fact of life, however, and a part of the real world of which we are all a part. The sooner we get down the road toward accepting and being a part of the real world, and not shutting it out and away from us, the sooner will these difficulties vanish from the scene.

I suspect that it would be impossible to arrange an affirmative action program in a racially neutral way and have it successful. To ask that this be so is to demand the impossible. In order to get beyond racism, we must first take account of race. There is no other way. And in order to treat some persons equally, we must treat them differently. We cannot—we dare not—let the Equal Protection Clause perpetrate racial supremacy.

So the ultimate question, as it was at the beginning of this litigation, is: Among the qualified, how does one choose?

A long time ago, as time is measured for this Nation, a Chief Justice, both wise and far-sighted, said:

> In considering this question, then, we must never forget, that it is *a constitution* we are expounding (emphasis in original). [*M'Culloch* v. *Maryland*, 4 Wheat, 316, 407 (1819)]

In the same opinion, the Great Chief Justice further observed:

> Let the end be legitimate, let it be within the scope of the constitution, and all means which are appropriate, which are plainly adapted to that end, which are not prohibited but consist with the letter and spirit of the constitution, are constitutional. [*Id.*, at 421]

More recently, one destined to become a Justice of this Court observed:

> The great generalities of the constitution have a content and a significance that vary from age to age. [B. Cardozo, The Nature of the Judicial Process 17 (1921)]

And an educator who became a President of the United States said:

> But the Constitution of the United States is not a mere lawyers' document: it is a vehicle of life, and its spirit is always the spirit of the age. [W. Wilson, Constitutional Government in the United States 69 (1911)]

These precepts of breadth and flexibility and ever-present modernity are basic to our constitutional law. Today, again, we are expounding a *Constitution.* The same principles that governed M'Culloch's case in 1819 govern Bakke's case in 1978. There can be no other answer.

DISCUSSION

Any court decision expresses a syllogism: The major premise is the law; the minor premise, the facts of the case.

Here, the University of California had established a quota under which, out of every 100 students accepted for medical school, 16 would be from minority groups. Thus, it rejected the application of Allan Bakke, even though his entrance scores were higher than those of some of the minority applicants. Bakke sued, claiming that he was discriminated against because he was white and that this violated the Fourteenth Amendment of the U.S. Constitution as well as Title VI of the Civil Rights Act of 1964. After the California Supreme Court ruled for him, the case was ruled on by the Supreme Court, which also supported Bakke.

The majority opinion of the Supreme Court (written by Justice Stevens) avoided the Constitutional question. It based its judgment on the Title VI statute, which provided a major premise:

> No person in the United States shall, on the ground of race, color, or national origin, be excluded from participation in, be denied the benefits of, or be subjected to discrimination under any program or activity receiving Federal financial assistance.

To this, Justice Stevens added a minor premise and a conclusion:

The University, through its special admissions policy, excluded Bakke from participation in its program of medical education because of his race. The University also acknowledges that it was, and still is, receiving federal financial assistance.

The plain language of the statute therefore requires affirmance of the judgment below.

In a minority opinion, Justice Blackman argued from the Fourteenth Amendment. He worked from the major premise that Bakke had offered to support his case:

No state shall make or enforce any law which shall abridge the privileges or immunities of a citizen of the United States, nor shall any state deprive any person of life, liberty, or property, without due process of law; nor deny to any person within its jurisdiction the equal protection of the laws.

A strict construction of this would seem to benefit Bakke. Instead, Justice Blackmun saw it as a basis for "special" rights of minority citizens. He argued that the Fourteenth Amendment embraces a "broader principle," that it should be interpreted in a dynamic way "consistent with the spirit of the Constitution."

Examine the relative merits of the majority and the minority syllogisms.

Paul L. Houts

THE SCORE AGAINST IQ

A Look at Some Test Items

Many of the articles in this book are illustrated with actual items from
the intelligence tests. Lest you be tempted to conclude that the authors
have deliberately selected the most outrageous examples from the tests,
we urge you to take the time to examine the major tests in their entirety.
Even with a generous selection of items, it is almost impossible to convey
just how inadequate the tests are. To see them whole is to feel the full
impact of the foolishness of trying to measure anything as complex as
"intelligence" with such instruments.

However, for those readers who may not have easy access to the
tests (and it is often needlessly difficult), we are including some additional selections here, with comment, both to provide a greater range of
items and to cite some deficiencies of the tests not always mentioned
elsewhere in this issue. It may be necessary to add that these items are
neither the worst nor the best examples of the tests, but generally—and

Reprinted from *The Myth of Measurability*, by Paul L. Houts, copyright 1977 Hart
Publishing Company, Inc.

unfortunately—typify some of the basic flaws of the so-called intelligence tests.

Something you see in your sleep is a . . .
☐ dream ☐ fairy ☐ wish ☐ dread

Iowa Tests of Basic Skills,
Primary Battery, Level 7, Form 5,
Vocabulary Subtest

Dr. Freud might answer *wish* or *dread,* and a kid who's lost a tooth and put it under the pillow might answer *fairy.* And anyway, *see* is a poor choice of verbs. Did *you* see a dream last night?

hand beater : electric mixer : :
   A broom : vacuum cleaner
   B flashlight : light bulb
   C sink : dish washer
   D wrench : vise

Cooperative School and College Ability
Tests, Series II, Form 3B, p. 3

If the relationship intended is that of a hand operated household item to an electrical household item that is used for the same purpose, then couldn't B and C also be acceptable answers?

You can't _____ him; he was just doing his job.
   R annoy S help T blame U find V trust

Cognitive Abilities Test, Form 1,
Levels A-H, Verbal Battery, p. 9

The answer wanted is *blame,* an excuse made famous by legions of low-level Nazis during the Nuremberg trials. In a Watergate government, the answer *trust* might be equally appropriate.

How tall is the average American man?
   Any answer from 5'7" to 5'11".
   (Do *not* give credit for 5'6½" or 5'11½".)

WISC-R, Manual, p. 68

It's hard to see how this question measures intelligence—or even intelligent guessing, if an answer that is off by half an inch is unacceptable.

Birds can fly.
Bats can fly.
Therefore, [1] a bat is a bird. [2] a bat is a mammal. [3] animals other than birds can fly.

California Test of Mental Maturity,
1963 Revision, Level 2, Test 9, p. 15

None of the answers are correct; without the additional statement that a bat is an animal, we cannot *logically* conclude that animals other than birds can fly.

When a dove begins to associate with crows, its feathers remain _____, but its heart grows black.
F black   G white   H dirty   J spread   K good

> Lorge-Thorndike, Multi-Level Edition,
> Level 3, Verbal Battery, p. 3

Not only is the statement itself erroneous, but think of the emotional impact of an item like this on a black child. (And, incidentally, not all doves are white.)

How the _____ roses flush up in the cheeks!
R white   S pretty   T small   U yellow   V red

> Lorge-Thorndike, Multi-Level Edition,
> Level 3, Verbal Battery, p. 3

The "correct" answer is *red*—but only if the cheek in question is white. Note also the quaint phrasing.

Grey hair is a sign of age, not of _____.
R color   S youth   T courage
U despair   V wisdom

> Lorge-Thorndike, Level 4, Form A,
> Verbal Battery, p. 3

Youth and *wisdom* are equally valid answers for this ambiguous question.

Where there is _____, let me sow love.
R suspicion   S friendliness   T hatred
U love   V hope

> Cognitive Abilities Test, Form 1,
> Levels A-H, Verbal Battery, p. 11

Another ambiguous question. Either *suspicion* or *hatred* would do, and—for those who need encouragement—so would *friendliness*.

dollar   peso   mark   lira
F change   G franc   H foreign
J purchase   K bank

> Lorge-Thorndike, Level 4, Form A,
> Verbal Battery, p. 6

This question might pose no difficulties for the well-traveled child, but it requires at least a smattering of global economics for the others.

kaiser   emperor   king   czar
R senator   S governor   T pope
U sultan   V general

> Cognitive Abilities Test, Form 1,
> Levels A-H, Verbal Battery, p. 17

If you've studied the Renaissance but not the history of the Middle East, *pope* might seem to be as good an answer as *sultan*.

> tie   cravat   stock   neckcloth
>   A bib   B collar   C scarf   D kirtle   E girdle

Lorge-Thorndike, Level 4, Form A,
Verbal Battery, p. 7

A, B, or C—and what, by the way, is a *kirtle?*

Find the drawing at the right that goes with the third drawing in the same way that the second goes with the first.

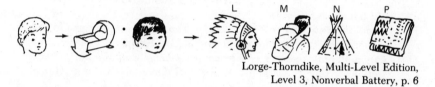

Lorge-Thorndike, Multi-Level Edition,
Level 3, Nonverbal Battery, p. 6

Ethnic stereotyping at its most unattractive, and outdated at that.

The pictures in the box go together in a certain way. We say: "Boy is to trousers as girl is to what?"

Otis-Lennon, Elementary I,
Form J, p. 5; Manual, p. 10

Most little girls wear blue jeans these days as often as they wear dresses.

In each row there is one picture that shows something which is the opposite of the first picture. Find it and mark its number.

California Test of Mental Maturity,
1963 Revision, Level 2, Test 1, p. 3

A "non-sense" question. What can the opposite of a pillow be, except a non-pillow? How can you tell from this drawing? What are 1 and 2? Is 4 a brick or a sponge?

TESTS CITED

California Test of Mental Maturity, 1963 Revision, Level 2. Elizabeth T. Sullivan, Willis W. Clark, and Ernest W. Tiegs (Monterey, Cal.: CTB/McGraw-Hill, 1963).

Cognitive Abilities Test, Multi-Level Booklet, Form 1, Levels A-H. Robert L. Thorndike and Elizabeth Hagan (Boston: Houghton Mifflin Co., 1971–72).

Cooperative School and College Ability Tests, Series II, Forms 1A-4B (Princeton, N.J.: Educational Testing Service, Cooperative Test Division, 1955–73).

Iowa Tests of Basic Skills, Primary Battery, Levels 7-8, Form 5. E. F. Lindquist and A. N. Hieronymous (Boston: Houghton Mifflin Co., 1972).

Lorge-Thorndike Intelligence Tests, Multi-Level Edition. Irving Lorge, Robert L. Thorndike, and Elizabeth Hagen (Boston: Houghton Mifflin Co., 1954-66).

Lorge-Thorndike Intelligence Tests, Level 4, Form A. Irving Lorge and Robert L. Thorndike (Boston: Houghton Mifflin Co., 1954).

Otis-Lennon Mental Ability Test, Elementary I Level, and Manual for Administration. Arthur S. Otis and Roger T. Lennon (New York: Harcourt, Brace, and World, 1967).

Wechsler Intelligence Scale for Children (WISC), and Manual. David Wechsler (New York: Psychological Corporation, 1949; revised edition 1974).

DISCUSSION QUESTIONS

1. The essay is, in fact, a syllogism with this major premise:
   No IQ test can measure intelligence if it asks obscure questions that lack necessary information, ambiguous questions that require arbitrary answers, or questions that reflect a cultural bias.
   Is this a reasonable major premise?
2. Are these questions offered as a representative sample of those asked on various IQ tests?
3. Examine the questions the author says are obscure, ambiguous, and culturally biased. Is he right? Do these questions impress you as "outrageous"?
4. What is your definition of "intelligence"? Take enough time to come up with a workable definition.
5. Isn't there in practically all the questions a fairly obvious "right" answer that the author has to reject or explain away?
6. Assuming your definition of "intelligence," would the person who routinely gave the "right" answer be more intelligent than one who did not?

Senator William V. Roth, Jr.
Representative Fortney H. Stark

PRO AND CON: A TAX CREDIT FOR COLLEGE TUITION?

Interview with Senator William V. Roth, Jr.

Republican, of Delaware

Q: Senator Roth, why do you favor a tax credit for college-tuition-expenses?

A: It's the easiest, simplest method of helping the big group that now gets no educational aid. Middle America is finding it increasingly difficult to send their children to college. This approach will help the greatest number for the least money.

Q: How would a tax credit work?

A: You would total up your federal income-tax bill and then subtract $250 if you spent that much on college tuition.

Q: What would that cost the government?

A: My proposal will cost roughly 1.2 billion dollars the first year. The cost would be around 2.4 billion dollars annually if the credit is increased to $500.

Q: Will that upset the budget?

A: No. As a matter of fact, my proposal costs exactly the same as the

Reprinted from *U.S. News & World Report,* April 3, 1978, pp. 61–62.

85

one the President has proposed to finance loans and grants to college students.

Q: Who would get help under your plan?

A: Like all tax credits, it would be available regardless of income, but something like 75 percent of the benefits will go to those making $30,000 or less. Even people who earn more than that are finding it difficult to send children to college.

Q: The President says any help should go to those most in need. Don't you agree with that?

A: The vast majority of federally backed loans and grants for education are now going to those making $12,000 or less. I've been a supporter of those programs because it's important to give those at the lower end of the economic scale the opportunity to go to college. But now middle America desperately needs help.

In the old days we had what we called upward mobility—where the average person could, by working a little harder, buy a better home, take a good vacation and send the children to college. Today, many of these people feel they are being pressed downward by mounting taxes and inflation, and they're getting angry. They say, "We're paying the bills, but the government has forgotten us."

Q: But isn't there an element of waste in giving aid to families earning more than $30,000?

A: There is waste in the present programs. These existing HEW [Health, Education and Welfare Department] programs waste hundreds of millions of dollars in administrative costs. In my tax-credit proposal, there is practically no administrative cost, and the money will all go to the people we're trying to benefit.

Middle America is entitled to have some benefits, too. The fact is, increasing costs are making it more difficult for middle-income students to go to college. At the same time, the enrollment in the upper and lower-income brackets has remained fairly stable.

Q: Why not simply broaden the availability of assistance under existing programs?

A: A tax credit involves a different approach. This is money families have earned and should keep rather than give to the government. The problem is people in Washington think all earnings belong to the government. In fact, the opposite is true.

All I am saying is: Let those who earn it keep more of their own money to spend on college expenses. They're not asking for a handout.

Q: Given the great expense of college these days, would a credit of $250 really help much?

A: One could always wish for more. I think $250 is a significant help. Most parents who write me look upon it as a step in the right direction, and over 7 million students would benefit.

Q: Won't the expense of your proposal mean that there will be less money available for subsidized loans and grants to students?

A: No, absolutely not. I think college loans and grants—the amount of money made available—will continue to rise in the future.

Q: Is it possible that colleges will simply increase tuition charges by $250 to skim off the credit?

A: It would not have that effect any more than would the President's proposal or any other federal-aid program. For every increase in college costs, there's a drop in enrollment. So you've got a restraint on college administrators to be competitive costwise.

Q: If a credit is allowed for college expenses, why not allow it for sending children to private elementary and high schools?

A: There is a proposal pending for tax credits for those expenses—which I also support.

Q: Should taxpayers who already pay for public schools also subsidize those who send their children to private schools?

A: People who use the private schools share the tax burden of public schools. This is just a matter of balancing things out. In the past, people had the choice of public or private schools, but taxes—not only at the federal but also at state and local levels—are so unrealistically high it is becoming increasingly difficult for families to exercise that option.

Q: Would the tax credit make it even more complicated than now for people to figure out their income-tax bills?

A: It will add one line to the IRS form. The most significant aspect of the tax-credit approach is simplicity.

First of all, you don't require people to fill out detailed forms and applications. You don't require them to disclose all their personal financial background. All you say is they can subtract $250 from their tax bill—very simple, compared with what they would be required to do under the grant-and-loan proposal.

Second, you don't require an army of bureaucrats investigating, reviewing and deciding who to help and not help—as you do under any plan with income restrictions.

Interview with Representative Fortney H. "Pete" Stark

Democrat, of California

Q: Representative Stark, why do you oppose giving families a tax credit for college-tuition expenses?

A: It's unfair and inequitable. It distributes too little to the people who need it, and may distribute a lot to people who don't need it or who, under the American tradition of paying your own way, shouldn't have it. It's also cumbersome, hard to administer and complicates the tax form.

Q: Wouldn't the tax credit help some people who can't qualify for federal loans and grants now but need help?

A: Sure, but the Senate version of the President's bill to help on tuition costs proposes making some grants available to families with incomes as high as $25,000, and loans without limit on family income. I think that's the direction in which we should move.

We can't take care of all the people who say they want help. We don't have that much money, without cutting the military budget in half. If we did that, you'd hear screams from the same people who are asking for the college aid that would far drown out the request for that.

Q: Wouldn't a tax credit for middle-income families be simpler and more direct?

A: Absolutely not. Doing things through the tax code has gotten to be terribly complicated. Anybody who believes you could claim a tax credit just by filling out one line on your tax return has never filled out his own return.

Tax credits are very cumbersome. The people who itemize their deductions and fill out complex tax forms have to fill out several lines to justify any kind of a tax credit, not just check a box.

Besides, we ought not give money away through the tax code. We should authorize it and appropriate it so we know exactly who's getting it and how much it's costing us. Once you bury something like this in the tax code, you'll never get it out.

The education committees in the House and Senate are the proper ones to be making these decisions, not the tax-writing committees. They understand education. They've studied it. They've been doing it for years.

Q: Compared with loans or grants, a tax credit would give a family more discretion in using the money it earns, wouldn't it?

A: You're absolutely right. It gives the family this much discretion: It allows a family whose children are out working their way through a community college, where the family is still deducting for that child, to take the 250 bucks and put it in their pocket and not help the child at all. That's too much discretion.

I'd want to see some strings attached to college aid. There's a need concept that's got to be maintained, which the tuition credit ignores. Why should we vote to give every man, woman and child in this country 250 bucks, whether they need it or not?

Q: Which would be more helpful to a family with an income of, say, $20,000 a year—the present system of loans and grants, or a new tax credit?

A: In many cases, the credit would offer less help. For one thing, loans go up to $2,500 a year, and a total of $7,500 for three years in college. Grants come to $1,600—and they would be increased under the President's plan.

What's more, a credit comes too late—six months after you spend the money for tuition. If you're short of cash, you need help in September and January when the bills come due, not in March or April when your income-tax refund arrives.

Q: What about using a tax credit to help families pay to send children to private elementary and high schools?

A: That would destroy the public-school system and help millionaire families as much as those who really need the help. It's true that parents who send their kids to private schools end up paying twice, but this is a voluntary decision on their part.

If we enact the tuition tax credit, parents with kids in public schools will pay twice involuntarily—once for public schools and once to subsidize private ones. That to me is patently unfair. Besides, there's a question whether a credit for those who send children to parochial schools would be constitutional.

Q: Haven't there been problems with the loans and grants for college education that you prefer—defaults, for example?

A: Not many. These are workable programs. They started with the veterans' benefits from World War II, which many of us went to college under. After that came loans and grants for other youngsters on the basis of need. Defaulted loans—mostly related with shoddy proprietary schools—have provided the only touches of scandal. Aside from that, the only complaint we've ever had is that there hasn't been enough money.

Q: But many families complain about the forms and the bureaucracy of the grant program. Doesn't that discourage people who need help?

A: The families that are complaining about the bureaucracy and the forms are exactly the families who want a handout. And they're mostly high-income families.

My point is: We don't give money away in the government. We provide assistance to those who need it, and we're charged with making sure that we do it in an orderly fashion that we can account for. And so, if you want to get government assistance, you necessarily must have the government supervising.

I think people want to make sure that their money is spent

honestly, and they don't want people ripping it off. So those who want the money have to subscribe to minimum limits.

Q: Do you think a tax credit might be cheaper than expanding the system of loans and grants?

A: Absolutely not!

The tax-credit scheme would be far more expensive. But more important, it's a question of who gets the money.

DISCUSSION QUESTIONS

1. Senator Roth's main argument can be resolved into a syllogism:
   A simple and efficient program that provides economic help to parents sending children to college should be passed into law.
   The proposed tax credit system is a simple and efficient program providing such help.
   The proposed tax credit system should be passed into law?
   How does Representative Stark challenge this syllogism?
2. Senator Roth is asked whether the tax credit program will "upset the budget" and whether it will make less money available for loans and grants. Are his answers to these questions consistent?
3. The spokesmen argue about the "simplicity" of the proposed program. Which is more persuasive?
4. What help would Representative Stark offer middle-American parents with children in college? How much relief would this give them?
5. The spokesmen differ about giving tax credits for parents sending children to private elementary and secondary schools. Are there broader issues here than in the debate about tax credits for college?
6. Representative Stark's final remarks establish a syllogism:
   Any program permitting individuals to "rip off" government money is unsatisfactory.
   The program of tax credits for college would permit this.
   The program of tax credits for college is unsatisfactory.
   Is this syllogism invulnerable?

Erich von Däniken

EASTER ISLAND—LAND OF THE BIRD MEN

The first European seafarers who landed on Easter Island at the beginning of the eighteenth century could scarcely believe their eyes. On this little plot of earth, 2350 miles from the coast of Chile, they saw hundreds of colossal statues lying scattered about all over the island. Whole mountain massifs had been transformed, steel-hard volcanic rock had been cut through like butter, and 10,000 tons of massive rocks lay in places where they could not have been dressed. Hundreds of gigantic statues, some of which are between 33 and 66 feet high and weigh as much as 50 tons, still stare challengingly at the visitor today—like robots which seem to be waiting solely to be set in motion again. Originally these colossuses also wore hats; but even the hats do not exactly help to explain the puzzling origin of the statues. The stone for the hats, which weighed more than ten tons apiece, was found at a different site from that used for the bodies, and in addition the hats had to be hoisted high in the air.

Wooden tablets, covered with strange hieroglyphs, were also found

Reprinted by permission of G. P. Putnam's Sons from *Chariot of the Gods?* by Erich von Däniken. English translation copyright © 1969 by Michael Heron and Souvenir Press.

on some of the statues in those days. But today it is impossible to find more than ten fragments of those tablets in all the museums in the world, and none of the inscriptions on those till extant has yet been deciphered.

Thor Heyerdahl's investigations of these mysterious giants produced three clearly distinguishable cultural periods, and the oldest of the three seems to have been the most perfect. Heyerdahl dates some charcoal remains that he found to about A.D. 400. It has not been proved whether the fireplaces and remains of bones had any connection with the stone colossuses. Heyerdahl discovered hundreds of unfinished statues near rock faces and on the edges of craters; thousands of stone implements, simple stone axes, lay around as if the work had been abandoned quite suddenly.

Easter Island lies far away from any continent or civilization. The islanders are more familiar with the moon and the stars than any other country. No trees grow on the island, which is a tiny speck of volcanic stone. The usual explanation, that the stone giants were moved to their present sites on wooden rollers, is not feasible in this case, either. In addition, the island can scarcely have provided food for more than 2000 inhabitants. (A few hundred natives live on Easter Island today.) A shipping trade, which brought food and clothing to the island for the stonemasons, is hardly credible in antiquity. Then who cut the statues out of the rock, who carved them and transported them to their sites? How were they moved across country for miles without rollers? How were they dressed, polished, and erected? How were the hats, the stone for which came from a different quarry from that of the statues, put in place?

Even if people with lively imaginations have tried to picture the Egyptian pyramids being built by a vast army of workers using the "heave-ho" method, a similar method would have been impossible on Easter Island for lack of manpower. Even 2000 men, working day and night, would not be nearly enough to carve these colossal figures out of the steel-hard volcanic stone with rudimentary tools—and at least a part of the population must have tilled the barren fields, gone fishing, woven cloth, and made ropes. No, 2000 men alone could not have made the gigantic statues. And a larger population is inconceivable on Easter Island. Then who did do the work? And how did they manage it? And why do the statues stand around the edge of the island and not in the interior? What cult did they serve?

Unfortunately, the first European missionaries on this tiny patch of earth helped to ensure that the island's dark ages stayed dark. They burned the tablets with hieroglyphic characters; they prohibited the ancient cults of the gods and did away with every kind of tradition. Yet thoroughly as the pious gentlemen went to work, they could not prevent the natives from calling their island the Land of the Bird Men, as they still do today. An orally transmitted legend tells us that flying men landed and lighted fires in ancient times. The legend is confirmed by sculptures of flying creatures with big, staring eyes.

Connections between Easter Island and Tiahuanaco automatically force themselves upon us. There as here, we find stone giants belonging to the same style. The haughty faces with their stoic expressions suit the statues—here as there. When Francisco Pizarro questioned the Incas about Tiahuanaco in 1532, they told him that no man had ever seen the city save in ruins, for Tiahuanaco had been built in the night of mankind. Traditions call Easter Island the "navel of the world." It is more than 3125 miles from Tiahuanaco to Easter Island. How can one culture possibly have inspired the other?

Perhaps pre-Inca mythology can give us a hint here. In it the old god of creation, Viracocha, was an ancient and elemental divinity. According to tradition Viracocha created the world when it was still dark and had no sun; he sculpted a race of giants from stone, and when they displeased him, he sank them in a deep flood. Then he caused the sun and the moon to rise above Lake Titicaca, so that there was light on earth. Yes, and then—read this closely—he shaped clay figures of men and animals at Tiahuanaco and breathed life into them. Afterward, he instructed these living creatures of his own creation in language, customs, and arts, and finally flew some of them to different continents which they were supposed to inhabit thenceforth. After this task the god Viracocha and two assistants traveled to many countries to check how his instructions were being followed and what results they had had. Dressed as an old man, Viracocha wandered over the Andes and along the coast, and often he was given a poor reception. Once, at Cacha, he was so annoyed by his welcome that in a fury he set fire to a cliff which began to burn up the whole country. Then the ungrateful people asked his forgiveness, whereupon he extinguished the flames with a single gesture. Viracocha traveled on, giving instructions and advice, and many temples were erected to him as a result. Finally he said good-bye in the coastal province of Manta and disappeared over the ocean, riding on the waves, but he said he intended to come back.

The Spanish conquistadors who conquered South and Central America came up against the sagas of Viracocha everywhere. Never before had they heard of gigantic white men who came from somewhere in the sky. Full of astonishment, they learned about a race of sons of the sun who instructed mankind in all kinds of arts and disappeared again. And in all the legends that the Spaniards heard, there was an assurance that the sons of the sun would return.

Although the American continent is the home of ancient cultures, our accurate knowledge of America is barely 1000 years old. It is an absolute mystery to us why the Incas cultivated cotton in Peru in 3000 B.C., although they did not know or possess the loom. The Mayas built roads but did not use the wheel, although they knew about it. The fantastic five-strand necklace of green jade in the burial pyramid of Tikal in Guatemala is a miracle. A miracle because the jade comes from China. The sculptures of the Olmecs are incredible. With their beautifully helmeted giant skulls, they can be admired only on the sites where they were found, for they will never be on show in a museum. No bridge in the country could stand their weight. We can move smaller "monoliths" weighing up to fifty tons with our modern lifting appliances and loaders, but when it comes to hundred-tonners like these our technology breaks down. But our ancestors could transport and dress them. How?

It even seems as if the ancient peoples took a special pleasure in juggling with stone giants over hill and dale. The Egyptians fetched their obelisk from Aswan, the architects of Stonehenge brought their stone blocks from southwest Wales and Marlborough, the stonemasons of Easter Island took their ready-made monster statues from a distant quarry to their present sites, and no one can say where some of the monoliths at Tiahuanaco come from. Our remote ancestors must have been strange people; they liked making things difficult for themselves and always built their statues in the most impossible places. Was it just because they liked a hard life?

I refuse to think that the artists of our great past were as stupid as that. They could just as easily have erected their statues and temples in the immediate vicinity of the quarries if an old tradition had not laid down where their works ought to be sited. I am convinced that the Inca fortress of Sacsahuamán was not built above Cuzco by chance, but rather because a tradition indicated the place as a holy spot. I am also convinced that in all the places where the most ancient monumental buildings of mankind were found, the most interesting and important relics of our past lie still untouched in the ground, relics, moreover, which could be of tremendous importance for the further development of present-day space travel.

The unknown space travelers who visited our planet many thousands of years ago can hardly have been less farsighted than we think we are today. They were convinced that one day man would make the move out into the universe on his own initiative, using his own skills.

It is a well-known historical fact that the intelligences of our planet have constantly sought for kindred spirits, for life, for corresponding intelligences in the cosmos.

Present-day antennae and transmitters have broadcast the first radio impulses to unknown intelligences. When we shall receive an answer—in ten, fifteen, or a hundred years—we do not know. We do not even know which star we should beam our message at, because we have no idea which planet should interest us most. Where do our signals reach unknown intelligences similar to human beings? We do not know. Yet there is much to support the belief that the information needed to reach our goal is deposited in our earth for us. We are trying hard to neutralize the force of gravity; we are experimenting with elementary particles and antimatter. Are we also doing enough to find the data which are hidden in our earth, so that we can at last ascertain our original home?

If we take things literally, much that was once fitted into the mosaic of our past with great difficulty becomes quite plausible: not only the relevant clues in ancient texts but also the "hard facts" which offer themselves to our critical gaze all over the globe. Lastly, we have our reason to think with.

So it will be man's ultimate insight to realize that his justification for existence to date and all his struggles to advance really consisted in learning from the past in order to make himself ready for contact with the existence in space. Once that happens, the shrewdest, most die-hard individualist must see that the whole human task consists in colonizing the universe and that man's whole spiritual duty lies in perpetuating all his efforts and practical experience. Then the promise of the "gods" that peace will come on earth and that the way to heaven is open can come true.

As soon as the available authorities, powers, and intellects are devoted to space research, the results will make the absurdity of terrestrial wars abundantly clear. When men of all races, peoples, and nations unite in the supranational task of making journeys to distant planets technically feasible, the earth with all its mini-problems will fall back into its right relation with the cosmic processes.

Occultists can put out their lamps, alchemists destroy their crucibles, secret brotherhoods take off their cowls. It will no longer be possible to offer man the nonsense that has been purveyed to him so brilliantly for thousands of years. Once the universe opens its doors, we shall attain a better future.

I base the reasons for my skepticism about the interpretation of our remote past on the knowledge that is available today. If I admit to being a skeptic, I mean the word in the sense in which Thomas Mann used it in a lecture in the twenties: "The positive thing about the skeptic is that he considers everything possible!"

DISCUSSION QUESTIONS

1. The central argument of this essay is deductive. Analyze these syllogisms:
   The Easter Island statues could not have been carved, moved, and erected by mere humans.
   The Easter Island statues were carved, moved, and erected.

The Easter Island statues were carved, moved, and erected by superhuman agents.

The Easter Island statues were carved, moved, and erected by superhuman agents.
Space travelers who could visit Earth must be superhuman agents.
The Easter Island statues were carved, moved, and erected by space travelers who visited Earth.

2. What implication does the author intend to convey with these lines?
    "None of the inscriptions on those [wooden tablets] still extant have yet been deciphered."
    "Thousands of stone implements, simple stone axes, lay around as if the work had been abandoned quite suddenly."
    "They could not prevent the natives from calling their island the Land of the Bird Men, as they still do today."
    "And why do the statues stand around the edge of the island and not in the interior? What cult did they serve?"
    What evidence supports these implications?
3. On what evidence does the author maintain that the island could not have more than 2000 inhabitants?
4. What is the author's purpose in telling the pre-Incan myth of Viracocha? Is this story significantly different from stories in classical and Christian traditions?
5. Consider the transition leading to the author's first mention of "unknown space travelers." How does he approach the subject?
6. How does the essay relate to these statements taken from the *Encyclopaedia Britannica* and from Father Sebastian Englert's *Island at the Center of the World* (1970)?
    "Easter Island . . . is about 11 mi. long and 15 mi. wide."
    "The writing engraved on wooden tablets . . . takes the form of symbols, strongly stylized, representing human beings, birds, fish, crustaceans, plants, ceremonial articles, and designs of a purely geometrical character."
    "The statues were cut from compressed volcanic ash, a soft and easily worked stone."
    "The usual height of the images on the *ahu* were from 12 to 20 feet."
    "A native account states that they were dragged into position (presumably with ropes, the native hemp and hibiscus fibre furnishing adequate materials) and that round pebbles were placed underneath to serve as rollers. Seaweed may also have been used to minimize friction with the ground."
    "The statues probably were erected on the *ahu* by being hauled up an incline made of earth or stones and then gradually up-ended into position by the withdrawing of the supporting material from under their bases."—*Encyclopaedia Britannica*

    "Judging by the many examples abandoned along roads, the statues appear to have been moved in a prone position and head first."
    "The topknots were carved in much the same manner as the statues, by ex-

cavating a channel around them and breaking them loose. Being cylindrical they could be rolled relatively easily to their *ahu* locations."

"Its purpose [that of carving large statues] appears to have been to commemorate illustrious ancestors of the various kin-groups, whose mana was thought to bring benefit to the communities."

"[The population of Easter Island] could never have exceeded 3000 or 4000."—Englert

Neither source mentions the island as the "Land of the Bird Men."

Argument by Authority

Believe a woman or an epitaph.
—Lord Byron, *English Bards and Scotch Reviewers*

Many of the things you believe—or are asked to believe—must be accepted simply on the authority of an expert. Your doctor says you have glaucoma. Your mechanic says the car needs a valve job. Your newspaper reviews *King Kong* and calls it awful. Scientific authorities say the universe is expanding. In such instances you are asked to accept a view on the basis of someone's testimony.

It is reasonable to credit such testimony if it fulfills two conditions: (1) The speaker must be a genuine expert in the subject at hand. (2) There must exist no reasonable probability of his being biased. When Zsa Zsa Gabor, for example, turns from her acting career to praise the effects of acupuncture, you can justly question her expertness in the area. And when Billie Jean King appears proclaiming the excellence of Colgate toothpaste, you know she is being paid for the advertisement and suspect a degree of bias.

You must remember, however, that these unreliable arguments are not necessarily false. Zsa Zsa Gabor may be expressing an important truth about acupuncture, and Billie Jean King may be giving her honest opinion about Colgate toothpaste. Nevertheless, it would be unreasonable to accept an argument—or to build a persuasive essay— solely on the authority of such speakers. You should relate their views to other evidence and to the word of other authorities.

EXPERT TESTIMONY

Many arguments raise the question of genuine expertness. The authority cited may be unnamed. (An advertisement for *The Illustrated Encyclo-*

pedia of Sex includes sterling recommendations from "A Doctor," "A Teacher," "A Judge," and "A Minister.") He may be unfamiliar. (*"Oblique Frame* is a provocative book—readable and profoundly informed."—Dr. Winston X. Montgomery) He may be known largely by his degrees. (A Kansas medico, in recommending goat-gland surgery to restore virility, signed himself "John R. Brinkley, M.D., C.M., Dr.P.H., Sc.D. . . .") And he may appear with magnified credentials. (A temperance circular quoting William Gladstone's condemnation of alcohol describes him as the "greatest prime minister in English history.")

Sometimes speakers of unquestioned authority express themselves in areas outside their competence. You hear physicists talking politics, evangelists discussing evolution, and movie stars recommending floor wax. One advertisement describes a star third-baseman, then adds, "His good judgment on the ball field holds true with his selection of wearing apparel. That's why he picks Munsingwear all the way." A religious newspaper headlines an article by L. Nelson Bell, M.D., "A Physician Looks at the Virgin Birth," then prints his biblical argument based solely on a reading of Isaiah, Matthew, and Luke. Dr. Bell offers no medical opinion at all. Such spokesmen must be judged on the quality of their evidence, not on their word as experts.

Religious Authority

Equally questionable as authorities are "God" and "everyone." Because the claim is not subject to hard evidence, one can affirm almost any opinion by saying it conforms to the divine will. At a 1956 California Democratic rally, for example, a clergyman announced that Adlai Stevenson was God's choice for President of the United States. A correspondent to the *Mobile Press,* in 1969, expressed confidence that the tragedies falling on the Kennedy family were divine justice answering their misdeeds. And a recent correspondent declared it would violate "Christ's plan for the world" if the United States gave up its holdings in Panama.

Christian spokesmen often quote passages from the Bible to declare the will of God, and thus open up a rich area of argument. As mentioned earlier, religious questions often do not lend themselves to meaningful discussion because people cannot agree on necessary definitions. Clearly, an argument involving biblical authority can be persuasive only when addressed to someone who already accepts the validity of Scripture and who interprets it in the same sense as the speaker. (Large differences exist, for example, among those who claim the Bible *is* the word of God, those who believe it contains the word of God, those who enjoy it as an anthology of great literature, and those who reject it altogether.)

Even where preliminary agreement exists, problems remain. Because the biblical texts were written over some 1300 years and represent a wide variety of authors, occasions, opinions, literary types, and translations, a spokesperson can find a passage or two to support any argument he or she chooses to make. (Bishop James Pike illustrated this by asking ironically: "How many persons have been reborn from meditating on the last line of Psalm 137: 'Blessed shall be he that taketh and dasheth the little ones against the stones'?") Consequently, facing a scriptural argument, you should take time to trace the references. You will find that authors often quote passages out of context (they might be championing the superficial counsel of Job's friends) and that, not uncommonly, they quote from an inaccurate memory and refer to lines scarcely related to the issue at hand. ("Only God can save America now. See Chronicles 7:14.")

Mass Authority

The authority of "everyone" is claimed in statements beginning, "They say," "Everyone knows," or "All fair-minded people agree." Such argument can be convincing in instances where "they" (some notable majority) have demonstrably committed themselves in an area they are competent to judge. Arguments announcing, "More women choose Simplicity than any other pattern" and "Budweiser—Largest Selling Beer in the World" are genuinely impressive because, in these areas, a mass authority is superior to that of any particular expert. (What renowned epicure is qualified to assure you that Jax is America's best-tasting beer?) It is important to remember that America's democratic procedures and its jury system both rely on the expertness of "everyone."

But mass authority can be distorted in a number of ways. It can be claimed arbitrarily. ("Everyone knows that John Kennedy stole the 1960 election.") It can be coupled with ambiguous language. ("More men get more pleasure out of Roi-Tan than any other cigar at its price.") And it can be invoked in areas that call for technical expertness. (A Gallup Poll reported that 48 percent of Americans believe that flying saucers are real.) In such instances, "everyone" is a dubious authority.

Still, mass opinion is worth listening to, especially when it becomes more or less unanimous. Remember the famous counsel: "If you can keep your head when all about you are losing theirs, probably you haven't grasped the situation."

Divided Authority

The word of a genuine expert will not, of course, settle all questions. Alexander Pope put the question best:

> Who shall decide when Doctors disagree,
> And soundest Casuists doubt, like you and me?

The plain fact is that many issues are complex and that, in these areas, experts hold opposing views. Legal authorities disagree whether certain eavesdropping measures violate constitutional safeguards. Psychiatrists appear in court arguing about the mental competence of particular defendants. Scientists dispute about the relative danger of D.D.T. pesticides. And sociologists cannot agree whether pornography contributes to criminal acts. Whose opinion should you accept?

In such cases, it is probably wise to credit the larger body of expert opinion or to withhold judgment and await further pronouncements in the area.

Critical Authorities

You should recognize that some authorities have more established reputations than others. Many periodicals carry reviews of books, plays, and movies, for example, but those of the major New York City newspapers, *The Christian Science Monitor,* and such national magazines as *Time, Newsweek, Harper's, Atlantic, Saturday Review,* and *The New Yorker* are generally thought most critically reliable.

If a book, movie, or play wins praise from these critics, the reviews may be quoted in magazine advertisements or on book jackets. If an advertisement quotes reviews from other sources, it strongly suggests that the work was not praised by the major critics. An advertisement for Ian Fleming's *On Her Majesty's Secret Service,* for example, boasts these reviews:

> "Packed with danger, mystery, crime, and wild pursuit . . . I can recommend it with confidence to readers who sat up late nights to finish the preceding 10."—Vincent Starret, *Chicago Tribune*
> "Hair raiser."—*Boston Herald*
> "Astonishing . . . ingenious."—*Diners Club Magazine*
> "The hottest sleuth in the suspense field, James Bond, really tops himself in this new Ian Fleming thriller."—*St. Paul Dispatch*
> "More fun than Tarzan and Superman combined."—*Denver Post*
> "Taut, instructive and artfully told."—*Chicago Daily News*
> "You can't argue with success."—Anthony Boucher, *New York Times Book Review*
> "A fine surge of adrenalin in our veins."—*Columbus Dispatch*
> "Solid Fleming."—*New York Herald Tribune Books*

Though it appears at first glance that authorities were unanimous in acclaiming this novel, such is scarcely the case. Only two of the reviews were from major critics, and those were notably less enthusiastic than the others. The *New York Times* declared it would not argue with general taste. And the *New York Herald Tribune* said the novel is a good example of the kind Fleming writes.

This is not to suggest that you should not enjoy Ian Fleming novels. You should, however, recognize the varying standards of critical authorities and not misread such advertisements as expressions of universal acclaim. You should be less than impressed, for example, when you see the paperback edition of Nancy Freeman's *Joshua Son of None* boasting rave reviews from the *El Paso Times*, the *San Gabriel Valley Tribune*, the *Macon Georgian*, and the *Oceanside Blade-Tribune*.

You should recognize these distinctions when writing a critical essay. If the book or movie you're championing was praised by the major critics, quote the reviews. If it found favor only with lesser authorities, probably you shouldn't mention the reviews at all.

BIASED TESTIMONY

Even when a spokesman is an admitted expert in the field under discussion, his argument should be examined for the possibility of bias. An argument is said to have a probable bias if the authority profits from the view he expresses or if he reflects the predictable loyalty or routine antagonism of a group. To dismiss the testimony of such a person is not to call him a liar or even to say he is wrong; it means that a condition exists which makes it unreasonable to accept a conclusion solely on his authority.

An authority profits from making an argument when it brings him money or prestige. The incentive is easy to recognize when Danny Thomas recommends Maxwell House Coffee, when Sybil Leek makes lecture tours proclaiming she is a witch, and when spokesmen for outdoor movies protest the unnaturalness of daylight-savings time. The effect of prestige is clear when individuals discuss their income, their reading habits, and their sex lives. In these areas, ego is threatened, and people lie. The impact of money and prestige on an expert is sometimes difficult to establish. Few genuine scientific authorities have affirmed the existence of the Loch Ness monster or the abominable snowman, for example; but these few have won a level of recognition—along with television appearances, speaking engagements, and book contracts—that they could never gain voicing more orthodox opinions. These experts may be expressing their honest judgments, but the resulting acclaim should be taken into consideration when you assess their testimony.

Predictable Judgments

Arguments by authority is presumed biased if it is totally predictable—that is, when it reflects the traditional loyalty or antagonism of a particular group. A definitive example occurred in 1977 when Alabama's football team was ranked second in the final AP and UPI national polls.

Thereupon the Alabama state legislature issued its own poll, and Alabama moved up to No. 1. Equally predictable are pamphlets on smoking and health distributed by the Tobacco Institute, and the publicized study of pain relievers produced by The Bayer Company.

This presumption of bias appears most notably in political argument. When *any* Democrat is nominated for president, the man and his platform will be praised in liberal periodicals (*Washington Post, St. Louis Post-Dispatch, Commonweal*) and condemned by conservative publications (*Chicago Tribune, Los Angeles Times, National Review*). When any President finishes his State-of-the-Union message, opposition spokesmen will call his program inadequate, wrong-headed, and potentially dangerous. You must judge these claims on specific evidence; such predictable views carry little authority.

DISTORTING QUOTATIONS

Besides a doubtful expert and a biased opinion, other misleading features attend argument by authority. Statements are sometimes abridged. (The advertisement of Kyle Onstott's *Mandingo* quotes a review from the *Dallas News*: ". . . like no other book ever written about the South. . . .") Assertions may be irrelevant to the present issue. (The paperback edition of *Nightmare in Pink* prints Richard Condon's opinion that "John D. MacDonald is the great American story-teller.") Quotations appear without source. (See *Hand in Hand*—"The Most Widely Praised Motion Picture of Them All!") Undated statements can be impressive. (Commonly in Presidential campaigns, opposition spokesmen will embarrass a candidate by quoting statements he made a decade or two earlier.) Exact quotations can be presented in a distorting context. (Under the heading "How L.B.J. Would Remake America," *Common Sense* printed a sentence from the President's 1964 State-of-the-Union message: "We are going to try to take all the money that we think is unnecessarily being spent and take it from the 'haves' and give it to the 'have nots' that need it so much." As the context of the speech made clear, Johnson did not advocate taking from the rich to give to the poor; he proposed taking money from the more heavily-funded federal programs and putting it in those with smaller appropriations.) And with the advent of the tape recorder, new techniques are possible. (In the 1972 campaign in Alabama, opponents spliced together separate parts of a taped interview and broadcast Senator John Sparkman's voice saying, "Will the cause of desegregation be served? If so, the busing is all right.")

Lies

Expert testimony can lend itself to bald misstatement of fact, on the part of either an authority or those who quote him. A national columnist attacked Quentin Reynolds as a communist, a womanizer, and a war profiteer. A U.S. Senator called newsman Drew Pearson a child molester. Many have circulated the story that three Pennsylvania students on LSD became blind from staring at the sun for several hours, and that a Michigan teacher took off all her clothes to demonstrate female anatomy to her coed sex-education class. All these sensational claims were lies.

Fictional quotations appear as evidence. For many years the statement "We shall force the United States to spend itself to destruction" has been attributed to Nikolai Lenin and used to ground American political argument. More recently, spokesmen have circulated a statement protesting the communist threat and concluding, "We need law and order"; they ascribe this to Adolf Hitler. Both quotations are wholly fictional. During the 1972 Presidential primary in Florida, letters were mailed on Senator Edmund Muskie's stationery accusing his Democratic opponents, Senators Humphrey and Jackson, of sexual indiscretions; the letters were written by Republican partisans intending to discredit all three men. Not long ago a news story proclaiming that marijuana may cure cancer quoted Dr. James H. Kostinger, director of research for the Pittsburgh Academy of Forensic Medicine, who had been conducting studies in this area for four years. Investigation later revealed that the Academy did not exist and that no medical school in Pittsburgh had ever heard of Dr. James H. Kostinger.

Though expert testimony can be misused by dishonest spokesmen, it remains a forceful element of legitimate argument. Where genuine authorities agree with you, quote them in your writing. Your case will be more persuasive.

EXERCISES

How reliable are these arguments from authority?

1. Fluoridation causes gum disease. Many eminent authorities, such as Dr. H. K. Box, University of Toronto, and Dr. G. C. Geiger, Florida State Dental Health officer, have observed a marked increase in periodontal (gum) disease where small amounts of fluoride occur naturally in water.

2. In the Song of Solomon (6:10), God describes a pure woman as being "fair as the moon, clear as the sun." I do not believe Our Lord will permit the fairness and beauty of the moon to be corrupted by sinful men seeking to establish bases from which they can spread military death and destruction.

3. *Shakespeare of London* by Marchette Chute. "The best biography of Shakespeare."—Bernadine Kielty, *Book-of-the-Month Club News.*

4. Banning marijuana establishes a frightening precedent, under which puritanical bias is more important to our legislators than experimentally determined fact. Dr. Philip Handler, board chairman of the National Science Foundation, bluntly told a House subcommittee investigating drug laws,

"It is our puritan ethics . . . rather than science" that say we should not smoke marijuana.

5. Review of the movie *Martin Luther.* "Although technically well produced and acted, I detected in it the writing and directing techniques of 'emphasis and omission' often employed by communist film propagandists."—William F. Mooring, *The Catholic Herald*

6. I think it's silly for this country to get into a patriotic fervor about an abstract issue. Remember that Dr. Johnson called patriotism the "last refuge of a scoundrel" and that Shakespeare said, "What is honour? A word . . . Air."

7. Officer, I want to confess to the violent sex crime that occurred in Detroit last month.

8. In almost no time, Aspen has become one of the most popular cars around. And for good reason. It's one of the best cars around. So, with so many happy and pleased Aspen owners across the country, Aspen has become less "unbelievable." And more believable. Just ask any believer who owns a Dodge Aspen.

   "I love the overall car. The size, handling, and visibility are excellent. And the price was very good. My family and friends just love it."

   "I like the way Aspen handles on the road. It's very comfortable for a small car. And you get a lot of car for the price."

   "I test-drove an Aspen, and that was it. I like the ride, the handling, and the looks."

9. In 1968, Pope Paul VI said that bones found beneath St. Peter's Basilica 18 years earlier, had been identified "in a manner we think of as convincing" as those of the apostle St. Peter.

10. Marlboro is America's largest-selling cigarette.

11. Two important medical research studies (one at a leading university and another at a major hospital) had proved that Excedrin is significantly more effective against pain than the common aspirin tablet.

12. "CHRISTIANS AWAKE—The Communists are trying to disarm you. Jesus told His disciples to arm themselves. Read St. Luke 22:36 and 37."— Whitehouse Gun-shop; Merced, California

ESSAY ASSIGNMENTS

Write an essay either affirming or opposing one of these statements. The arguments you encounter in your background reading will include expert testimony, and so should your essay.

1. Marijuana smoking should be legalized.
2. Vitamin C pills are necessary for good health.
3. Speaking in tongues is a genuine spiritual gift.
4. Flying saucers are here.
5. Fluoridation of drinking water is dangerous.
6. A faith healer can help you.
7. To remain healthy, one should avoid X. (Fill in the X.)

Jeanne Schinto

IS OUR DIET
DRIVING US CRAZY?

*Let thy food be thy medicine and thy medicine be thy
food.*

—*Hippocrates*

Drastic changes in our eating patterns since the turn of the century have
played havoc with our physical well-being. Diabetes, hypertension, heart
disease, and cancer are among the major health problems identified as
nutrition-related. Less certain is how a diet that includes more than 126
pounds of sugar and nine pounds of additives each year has affected our
mental well-being. A growing number of scientists and physicians are
convinced that many of the 6.4 million Americans now under some form

of mental health care—as well as the estimated 13.6 million in need of such care—could be cured by better nutrition.

When Benjamin F. Feingold, chief emeritus of the Department of Allergy at the Kaiser-Permanente Medical Center in San Francisco, eliminated artificially dyed and flavored foods from the diets of his hyperactive patients, 40 to 50 per cent showed improvement. Dr. Feingold's hypothesis, first advanced in 1973, is that many of the one million to five million American schoolchildren diagnosed as hyperkinetic are actually displaying a syndrome of behavioral toxicity, due to excessive ingestion of these substances. There are now 100 "Feingold Associations" in twenty-five states, and they claim great success in applying his findings.

When therapists eliminated sugar from the diets of children diagnosed as "hyperactive" and "learning disabled," many improved. The New York Institute of Child Development reports an improvement rate of up to 73 per cent.

Abram Hoffer, a biochemist and physician in Saskatchewan, suggests that 70 per cent of the inmates imprisoned there for serious crimes have vitamin deficiencies which were the primary cause of their aggressive behavior. His research also indicates that about 90 per cent of convicted murderers diagnosed as paranoid schizophrenic suffer from vitamin deficiencies or low blood sugar (hypoglycemia).

Historically, mental illness attributable to nutrient deficiencies has been extensively demonstrated. Michael Lesser, a Berkeley psychiatrist, cites the example of pellagra: "Less than forty years ago, upwards of 10 per cent of the population of some Southern mental hospitals were suffering from pellagra, a B-vitamin deficiency caused by eating a high-corn, low-protein diet, inadequate in niacin. Until it was discovered that these persons were suffering from malnutrition, they were considered schizophrenic. When they were placed on a corrective diet, their sanity returned."

That poor nutrition causes some mental health problems was also the conclusion of the Senate Select Committee on Nutrition and Human Needs after hearings on Mental Health and Mental Development were held last June. Committee Chairman George McGovern noted, however, that "achieving recognition of the relationship between nutrition and mental health is still very much a struggle. Established scientific thinking remains weighted against those few scientists and practitioners who are striving to understand the complex links between the foods we consume and how we think and behave as individuals."

Frederick J. Stare, a founder and chairman of the Department of Nutrition at Harvard University's School of Public Health, remains one of the country's leading defenders of sugar in our diet. He thinks the substance has been "unduly maligned." He applauds it as "the least expen-

sive important source of calories" and "an important nutrient and food."
Dr. Stare also believes as much as 30 per cent of our total calories can be
sugar. Yet the McGovern Committee's controversial "Dietary Goals for
the United States," released in February 1977, suggests a sugar intake of
no more than 15 per cent to protect health.

The American Medical Association and the American Academy of
Pediatrics, skeptical of the Feingold hypothesis, are closely allied with
the drug industry, which obviously believes hyperactivity is best treated
with amphetamines. General Foods Corporation, the second-largest user
of sugar in the country, paid for the Nutrition Research labs at Harvard's
School of Public Health. Other contributors to Harvard's Department of
Nutrition—Amstar, Domino Sugar, Coca-Cola, Kellogg, the International Sugar Research Association, and the Sugar Association—are no
more eager for the true sugar story to emerge. (See "Professors on the
Take," by Benjamin Rosenthal, Michael Jacobson, and Marcy Bohm, in
the November 1976 issue of *The Progressive.*)

In the face of such self-interested opposition, it is difficult to locate
pockets of real scientific inquiry into the matter, but they do exist. Some
scientists can show that severe malnutrition will cause brain damage. But
Michael C. Latham, a professor at Cornell's Graduate School of Nutrition, claims that iron-deficient children, one subgroup, score poorly on
intelligence tests not because the deficiency directly affects the brain,
but because of low energy.

K. E. Moyers, a professor of psychology at Carnegie–Mellon University, says food allergies, not excesses, will "lead to beating, biting, and
battle." In his book, *The Psychobiology of Aggression,* Dr. Moyers includes this letter from a mother whose son, he believes, has a food allergy: "You wouldn't believe bananas. Within twenty minutes of eating a
banana the child would be in the worst temper tantrum—no, seizures—
you have ever seen. I tried this five times because I couldn't believe my
eyes. He reacted with behavior to all sugars except maple sugar."

Since all aspects of the relationship between diet and mentality are
still highly speculative, many years of research will be needed to unravel
the tapestry of cause-and-effect. However, the mental health link is the
least funded area of nutrition research, according to the McGovern
Committee. The National Institute of Mental Health is currently funding
only one project in the field: a $118,000 study of the Feingold hypothesis.

Government, in its own estimation, has been bungling the job of nutrition research in general. According to a report by the Office of Science
and Technology Policy (OSTP), "There is little formal coordination of
research planning or joint conduct of nutrition research" among various
Federal agencies concerned.

Some steps have been taken to achieve coordination, but they seem
only to have caused more confusion. The OSTP report, for example,

while a good and useful project, was almost identical to reports on the same subject—the state of Government nutrition research—made by the General Accounting Office and the Department of Health, Education, and Welfare. In another instance, while the National Institutes of Health have long been mandated to conduct research on the role of nutrients in major diseases (and, doing so, spent almost 70 per cent of the total $116.6 million budgeted in fiscal year 1977 for all nutrition research), the Food and Agriculture Act of 1977 just recently designated the Department of Agriculture as the lead agency in nutrition research.

Government administrators would have us believe that the bungling and neglect of the mental health link are the inevitable result of the interdisciplinary nature of nutrition. But space exploration encompasses as many sciences as nutrition, and no similar interdisciplinary problems seem to hamper the National Aeronautics and Space Administration. Whatever the reality—honest bureaucratic mismanagement or a calculated shell game—the fact that the research gap exists raises other political questions.

For example, how much adverse scientific information about a product does the Government need before it proposes restrictions? In the case of saccharin, not very much; in the case of sugar, evidently more than we have right now. And how political are these decisions to ban a product, warn against, it, or leave it alone? If they are largely political, how can we defend the process and the damage it inflicts?

And what should the Government's policy be in the meantime? The New York City Board of Education announced last December that it would soon introduce such fast foods as tacos, pizza, french fries, cheeseburgers, and milk shakes into three of its large high schools in an effort to appeal to "student tastes" and thus avoid waste. The Las Vegas School Board has already put such a plan into action for the same reasons. These items, it is said, will be "enriched" and will meet current nutrition requirements, but the idea that their less nutritious counterparts are healthful will be unavoidable.

Because the Government is in the formidable position of legislating diet through its Federal food assistance programs—some 44.8 million children are eligible for the National School Lunch Program—that diet should reflect our most recent nutrition information, rather than the questionable products pushed by an industry whose top concern has never been the nation's health.

In addition to enforcing a much sounder nutritional policy for its food assistance programs, the Government should allocate more funds to effective research into the mental health link. Dr. Michael Lesser of Berkeley proposes that we develop community health care systems where we could also do research: "I think it is wrong to do our research in the lab," he told the McGovern Committee. "We are talking about human reactions. When you are studying humans, the research needs to be done in the field. . . . And when you're using nutrients and nutrition, you're using safe substances so it is not dangerous to do clinical research in this area."

Finally, what is the role of the medical community in all this—not researchers, but practicing physicians? Historically, nutrition was a physician's first line of defense against both physical and mental ills. Now, according to a survey of 114 medical schools by the AMA's Department of Foods and Nutrition, only 63 per cent of the responding schools *offered* nutrition courses, and only 23 per cent *required* a nutrition course.

"The students in medical schools are taught to use drugs, not vitamins," laments Dr. Lesser. He views using drugs to treat mental illness as highly destructive. While tranquilizers may gold-plate the drug industry, they are "a chemical strait jacket" for the mentally ill. Nutrients, on the other hand, come closer to treating the mental disease where it starts, according to Dr. Lesser, who adds, "Nobody has ever claimed that mental illness is due to a deficiency of thorazine or valium."

If we are ever going to find the nutritional keys to mental health, a sound Governmental structure that will not be swayed by the special interests of the food or drug industries is needed. We must also demand of the medical community a greater emphasis upon nutritional counseling. If these steps sound basic, it is because good food and health are such basic human rights. That we have let them slip away from us is tragic, but we can get them back.

DISCUSSION QUESTIONS

1. Judge the relative expertness of the authorities cited by the author:
   Benjamin Feingold
   100 "Feingold Associations"
   therapists
   New York Institute of Child Development
   Abram Hoffer
   Michael Lesser
   Senate Select Committee on Nutrition and Human Needs
   George McGovern
   Frederick J. Stare
   American Medical Association
   American Academy of Pediatrics
   Harvard's School of Public Health
   Michael C. Latham
   K. E. Moyers
   National Institute of Mental Health
   New York City Board of Education
   Las Vegas Board of Education

2. How many of these authorities support the author's contention that sugar and food additives contribute significantly to impaired mental health?
3. Specifically, what do Dr. Hoffer and Professors Latham and Moyers contribute to her case?
4. How does the author explain away the authorities who differ with her?
5. Complaining that the "mental health link is the least funded area of nutrition research," the author cites examples of government "bungling and neglect." What does she mean when she mentions all this might be a "calculated shell game"?
6. Taking information solely from this essay, make the best case against sugar that you can. How persuasive is that case?
7. Do all of the statistics in this essay seem equally reliable?

David A. Noebel

HEROIN, MARIJUANA, AND LSD

Narcotics, of course, are dangerous even when administered under the care of a physician. Both heroin and marijuana are exceedingly dangerous. Heroin is the strongest and most addictive opium derivative and is either sniffed into the nasal passages through the nose or mixed in water and heated to form a solution and injected intravenously with a hypodermic directly into the bloodstream. Marijuana is a derivative from the hemp weed, which affects the nervous system and the brain of the user, causing mental unbalance for varying periods of time and in which a sufficient dose of the active substance—tetrahydrocannabianol—is capable of producing all the hallucinatory and psychotic effects relative to LSD (which is conceded to be one of the most powerful drugs known).

Repeated use of heroin produces psychological and physical dependence in which the user has an overwhelming compulsion to continue using the drug. Under heroin the body develops a tolerance for it in the

Reprinted from *The Beatles: A Study in Drugs, Sex and Revolution* (Tulsa, Okla: Christian Crusade Publications, 1969), pp. 13–17.

bloodstream and virtually all bodily functions are attuned to that presence. Of course, once the victim has the habit, he stops at nothing to satisfy it, and since heroin is considered incurably addictive, when the narcotic is no longer in the body, death can result even during the withdrawal process.

Marijuana, on the other hand, is no less to be desired. In a timely article on narcotics, Dr. Susan Huck, in a personal interview with the noted geneticist, Dr. Louis Diaz de Souza (who has spent 18 years investigating the effects of marijuana on the human body) found that "even one smoke of marijuana does calamitous damage to the chromosomes." The doctor told her that damage to one chromosome, "may mean that the child will be hemophilian, or mongoloid, or afflicted with leukemia. The chromosome may pass from one generation to another. The child of the marijuana user may show this damage or his child may show it."[1]

Unfortunately, a semantical argument has developed over the usage of the word "addictive" and "dependent." Some argue the drug is not addictive, but rather the user only becomes dependent on it. Others, e.g., Dr. Hardin Jones, of the Donner Laboratory at the University of California (Berkeley), maintains that marijuana is habit-forming and with continued use it is addictive. Naturally, the argument makes little difference since (1) few are so sophisticated as to see any difference between "addictive" and "dependent" and (2) since it takes the user away from reality and removes his normal inhibitions, marijuana is harmful apart from either word. Smith, Kline & French Laboratories, in a special report prepared primarily for educators, found marijuana not only impairing the user's ability to drive an automobile, but producing such physical effects as dizziness, dry mouth, dilated pupils and burning eyes, urinary frequency, diarrhea, nausea and vomiting.[2]

Dr. Hardin Jones in his research found marijuana not only habit-forming and addictive with continued use, but also reported (1) that although it does not lead to the use of harder narcotics through chemical addiction, it promotes a curiosity about the harder drugs; (2) that its effect is cumulative, witness that a neophyte needs several joints to "turn on," whereas a professional can get high on one; (3) that it interferes with normal perceptions; (4) that its cumulative impact brings repeated hallucinations that disturb the reference memory, causing (5) wholesale abandonment of goals and ambitions.

Jones goes on to say that marijuana and other drugs are in a very real sense sexual stimulants. Marijuana is a mild aphrodisiac. "It enhances sensitivity and makes a person more receptive to sensual stimuli," he

[1] *American Opinion,* May 1969, p. 58.
[2] *Tulsa Daily World,* May 5, 1967, p. 8.

says, "but this condition only lasts a short period of time and chronic marijuana users find that sex activities without the drug are difficult and confusing."[3]

And the world-famous authority on marijuana, Dr. Constandinos J. Miras, of the University of Athens, who has been studying man and marijuana for over twenty-five years, found marijuana users to have abnormal brain wave readings and marked behavioral changes. Longtime users, for example, revealed chronic lethargy and loss of inhibitions for two years after their last usage. Many of his subjects were slipping into less demanding jobs as the habit got a firmer grip on them and were variously depressed and exalted, not always sure when they were having hallucinations. Others went through a rapid succession of physical changes—crying, laughing, sluggishness, hunger for sugar, hallucinating. The idea of the so-called harmless use of marijuana is either ignorance or deception. And one State official in Maryland remarked that marijuana not only induces a lethargy in most people, but a dangerous attitude toward the community.

The hallucinogens which are popularly known as psychedelics (since they produce sensations distorting time, space, sound and color) include LSD, STP and DMT. All hallucinogens create hallucinations which lessen the user's ability to discriminate between fact and fancy, and studies indicate that LSD may cause chromosome damage which could result in mental deficiencies and blood diseases in children born to users. One of the foremost authorities in the United States on LSD is Dr. J. Thomas Ungerleider. He states that, "LSD has been called a consciousness-expanding drug. In fact, it is quite the reverse. It decreases one's ability to select and pay attention. Therefore, it decreases conscious functions. Sensations do become intensified. Perception, however, is not enhanced, and visual and auditory acuteness are not revolutionized, but rather are distorted." Since LSD dulls the user's objective judgment, which is replaced by purely subjective values, Dr. Ungerleider says, "LSD seems to affect a person's value system."[4]

Then, too, both the amphetamines and barbiturates are danger drugs. Amphetamines, often called pep pills, produce a feeling of excitation which usually manifests itself in appetite loss with an increasing ability to go without sleep for long periods of time. The most common amphetamines are Benzedrine (called Bennies), Dexedrine (called Dexies) and Methadrine (referred to as crystal or speed). The danger, of course, with amphetamines as well as barbiturates is the psychological desire to continue using the drugs. The most common barbiturates are Amytal (referred to as Blue Heavens), Nembutal (or Yellow Jackets) and Seconal (called Red Devils or Red Birds). In the jargon of drug addicts,

[3] *Tulsa Daily World*, September 25, 1969, p. 16A.
[4] *Tulsa Tribune*, February 24, 1967, p. 14.

barbiturates in general are referred to as "goofballs" and affect the central nervous system and the brain by slowly depressing the mental and physical functions of the body. A person under the influence of a barbiturate will be disoriented to time, place and person and may experience delusions and hallucinations.

Obviously, such drugs cannot be equated with apple pie and vanilla ice cream. And any drug—marijuana, for example, which at one moment makes a person feel so tiny he is not able to step off an eight-inch curb, and yet an hour later makes him feel so huge he could step off a ten-story building—is dangerous. Any individual, who under the influence of marijuana can barrel down the highway at 80 mph and assume he is only traveling 20 mph, or drive through a red light which appears to be green and smash into a row of cars which appeared to be a mile away, is dangerous. And, any drug—LSD, for example, which makes a person feel he can fly like a bird and so take off from a four-story building only to discover he is flying to his death—is not safe.

DISCUSSION QUESTIONS

1. Because no experimental studies are described in the essay, the reader must judge on the basis of the testimony of a number of authorities. Compare and evaluate them:
   a. David A. Noebel
   b. Dr. Susan Huck
   c. Dr. Louis Diaz de Souza
   d. *American Opinion*
   e. some [who] argue the drug is not addictive
   f. others
   g. Dr. Hardin Jones
   h. the Donner Laboratory at the University of California (Berkeley)
   i. Smith, Kline & French Laboratories
   j. a special report prepared primarily for educators
   k. *Tulsa Daily World*
   l. Dr. Constandinos J. Miras
   m. the University of Athens
   n. one State official in Maryland
   o. Dr. J. Thomas Ungerleider
   p. *Tulsa Tribune*
   q. Christian Crusade Publications
2. Are all the experts speaking within the area of their competence? What kind of tests, for example, could the Donner Laboratory perform to permit Dr. Jones to claim that marijuana leads to "wholesale abandonment of goals and ambitions"?
3. The author writes that, "Narcotics, of course, are dangerous even when . . ."; that, "The danger, of course, with amphetamines as well as barbiturates is . . ."; that, "heroin is considered incurably addictive"; that, "such

drugs cannot be equated with apple pie"; and so on. Comment on the argumentative value of this technique.

4. In the statements taken directly from *American Opinion*, who is being quoted?

5. Why would anyone smoke marijuana if, as the author says, it produces "such physical effects as dizziness, dry mouth, dilated pupils, and burning eyes, urinary frequency, diarrhea, nausea and vomiting"?

Ruth Adams
Frank Murray

VITAMIN E IN THE HANDS OF CREATIVE PHYSICIANS

Of all the substances in the medical researcher's pharmacopoeia, perhaps the most maligned, neglected and ignored is vitamin E. In spite of this apparent ostracism in the United States, however, some of the world's leading medical authorities are using alpha tocopherol—more commonly known as vitamin E—to successfully treat and cure a host of mankind's most notorious scourges.

For those medical researchers who are at work trying to treat and prevent heart attacks—our No. 1 killer—and to help many more thousands who are dying of related circulatory disorders, vitamin E is playing a major role. And for many athletes, vitamin E (in the form of wheat germ oil, specially formulated oils for stamina and endurance, vitamin E capsules and perles, etc.) has long been as indispensable as calisthenics.

"There are over 570,000 deaths from heart attacks each year," says a publication of the American Heart Association, "many thousands of

Reprinted from *Vitamin E, Wonder Worker of the '70's?* (New York: Larchmont Books, 1972), pp. 17–26, 31–32.

them among people in the prime of life—and growing indications that heart disease may be a disease of prosperity."

In scientific minds, vitamin E may be related to fertility and reproduction, said an article in *Medical World News* for April 18, 1969. But a famous ball player, Bobby Bolin of the San Francisco Giants, credits the vitamin with keeping his pitching arm in condition. He developed a sore shoulder in 1966, resulting in a poor pitching season for two years. He began to take vitamin E. The article said that he expected to be a "regular starter" at the beginning of the 1969 season, and that vitamin E was responsible for the good news.

It isn't surprising that many athletes have discovered the benefits of taking vitamin E regularly. The vitamin is in short supply in most of our diets. Vitamin E is an essential part of the whole circulatory mechanism of the body, since it affects our use of oxygen. When you have plenty of vitamin E on hand, your cells can get along on less oxygen. This is surely an advantage for an athlete, who expends large quantities of oxygen. And, according to recent research at the Battelle Memorial Institute, which we will discuss in greater detail in a later section of this book, vitamin E, along with vitamin A, are important to anyone who lives in the midst of constant air pollution.

From *The Summary,* a scientific journal published by the Shute Institute in Canada, a publication we will frequently refer to, we learn additional facts about vitamin E. Dr. Evan Shute, who heads the clinic, and Dr. Wilfrid E. Shute, his brother, have pioneered in work with vitamin E for more than 20 years. *The Summary* condenses and abstracts for doctors and medical researchers some of the material on relevant subjects that has appeared in medical journals throughout the world.

For instance, a Hungarian doctor reports on the encouraging effects of vitamin E in children born with certain defects. Of all vitamin deficiencies, she believes that vitamin E is the most important in preventing such occurrences. She has given the vitamin with good results in quite large doses to children who would otherwise be almost incapacitated. Mothers, too.

She tells the story of a woman who had three deficient children, two of them with Down's Syndrome or mongolism. When she was pregnant for the fourth time, the physician sent her away for a rest—"tired, aging, torpid" as she was, with "a diet rich in proteins, liver, vegetables and fruit with large doses of vitamins, especially vitamin E, and thyroid hormone." She returned in six weeks to give birth to a perfectly healthy baby!

As for another insidious disorder—chronic phlebitis—Dr. Evan Shute says that most doctors have no idea of how common this condition is. It should be looked for in everyone, he says, certainly every adult woman. After describing the symptoms—a warm swollen foot and an ache in the leg or foot which is relieved by raising the feet higher than the head—he tells his physician readers, "Look for chronic phlebitis and you will be astounded how common it is. Treat it with vitamin E and you will be deluged with grateful patients who never found help before."

Describing a symposium on the subject of vitamins E, A and K, Dr. Shute tells us that speakers presented evidence that vitamin E is valuable in doses of 400 milligrams daily for treating claudication—a circulatory condition of the feet and legs—and that a similar dosage helps one kind of ulcer.

High dosage of vitamin E improves survival time of persons with hardening of the arteries and should always be given to such patients, according to Dr. Shute. He adds that there are some 21 articles in medical literature, aside from the many he himself has written showing that vitamin E dilates blood vessels and develops collateral vessels—thus permitting more blood to go through, even though the vessel is narrowed by deposits on its walls.

An article that appeared in *Postgraduate Medicine* in 1968 by Dr. Alton Ochsner, a world-famous lung surgeon, states that he has used vitamin E on every surgical patient over the past 15 years and none has developed damaging or fatal blood clots.

Dr. Shute goes on to say that at the Shute Clinic all surgery patients are routinely given vitamin E both as a preventive and as a curative measure.

He quotes an article in *Annals of Internal Medicine,* saying that thrombosis or clot formation "has become the prime health hazard of the adult population of the Western world." Dr. Shute adds these comments: "Here is a real tragedy. Twenty years after we introduced a simple and safe clotting agent, alpha tocopherol, to the medical world, everything else is tried, including (dangerous drugs) and the anti-coagulants, with all these the results are extremely unsatisfactory. When will the medical profession use vitamin E as it should be used for this condition?"

He quotes a statement from the *Journal of the American Medical Association* showing that the average teenage girl or housewife gets only about half the amount of iron she should have from her diet in the United States. Then Dr. Shute says, "Another nutritional defect in the best fed people on earth! In one issue the *JAMA* shows the average American is often deficient in iron and vitamin A. Now what about Vitamin E?" He, of course, has pointed out many times that this vitamin is almost bound to be lacking in the average diet. As we mention elsewhere, up to 90% of the vitamin E content of various grains is lost during the flaking, shredding, puffing processes that are used to make breakfast cereals.

Dr. Shute then quotes a newsletter on the U.S. Department of Agriculture survey revealing that only half of all American diets could be called "good." He comments thusly, "One continually reads claptrap by nutritionists contending that the wealthiest country in the world feeds everybody well. This obviously isn't true. It is no wonder that deficiency of vitamin E is so common when even the diet recommended by the National Research Council of the U.S.A. contains something like 6 milligrams of vitamin E per day before it is cooked!"

In another issue of *The Summary*, we learn how two Brazilian researchers are working on heart studies done on rats that were made deficient in vitamin E. Of 26 rats, only six normal ones were found. All the rest showed some heart damage when they were tested with electrocardiograms and other devices.

Two German researchers report on the action of an emulsified vitamin E solution on the heart tissues of guinea pigs. They found that the vitamin protects the heart from damage by medication, and helps to prevent heart insufficiency. Dr. Shute adds that this paper indicates that vitamin E should be investigated further in hospital clinics.

Animals deficient in vitamin E produced young with gross and microscopic defects of the skeleton, muscles and nervous system. They had harelips, abdominal hernias, badly curved backs and many more defects. This was reported in *The Journal of Animal Science*, Volume 22, page 848, 1963.

Two American obstetricians report in the *American Journal of Obstetrics and Gynecology* that they know of no way to prevent serious damage and death for many premature infants. Dr. Shute comments, "These authors apparently have not seen our reports on the use of vitamin E in the prevention of prematurity." He goes on to say, "No comparable results have been reported."

A report in the journal, *Fertility and Sterility*, indicates that in six percent of patients studied, the cause of abortion and miscarriage lay in the father's deficient sperm, not in any deficit of the mother's. The authors studied carefully the medical histories of many couples who had been married several times. Dr. Shute comments, "We have long advocated alpha tocopherol for poor sperm samples, especially in habitual abortion couples."

A Romanian farm journal reports that extremely large amounts of vitamin E, plus vitamin A, were given to 77 sterile cows. Within one to one and a half months, their sexual cycles were restored and 70 percent of them conceived.

A German veterinarian reports in a 1960 issue of *Teirarztliche Umschau* that he uses vitamin E for treating animals with heart conditions. A one-year-old poodle with heart trouble regained complete health after 14 days on vitamin E. A three-year-old thoroughbred horse with acute heart failure was treated with vitamin E for two weeks, after which time its electrocardiogram showed only trivial changes even after exercise. The vet uses, he says, large doses of the vitamin.

And an Argentinian physician reports in *Semana Med.* that vitamin C is helpful in administering vitamin E. It works with the vitamin to retain it in body tissues. Dr. A. Del Guidice uses the two vitamins together in cases of cataracts, strabismus and myopias. He also noted that patients with convulsive diseases are much helped by vitamin E—massive doses of it—so that their doses of tranquilizers and sedatives can be lessened.

A letter from Dr. Del Guidice to Dr. Shute tells of his success in treating mongolism in children with vitamin E. For good results, he says, it must be given in large doses from the age of one month on. He continues his treatment for years sometimes, and claims that spectacular results can be achieved in this tragic disease.

Two Japanese scientists report in the *Journal of Vitaminology* that hair grew back faster on the shaven backs of rabbits when they applied vitamin E locally for 10 to 13 weeks.

And again from Argentina comes word of vitamin E given to 20 mentally defective children in large doses. In 75 percent, the intelligence quota was raised from 12 to 25 points, "with improved conduct and scholarly ability. Less attention fatigue was noted in 80 percent, and 90 percent had improved memory." A short experience with neurotic adults showed that vitamin E brought a definite reduction in phobias, tic, obsessions and other neurotic symptoms.

In one issue of *The Summary*, Dr. Shute prints a letter of his to the editor of the *British Medical Journal* (July 1966) urging this distinguished man to consider vitamin E as a treatment for pulmonary embolism. He says, "I have used nothing else for years and no longer even think of embolism (that is, blood clots) in my patients, even in those with records of previous phlebitis. Dosage is 800 International Units a day." He adds a PS to readers of *The Summary:* "The Editor could not find space for this letter unfortunately."

A *British Medical Journal* editorial comments on our present methods of treatment for blood clots in leg veins. Raising the foot of the bed, bandaging the legs and getting the patient on his feet doesn't seem to be very helpful, says the editor. Using anticoagulants seem to help some, but we should speedily develop some new methods of treatment. Dr. Shute comments that one would think that vitamin E has a clear field, since nothing else is very effective. It is easy to use, he goes on, safe and effective.

Each issue of *The Summary* contains many articles that have appeared in world medical literature on vitamin E and related subjects. In other countries, vitamin E is treated quite seriously in medical research, is routinely used in hospitals and clinics. In our country, such use is rare.

These are just a few of the case histories that Dr. Shute reports, at his own expense, in *The Summary*. The book is not available for nonmedical people, since it is written in highly technical terms. However, we suggest that you recommend these publications to your doctor, if you or someone you know is suffering from a disorder that might be treated successfully with vitamin E. The address is: Dr. Evan Shute, Shute Foundation for Medical Research, London, Ontario, Canada.

DISCUSSION QUESTIONS

1. The case for vitamin E is supported by reference to a range of authorities:
    a. a publication of the American Heart Association
    b. an article in *Medical World News*
    c. Bobby Bolin of the San Francisco Giants
    d. many athletes
    e. recent research at the Battelle Memorial Institute
    f. *The Summary*
    g. The Shute Institute in Canada
    h. Dr. Evan Shute
    i. a Hungarian doctor
    k. speakers at a symposium on the subject of vitamin E
    l. 21 articles in medical literature
    m. an article in *Postgraduate Medicine*
    n. Dr. Alton Oschner
    o. an article in *Annals of Internal Medicine*
    p. a statement from the *Journal of the American Medical Association*
    q. a newsletter on a U.S. Department of Agriculture survey
    r. The National Research Council of the United States
    s. two Brazilian researchers
    t. two German researchers
    u. *The Journal of Animal Science*
    v. two American obstetricians
    w. *American Journal of Obstetrics and Gynecology*
    x. a Romanian farm journal
    y. a German veterinarian
    z. *Teirarztliche Umschau*
    aa. an Argentinian physician
    bb. *Semana Med.*
    cc. Dr. Del Guidice
    dd. two Japanese scientists
    ee. *The Journal of Vitaminology*
    ff. an editorial in the *British Medical Journal*
    Evaluate the relative authority of these.
2. A number of consecutive paragraphs give quotations from respected medical journals along with Dr. Shute's commentary. Do these usually say the same thing?
3. The authors begin by noting that vitamin E has been "maligned, neglected, and ignored" by American doctors. How can this occur if the vitamin has been so successful in tests and studies?
4. Studies do show that animals and humans deficient in vitamin E improved

significantly when given the vitamin. Does this prove that vitamin E should be added to most people's diet?

5. Who publishes *The Summary?*
6. How successful a pitcher was Bobby Bolin in 1969?
7. Make a list of the varying maladies the essay suggests may be cured by vitamin E. Do the wide-ranging claims for the vitamin make the case for it more or less persuasive?

Martin E. Marty

ANITA BRYANT
READS THE BIBLE

SPEAKING LITERALLY

The Dade County, Florida, referendum on homosexuals' rights belongs
to history by now—to such ancient history that I'd ordinarily let its
records yellow in the archives. But both sides keep its issues alive, and
these we shall be confronting again and again. Therefore, with an eye on
the future, let me venture into unfamiliar territory. I'm "booked solid,"
so far as crusades are concerned, and don't plan to make either side of
this campaign one of mine. For that matter, I don't know much about homosexuality; this is written out of vast pools of ignorance. Still, I do have
a Bible, which both sides are getting me to reread.

First, it was interesting to me that the antiordinance people who
agitated, demonstrated, lobbied, sought votes and called for church sup-

port in the political and social sphere were precisely the conservative Protestant clerics and lay leaders who all through the 1960s vehemently opposed those who agitated, demonstrated, lobbied, sought votes, and called for church support in the political and social sphere. Welcome to the club.

Second, I agree with them that every one of the relatively few biblical references to homosexuality is negative and condemning. Anything said on the other side has to reckon with that statistical fact. But the reckoners do have some things to say that the Florida Orange Juice antirightsers, led by singer Anita Bryant, have to reckon with as well. I think the prorights people should call the opponents to face up to these.

The claim that homosexuals should be punished, we are told, results from a literal reading of the Bible by literalists. If so, they are very bad at literalism. In Leviticus 20:13 the Bible just as literally commands people who act as homosexuals to be put to death, and I didn't hear the Bryanites, even in their bloodthirstiest moments, willing to be the literalists they claimed to be. They only wanted to Save Our Children, which is not Leviticus' concern.

Nor will I take seriously any literalist who has not weeded out the married males who have had sexual relations with menstruating wives (Lev. 18:19) (an excommunicating act that would no doubt rule out most male communicants), or the literalist who has not "cut . . . off from among God's people" any of the leftover members who "eat any blood" (Lev. 17:10, 12 f.) (which takes care of all but the vegetarians). In other words, I am interested in hearing about literalism only from conservative women vegetarians. The others are inconsistent, while Leviticus is consistent.

In Romans 1:26 f. Paul says that certain people were idolators and that therefore God gave them up to a life of homosexual actions. Anita and Company should and must first demonstrate that the people she opposes were idolators in ways that heterosexuals in their churches are not. That's literalism.

Finally, in Ms. Bryant's own favorite Bible verse, I Corinthians 6:10, homosexuals are told that they will not "inherit the kingdom of God." Nor will "the immoral, nor idolaters, nor adulterers . . . nor drunkards . . . nor robbers," all of whom make life easy in the conservative Orange Juice churches because, of course, there are none of such. But those dots also mark the omission of the word "revilers."

Revilers won't inherit the kingdom. And while Anita often stuck to the text, her husband, Bob Green, did some macho reviling of homosexuals. Out he goes. Now I'd better quit, stopping just short of reviling *him*. Otherwise the kingdom will have to get along without both Bob Green and me.

VENGEANCE IS MINE, SAITH ANITA

Dear Anita and Bob: This is my second and final attempt to help set you straight on the issue of biblical literalism. How else can I make a contribution to the "Battle for the Bible" except to ask literalists to be literally literal? This letter comes, then, in support of our new drive called "Save Our Scriptures" (SOS). You may have heard about our first effort, occasioned by the inconsistencies you showed as Bible-quoters back in Dade County. A column from that period produced many letters from your followers, who mistakenly thought it was written in defense of gay rights, homosexuality, and the losing side in Dade County. Not at all. Let us repeat ourselves and then try again by reference to a new incident.

Last time we dealt with our favorite Bible verses. From the Old Testament you are always quoting Leviticus 21:13: "If a man lies with a male as with a woman . . . they shall be put to death." Come now, how can we take you credibly as literalists until you follow the Bible and demand capital punishment for homosexuals? From the New Testament your pet Scripture is I Corinthians 6:9 f.: "Neither . . . homosexuals . . . nor revilers . . . will inherit the Kingdom of God." You are only half-literal, Bob, because you were reviling and you keep on reviling, but you and your followers do not worry about the possibility that you will be dropouts from the Kingdom.

In the newer incident we thought you really were getting your literalism right. In the Des Moines event, the pie-in-Anita's-face occasion, you were quick and secular, Anita, and that was fine: "At least it's a fruit pie." Then you turned Christian about it and both prayed for your assailant. "Let him go!" were Bob's words, and they follow Matthew 5 literally. You both prayed for forgiveness for thrower Thom Higgins, and that follows literally the Sermon on the Mount script. SOS was going to reward you, since we ourselves find pie-throwing no humorous irritation but a major human indignity. Were I as strong as you, Bob, I'd make no pretense of following the gospel at such a point. Retribution is too tempting.

So, I find out later, was it for you. *Newsweek* fills in what the papers did not: "Later in the parking lot, Bryant grabbed a pie from one of Higgins's companions, squashed it in the companion's face and said, 'How do you like it, fella?' " We do not care how he liked it. Your fellow literalists are our concern. Do you see what you are doing with Scripture and your approach to it by waiting until you get offstage, off-camera and out of the spotlight to violate the verses you profess to follow? You get the Brownie points for praying in public and the human thrill of retribution in private. Since we cannot change you, let us change the Bible. Here is Matthew 5, Bryantized and thus literally followable:

You have heard that it was said, "An eye for an eye and a tooth for a tooth." But I say to you, Do not resist one who is evil. But if any one strikes you on the right cheek, turn to him the other also. Later, off-camera, you can return evil for evil. And if any one would sue you and take your coat, let him have your cloak as well. You do not need it in Florida, it looks good in the press, and you can get it back later anyhow, because you are bigger than that fruit. And if any one forces you to go one mile, go with him two miles. Eventually you will come to a dark parking lot where you can belt him. And great will be your reward in heaven. Literally.

DISCUSSION QUESTIONS

1. Judging from the tone of the essay, what kind of person does the author seem to be? Does this expressed quality of his personality contribute to the effectivenss of his argument?
2. Does the author seem to be affirming or rejecting the authority of the Bible?
3. The author responds to Miss Bryant's "Save Our Children" program by mentioning his new drive to "Save Our Scriptures." What seems to be his attitude toward the "Save Our Children" program?
4. If a Christian cannot reasonably use Leviticus and the epistles of Paul, what attitude can he have toward homosexuals?
5. What opinion does the author express toward homosexuality itself?
6. What does he seem to think is the main characteristic of Christian life?

Semantic Argument

It depends what you mean by cows.
—Graham Greene, *The Potting Shed*

Semantic argument tries to make a persuasive point not by presenting or arranging evidence, but by using impressive language. It should convince no one.

Semantic argument always sounds good. Its effectiveness derives from the nature of words. A word can have two levels of meaning. It has a denotative meaning—that is, some specific thing or condition to which it refers ("mailman," "swim," "beige"). And it can have a connotative meaning—that is, certain emotional responses that it arouses. Connotations can be negative ("politician," "deal," "filibuster") or affirmative ("statesman," "negotiation," "right of unlimited debate"). Semantic argument consists in using connotative words to characterize an issue or to enhance the tone of a discussion.

SNARL WORDS AND PURR WORDS

Connotative words (sometimes called "purr words" and "snarl words") do not prove anything; they simply label a thing as good or bad. American politicians of both parties regularly run for office, for example, on a program favoring *obedience to God, family, and country; adherence to law and order; separation of powers; personal integrity; economic progress without inflation;* and *faith in the American dream.* They oppose *absenteeism, wasteful spending, communism, flag burning, anarchy, economic floundering,* and *stagnation.* The essence of such argument is its vagueness—and its usefulness. When asked his opinion on a controversial issue like busing, for example, a candidate can resort to language:

I'm glad you asked that question because I share your concern in this matter. My record shows I have always fought for the cause of education. I recognize the profound complexities in this area and the honest differences presently existing between good men. I assure you I will work for an effective, fair, and democratic solution. Trust me.

What is the speaker's view on busing? You can't even guess.

This kind of argument can praise any entity—a party platform, a current novel, a union demand—as *authentic, just, reasonable, natural,* and *realistic* or condemn it as *irresponsible, asinine, phony, dangerous,* and *superficial.* It can praise any citizen as a *Samaritan,* a *patriot,* and an *independent thinker* or reject him as a *do-gooder,* a *reactionary,* and a *pseudo-intellectual.* (One man's academic freedom is another man's brainwashing.) Such terms have little specific meaning. A rich collection highlighted the 1978 Alabama elections. There Fob James, a little-known candidate, won the governorship with a campaign affirming the *politics of compassion* and a *renaissance of common sense.*

Semantic language depends on its emotional associations. An automobile is more appealing when named *Thunderbird,* a bill when called a *right-to-work law,* and a military settlement when termed *peace with honor.* A hair preparation can be discredited as *greasy kid-stuff,* a business practice as *payola,* and a senator as part of a *military-industrial complex.* Advertisers have called up an impressive range of associations to offer: *Blue Cross, Lemon-fresh Joy, Cashmere Bouquet, Old Grand-Dad,* and *Lincoln Continental Mark V*—plus *Lark, Hustler, GL-70, English Leather,* and *Brut 33 by Fabergé.* The contrasting technique is to qualify dramatic events by using language that avoids emotional connotations. Government spokespersons have been effectively bland, for example, in describing a lost H-bomb as a "military artifact," massive bombing missions as "protective reaction strikes," and false statements about political espionage as "inoperative."

Names

Even names of people carry meaningful associations. In comic fiction, for instance, you know immediately that Mary Worth is good and that Snidely Whiplash is bad. And real-life examples demonstrate American rejection of vague or aristocratic names. Hollywood hired an actor named Leroy Scherer and starred him as Rock Hudson. (An actress named Doris von Kappelhoff became Doris Day.) Household Finance Corporation has loan officers across the country who are presented to the public as "friendly Bob Adams." John Varick Tunney had always been called Varick until he chose to enter politics; after Opinion Research of California polled citizen-response to the name Varick, he reverted to his unused first name and became Senator John Tunney. It is notable that the serious candidates for the Presidency in 1976 (Senators Udall and Jackson, President Ford, Governors Reagan and Carter) were introduced as Mo, Scoop, Jerry, Ron, and Jimmy.

INDIRECT STATEMENT

Semantic argument can also work indirectly. That is, in particular contexts, a purr word expressed is also a snarl word implied—and vice versa. To advertise "Oil Heat Is SAFE," for example, is to imply that gas and electric heat are dangerous. To describe a movie as "not recommended for immature audiences" is to boast that it is impressively sexual or violent. When political advertisements repeatedly praise a candidate as a devoted family man, there is a strong possibility that his opponent is either divorced or a free-living bachelor. Senator Ted Kennedy's next opponent probably will be too civilized to mention the Chappaquiddick accident, but the candidate's spokesmen will describe him as solid, stable, resolute, and responsible. In such instances you are expected to recognize the implications of the surface argument.

Often, however, semantic claims are not meant to be penetrated. This is especially true when impressive language is used to mask a negative admission. For example, when government economists announce that the inflation rate is slowing down, they wish to communicate optimistic reassurance rather than what the words really say, that prices are still high and are still climbing. When manufacturers label a garment as shrink-resistant, they want to suggest that it will not shrink, not what the term literally says, that the garment will resist shrinking and thus that shrinking will certainly occur. Advertisers for an inexpensive portable radio wish to imply that it is powerful and can pull in signals from distant stations, but what they say is, "You can take it anywhere."

PERSUASIVE STYLE

The attempt to communicate more than is literally said occurs also when a spokesman uses impressive language to add character to his argument. Couching his views in religious allusions, folksy talk, or esoteric jargon, the advocate argues more with manner than with facts. In a letter to *Saturday Review*, for example, Gelett Burgess maintained that Shakespeare of Stratford did not write the plays attributed to him. His style was impressive.

> Sir: My recent communication relative to Oxford-is-Shakespeare elicited responses which evince and hypostatize the bigoted renitency usual in orthodox addicts. For the Stratfordian mythology has engendered a strange nympholepsy like a fanatical religion which is not amenable to reason or logic and abrogates all scientific method.

Here the writer said more than that his earlier letter received much silly comment. He used pedantic language to make it clear that his response and his whole Shakespearean argument derived from a profoundly learned individual.

You should, of course, judge an argument solely on the evidence brought forward to support a conclusion, not on the effect of connotative language. Similarly, in writing argument, fight the temptation to overuse snarl and purr words. Avoid pedantic language and high-sounding phrases. Your reader will think, perhaps rightly, that you are compensating for weaknesses in your case.

Connotative language defies meaningful analysis. Is it true that "Education without God produces a nation without freedom," that Nike running shoes are "faster than the fastest feet," that Fleischmann's Gin is " Clean . . . Clean . . Clean"? Who can say? Until the claims are clarified and documented, such vague language can produce only empty and repetitive argument. Fleischmann advertisements, it should be noted, once offered to explain "What do they mean CLEAN . . . CLEAN . . . CLEAN?" The answer: "They mean the crispest, brightest drinks under the sun are made with clean-tasting Fleischmann's Gin." This is about as meaningful as semantic argument gets.

EXERCISES

How effective are these semantic arguments?

1. Look morning-lovely all day long. Use Revlon "Love-Pat."
2. Advertisement for *Valley of the Dolls:* "Any similarity between any person living or dead and the characters portrayed in this film is purely coincidental."
3. The Russian purges of the 1930s have been too emotionally depicted. What really occurred was a transfer of population, a rectification of frontiers, and an elimination of unreliable elements.
4. Some automobiles have it from the beginning. An indefinable combination of character and substance that gives them an immediate appeal. And makes them more than a mere necessity. Cordoba, from the beginning, has been such an automobile.
5. Every dogma has its day, and the dogma *du jour* is that Women Are Oppressed. This notion seems to elicit favorable noises from the least likely people, including such feminist bogeypersons as Pope Paul and Hugh Hefner.
6. The conclusion of President Nixon's first Watergate speech:

   I want these to be the best days in America's history because I love America. I deeply believe that America is the hope of the world, and I know that in the quality and wisdom of the leadership America gives lies the only hope for millions of people all over the world that they can live their lives in peace and freedom.

We must be worthy of that hope in every sense of the word.

Tonight, I ask for your prayers to help me in everything that I do throughout the days of my Presidency to be worthy of their hopes and of yours.

God bless America. And God bless each and every one of you.

7. Concerned about Foreign Aid Give-a-ways, and Communist Infiltration? Beat the Washington Crowd! Vote for JIM ALLEN—Alabama's Candidate for the U.S. Senate.

8. I can't decide what brand to smoke. I'm choosing between True, Fact, Real, Now, More, and Benson & Hedges Menthol 100's.

9. The human organism is a homeostatic mechanism, that is, all behavior is an attempt to preserve organismic integrity by homeostatic restoration of equilibrium, as that equilibrium, is distributed by biologically significant organizations of energies in the external or internal environments of the organism.

10. For a great light beer, try Anheuser-Busch Natural Light. Just ask for "a Natural."

11. When a correspondent wrote *Personality Parade* asking whether Elvis Presley had learned to act, columnist Walter Scott responded, "Mr. Presley has always been good to his mother."

12. I can't decide which car to buy. I'm choosing between a Dodge St. Regis, an Olds Cutlass Salon, a Caprice Silver Classic, and a Chevelle Malibu Classic Estate.

ESSAY ASSIGNMENTS

Write an essay either affirming or opposing one of these statements. The material you encounter in your background reading will include a good deal of semantic argument, and so should your essay.

1. Abortion is murder.
2. Feminist organizations want to destroy American family life.
3. Who needs poetry?
4. Capital punishment is necessary.
5. The publishers of *Hustler* and *Penthouse* should be sent to jail.
6. America needs some old-fashioned patriotism.
7. X should be abolished. (Fill in the X.)

William A. Nolen, M.D.

THE BABY IN THE BOTTLE

The abortion problem is still with us and, as a matter of record, is grow-ing in magnitude. Abortion is now the most common of all surgical oper-ations, more common than the tonsillectomy. In 1976, as mentioned previously, 25 percent of all pregnancies ended in abortion. In Minne-sota, a state which is, as I can testify from experience, relatively a bastion of conservatism, the abortion rate rose by an astounding 34 percent—from 10,565 to 14,124—between 1975 and 1976. To say that these figures are impressive would be a gross understatement.

I am not arguing that unwanted pregnancies are always, or even primarily, the result of careless, promiscuous behavior by teen-age girls. Poor women who can barely feed the children they already have find themselves with unwanted pregnancies. So do older women who have al-ready raised families and are looking forward to a few well-earned years of relative relaxation. So do women who are struggling to give their chil-dren the education they themselves could never afford. And so do women who are unmarried and, because they forgot to use a contraceptive (or the contraceptive failed, as contraceptives sometimes do), find themselves pregnant and feel they are either incapable of raising a child as a single parent or are convinced that to do so is unfair to the child.

Unwanted pregnancies are not uncommon now, but they were far more common twenty-five years ago when contraceptive methods were crude in comparison to what is available in 1977 and contraceptive information was difficult, if not impossible, to obtain. I felt sorry for those women twenty-five years ago—many of whom were friends or wives of friends—and I feel sorry for these women today. I only wish—as I'm sure that women then and women now do—that unwanted pregnancies never occurred. I also wish, as again, I'm sure they do, that abortion might never have to be utilized as the solution to an unwanted pregnancy. But human nature being what it is—and as the father of six living children, with a wife who has not only borne these six children but also suffered through two miscarriages and given birth to a seventh child who lived only an hour, I am fully cognizant of the temptations of the flesh that are part of human nature—I realize that unwanted pregnancies are going to occur. And I agree that, for those who choose abortion (probably with reluctance) as the answer to that unwanted pregnancy, abortion should be safely, conveniently, inexpensively available.

But I also know that—except in those rare instances such as rape or pregnancy in a mentally deficient person—the person who gets pregnant is responsible to some degree for that pregnancy. In some early civilizations the fact that pregnancy resulted from intercourse was not known; after all, nine months routinely elapsed between the two events, and the cause and effect relationship was not immediately clear. But the relationship between the two—with very few exceptions—is now general knowledge. When we indulge in intercourse, we know that pregnancy may result (assuming, of course, that neither party has been sterilized). Which means, of course, that in virtually all pregnancies women (and men) must logically assume some responsibility for the existence of that pregnancy.

So, I agree, the woman who wants an unwanted pregnancy terminated should have that right. Nor would I presume to classify the motive for her choice as good, bad or indifferent. No one can know another person well enough to make that judgment.

Obviously, abortion has—despite the protestations of the antiabortionists—achieved not only legal but moral acceptance, and not only in the United States but in most other countries of the world. The United States rate of abortion is twenty-two per thousand women of reproductive age. In Denmark the comparable figure is twenty-seven; in East Germany, twenty-nine; Finland, twenty-one; Norway, twenty; Sweden, twenty; England, eleven; Canada, ten; and Scotland, eight.

In view of these figures it is futile to argue that abortion is no longer acceptable, at least under some circumstances, to a large segment of the population. It is, however, possible to argue that abortion is immoral. That argument, as we are all aware, has vigorous, vociferous support. While doing the research for and writing of this book, I sought, as I said in my preface, to learn all I could from the Edelin trial in the hope that I might then be able to make some helpful suggestions as to how our society might best cope with the problem of abortion. This I shall now attempt to do.

First, let me say that to a doctor—certainly, to this doctor—abortion seems a mockery of all of the other things I do in my work. Much of my time—most of my working hours—are devoted to trying as best I can to keep people alive. Abortion, rationalize the procedure as you may, is an act in which the doctor terminates a potential life.

And not only does he (or she; I use "he" to stand for doctors since the majority of doctors in this country are still male) terminate the life or the potential life of an infant (or fetus or baby) but he is terminating (terminate is an euphemism for kill or destroy) a life which, in 1978, may be expected to last, on an average, 72.8 years.

On the other hand, the lives we physicians struggle to save are, with growing frequency as the average age of our population increases, those of people already in their 70s or 80s who have at most a life expectancy of ten or fifteen years. It would seem reasonable that what we ought to do is let die the 70- and 80-year-old people who, assuming they survive our operations, medications and X-ray treatments, will probably have to settle for less than optimum health. It is very expensive to keep them alive. On the other hand, to keep a twenty-week-old fetus alive so that in another eighteen weeks it will emerge from its mother's womb, presumably hale and hearty, ready to enjoy a long healthy, happy life, is not an arduous or expensive task. All we have to do is do nothing. Nature will do the job for us.

I am being a little bit facetious but not entirely so. Perhaps my suggestion will seem less unrealistic if I put it another way. Our society has a limited amount of money to spend on health care. Assume I have as a patient an eighty-year-old woman with extensive cancer whose life I can prolong for several months only by performing an expensive operation. (About one-fourth of the expense will be my fee; the other three-quarters will be hospital charges.) I have another patient, a pregnant woman, who needs a Caesarian section so that her fetus can become a baby. In this hypothetical case there is money (or hospital equipment or medical staff) sufficient to treat only one of these patients. Which patient should we treat? I think we would find few people who would say, "Treat the eighty-year-old woman"; I would expect that even the eighty-year-old woman might say, "Go ahead and save the infant's life. Let me die." With medical expenses increasing rapidly, and likely to continue to do so, we may be forced to make choices not unlike this hypothetical one in the near future. In fact, in deciding which recipients will receive available donor kidneys, we are already choosing which patients we will save and which we will let die.

Now, admittedly, when we perform abortions we are dealing with unwanted babies, if we define "unwanted" in terms of the mother. In all probability, since there are currently long lists of people waiting to adopt babies, the baby would be "wanted" by someone. But perhaps, since the baby is unwanted by its mother, it does not deserve the care and attention a wanted baby would get; perhaps, since it is unwanted, it is proper to destroy it. This is the position you must defend if you are in favor of granting women a virtually unrestricted right to have an abortion.

But let us not pretend to ourselves that that is what the unwanted baby wants. I know, personally, hundreds of children and adults who were, before their births, unwanted. (For all I know, I may fall into that category; I've never asked my mother if I was wanted or unwanted and I don't intend to ask her. Nor do I want any of our six children to ask that question of Joan and me.) Most of these unwanted children are now "wanted" by their parents. And even the few who may still be "unwanted" don't show any great desire to oblige their parents by committing suicide. Given a choice, they, like most human beings, prefer life to death. The "unwanted" hang on to life as tenaciously as do the "wanted."

We may as well also make it clear now that all this nonsense about "unwanted" babies ending up as "battered children" is just that: nonsense. I have never seen any figures to demonstrate conclusively that even a minimal correlation exists. Wanted children are battered by their parents with approximately the same frequency as unwanted children. Children are battered by a parent because the parent is permanently or temporarily deranged. The derangement has nothing to do with whether the child was, before birth, wanted or unwanted.

Dr. Ira S. Lourie, coordinator of child abuse programs for the National Institute of Mental Health, told me, "We are in an era where the incidence of reporting of child abuse is skyrocketing. There are so many factors that contribute to child abuse that statistics that show any reduction in the incidence of child abuse due to liberalization of the abortion laws are simply not available."

Dr. Michael Bazerman, associate professor at the University of Minnesota's Center for Youth Development and Research, put it another way. "People who really know about child abuse," he said, "would never get caught saying 'the unwanted child is more likely to be battered than is the wanted child.' The whole problem of child abuse is far too complicated for such generalizations."

Dr. Robert tenBencel, professor of pediatrics and director of the Department of Maternal and Child Health at the University of Minnesota Medical School, told me, "Actually, there are some studies which show that it's the child who is most wanted who is most likely to be battered by the parents. These studies show, for example, that among battered children there is a high incidence of children who are named after their parents and that the mothers of battered children tended to wear maternity clothes earlier than the average mother because they were so pleased to be pregnant.

"What happens, of course, is that the parents have unrealistic expectations with which they burden their children, and when the children don't live up to expectations, they are battered.

"There's certainly no evidence that liberalized abortion laws have resulted in a decrease in the number of battered children. It may well be that just the opposite is true."

As Dr. Joseph Stanton had testified at Dapper O'Neil's hearing, the incidence of child abuse in New York "soared" after the introduction of liberal abortion policies in 1972. (Though, in fairness to the proabortion group, the increased incidence of child abuse is probably not due to the liberalized abortion policy as much as it is to our increased awareness and reporting of such cases.)

However, clearly—and this is the point—liberalized abortion policies have not reduced the number of cases of child abuse. The obstetricians who advance as an argument in favor of abortion the theory that the unwanted child will probably become a battered child do not have a statistical leg to stand on.

Lest I be thought of as a rigid conservative, let me, before we get deeper into my suggestions regarding a proper approach to abortion, quote two paragraphs from a journal which is universally and deservedly classified as liberal and which has been and is a staunch defender of the rights of women to have abortions as they please—within, of course, the limits stipulated by the Supreme Court in *Roe* v. *Wade*. These paragraphs are from an editorial in the July 2, 1977, issue of *The New Republic*, an editorial provoked by the Supreme Court's decision that states did not have to provide funds for indigent women who wanted elective abortions.

'Roe v. Wade' killed off the movement for abortion reform, by making it seem superfluous. But this was the moment life began—conception, "quickening," viability, birth: Choose your own metaphor—for the right to life movement. In four years it has become one of the most powerful political lobbies in the country. The power is based not on numbers but on passion. It is inspiring, in a way. Since the end of the antiwar movement, these misguided [sic] people represent the only major pressure group on the political scene whose cause is not essentially self-interest.

They speak for what is in their minds a truly unrepresented minority: fetuses.

I have called attention to the word "misguided" because I think that word makes explicit the fact that *The New Republic* is unquestionably proabortion. Even though an editorial is, by definition, an expression of opinion, it seems to me that for modesty's sake, if for no other reason, the author of the editorial might have qualified "misguided" by inserting "in our opinion," either before or after the word.

However, the paragraph from the same editorial which I thought most interesting, with which I agree wholeheartedly and which I expect proabortionists are going to find very difficult to swallow, is this:

> Those who believe a woman should be free to have an abortion must face the consequences of their beliefs. Metaphysical arguments about the beginning of life are fruitless. But there clearly is no logical or moral distinction between a fetus and a young baby; free availability of abortion cannot be reasonably distinguished from euthanasia. Nevertheless we are for it. It is too facile to say that human life always is sacred; obviously it is not, and the social cost of preserving against the mother's will the lives of fetuses who are not yet self-conscious is simply too great.

When I read that paragraph I wanted to stand up and cheer. At last someone—a proabortion, liberal someone—had said what needed to be said. We have an obligation to stop playing games, hiding behind euphemisms, aruging over shades of meaning of the word "viability" and face a very distasteful fact: when we perform an abortion, we are destroying a life. We may choose to do that—some of us do choose to do it—but abortion is murder and there is no way we can, if we are honest, deny that revolting fact. (I do have one quibble with the paragraph I applaud. *The New Republic* refers to fetuses as "not yet self-conscious." To make that claim is, I think, an example of the kind of rationalizing that *The New Republic* advises us to avoid. On what grounds does *The New Republic* say that fetuses are not "self-conscious"? A sixteen-week-old fetus will kick and squirm if prodded by a needle. That, it would seem to me, is very simple evidence that the fetus is self-conscious. Perhaps a sixteen-week-old fetus does not spend time, as it bobs around in the amniotic sac, thinking about the meaning of life or musing on the works of Plato, but neither does a two-year-old toddler.

Dr. Fernando Torres, an expert in the field of electroencephalography, told me, "The electroencephalogram of a twenty-week-old fetus is virtually identical with that of a new-born infant, except that in the twenty-week-old fetus there are periods of inactivity which alternate with the periods of activity." This certainly suggests that a twenty-week-old fetus and a newborn are about equally self-conscious.

But insisting that abortion is murder (not legally, perhaps, but morally) does not really change things, as the statistics I quoted earlier show. Abortion is unquestionably acceptable to many if not most human beings. According to that previously quoted editorial in *The New Republic,* the percentage of Americans who favor abortion on demand runs, depending on which polls you accept, somewhere between 67 and 81 per cent.

DISCUSSION QUESTIONS

1. The author notes that "abortion has . . . achieved not only legal but moral acceptance, and not only in the United States but in most other countries of the world." He then adds, "It is, however, possible to argue that abortion is immoral." Is this a contradiction?
2. Considering the author's statements that the pregnant woman is "responsible to some degree for that pregnancy," that "abortion seems a mockery of all of the other things I do in my work," and that the potential baby is neither "unwanted" nor especially vulnerable to child abuse—what seems to be Dr. Nolen's standard of "morality"?
3. The abortion issue is always defined in particularly emotional language. Consider the implications of these words and phrases:
   a. fetuses
   b. a baby
   c. a twenty-week-old fetus
   d. child abuse
   e. battered
   f. elective abortions
   g. conception
   h. viability
   i. life
   j. these misguided people
   k. sacred (referring to life)
   l. destroying a life
   m. a two-year-old toddler
   n. murder
   o. a newborn infant
   p. a potential life
   q. terminating a pregnancy
4. The author says that "for those who choose abortion (probably with reluctance) as the answer to that unwanted pregnancy, abortion should be safely, conveniently, inexpensively available." Later he insists that "abortion is murder and there is no way we can, if we are honest, deny that revolting fact." Is this a contradiction?

Richard A. Snyder

WE'RE FALLING OFF YOUR LOG, MARK HOPKINS

You must be aware that lawmakers know little about the theory of education. We have heard of John Dewey, for better or worse. We know James B. Conant should be mentioned with respect. Also, that John Amos Comenius was a great educator and, presumably in gratitude, was *exiled*. Further, that Thaddeus Stevens, in spite of a bad leg, saved the common school system for Pennsylvania. But that's about it.

So when Jack Loose asked me to compare the images and realities of education for your fraternity of educators, as seen from the legislative standpoint, I was flattered but puzzled. How do you string out a few random facts to respectable length?

President Garfield's tribute to a great teacher—that all he needed was Mark Hopkins on one end of a log and himself on the other—does lead to a modern conclusion of sorts, however. For one thing, the educational fraternity has been trying to get that pupil-teacher ratio down to

Address delivered by Pennsylvania State Senator Richard A. Snyder to the Millersville Field Chapter, Phi Delta Kappa, Millersville, Pennsylvania, February 16, 1978. Reprinted from *Vital Speeches of the Day*, April 1, 1978, pp. 358–362.

1-to-1 apparently, and state budgets feel the impact. Furthermore, a lot of other worries cluster about that intellectual log. Let me begin.

For a long time, all of us willingly voted a general fund budget in which 50 percent went for education. In the words of long ago, "the scholars" were well-behaved, acquired a practical use of the English language, knew some math, some historical dates, and so forth. H. G. Wells said civilization was a race between education and catastrophe and everyone preferred education. God bless our children.

But now the Standard Achievement Test Scores are going down almost as fast as the budget costs are going up. Both in the wrong direction. Blackboard jungles in the cities. Truancy rampant and cover-up of truancy. Moreover, strange sounds from the campus. All of which prompts the question: Are we getting our money's worth? This state spends 2.7 billion in the current budget on public and higher education; and in the 50 states, collectively, we spend $75 billion a year for primary and secondary education alone.

George Bernard Shaw wrote that "Every profession is a conspiracy against the laity."

As the devil's advocate, let me proceed on that assumption, hunting wrinkles on the face of pedagogy, and tell frankly how it seems to a layman who has never taught a class or sat in a principal's office trying to draft a school bus schedule. In other words: What is wrong? And: What can be done about it?

I. ANARCHY IN THE CLASSROOM

Alexander Pope wrote that "order is heaven's first law." He might have said the same for a hospital operation room, an automobile assembly line, or a schoolroom. Unfortunately, too exquisite a refinement of "rights" of unruly lugs get in the way of pupils who want to learn, and thereby denies *them* their "rights."

It must be apparent by now, for example, that many oversize boys enrolled in the Philadelphia system either play hooky frequently or are unmanageable when they do attend. From a most surprising source, we have a suggested remedy: Spencer Coxe, of the Civil Liberties Union there, says: Set them free. They're not learning. They never will, at least not now. Further, they are impeding progress for the rest.

You may have a social worry about what will happen to these boys. The most plausible solution would be modification of the minimum wage laws—if only we could persuade the AFL–CIO—so that these youths could get into the labor force in some capacity, and from there we hope for the best.

But what of discipline in the rest of the system in this Spock-marked generation? This obviously worries the Department of Education, Caryl

Kline presiding, and the Senate Education Committee, which held four hearings on the subject recently. Looking over reports and the transcripts on such efforts, there does not seem much new. When it comes to innovation in the discipline field, no one has much imagination. What is proposed is more of the same: conferences, group therapy, or whatever.

At the risk of seeming hopelessly illiberal, let me suggest that a necessary element in maintaining order is fear, whether in an army factory, office or schoolroom. Not abject, cringing horror, but at least the knowledge that if something wrong is done, something unpleasant will be the penalty. Out-of-step in the Army, and you get KP. Foul up the assembly line at the factory, and you lose the job.

Rebecca West, in contrasting the occupation zones in Germany after the war, said the French came in like avenging dervishes, with expletives loud and imaginative, animated by the "rudest of verbs." British and Americans by contrast were almost antiseptic in their do-goodism to the fallen foe. Who was better understood in the long run by the Germans? The *French*. Indeed, in the end Rebecca West thinks they were better *liked*. There was a certain logic to the relationship, human nature being what it is. If you lose a war which you never should have begun, you can expect trouble.

The Pennsylvania Schoolmaster, published by the Association of Secondary School Principals, had a refreshing article by its editor, Joseph Mamana, in the December issue. He said behavior in schools resembles a "mini-nuthouse" and corporal punishment is an appropriate solution, quoting several principals, including Robert Kearn, of Easton Area Middle School, who has an especially appealing technique in administering it. Let me quote:

> The American flag that stands beside his desk is purposely planted there for parents and pupils to realize that his office is a refuge of law and order. . . . Moreover, to reinforce the concept that authority is absolute, Mr. Kearn has a beautiful, family size Holy Bible on his desk, hinting that his authority for school welfare is vested in him as a sacramental duty. . . . He has more students reporting back to him after graduation than all the self-appointed authorities who disavow corporal punishment put together.

II. THE AMORAL ATMOSPHERE

When the Supreme Court outlawed prayer in the schools, the symbolism was more damaging than the banishing of prayer itself. Somehow, it connoted the idea that there was something wrong with religion, and this was not lost on the young folk. So, with the cackling of an atheist or two, joined by a henhouse of way-out liberals anxious for a cause, fortified by those who would seize on anything to make trouble, you immobilize the greatest inspirational force known to man.

It is too late to reverse field now, but I heartily concur with former Dean Erwin Griswold. He wrote in the Utah Law Review that on such matters as the school prayer cases the Supreme Court would have been wiser to deny hearing of the appeal and leave the whole issue to local determination. It may have brought an illogical and spotty result, but on the whole it would have been better for the students and society, the grumblings of a few atheists notwithstanding.

We must worry about what rushes into this vacuum.

The current issue of *The Public Interest* tells how this gap in moral education would be filled if Sidney Simon of the University of Massachusetts, or Lawrence Kohlberg of Harvard, have their way. Simon urges something called "values clarification" and Kohlberg's nostrum is "cognitive moral development." If the samples in the article are accurate, these seem worse than nothing. They reject indoctrination of traditional values and put great emphasis on the child's wants and rights.

As it stands now, the parochial and Christian day schools have a strong appeal vis-à-vis the public schools. They can teach the virtues, and morality, and religion, with the authority of scriptural references, without walking on eggs. The growing interest in a voucher system arises in part from this, I am sure. What can the public schools do? At least they can offer silent meditation, as in New Jersey; and I see nothing wrong with urging *loyalty*—to the church or synagogue of your choice—in the classroom. After all, loyalty is an understood virtue: to the football team, for example. Why not to religion?

III. BIGNESS, OPENNESS, AND ALL THAT

A generation ago we were all out for consolidation and big schools, and big districts. Is bigger better? William Howard Taft, who weighed 300 pounds, thought so; but second thoughts are emerging. What we saved in central school administration and in specialty studies and whatnot, we are spending in buses and the time lost by all that transportation.

Moreover, isn't the individual lost in the crowd? His or her chances of being head cheerleader, or first violinst or varsity player are obviously diminished. If what we want is leadership or a sense of happy accomplishment, we are dividing and subdividing the hopes of thousands of pupils. All of which causes me to ask: Why were we all so convinced of the wisdom of consolidation, statewide, nationwide? Who sold us this bill of goods? Where are they now? What nostrums are they cooking currently? Buyer, beware!

As for "open classrooms," I enjoy the comments of Dr. Max Rafferty, the jolly educator from California:

Individual classrooms were done away with in favor of vast, barnlike open stretches of sheer space. In this educational version of Home on the Range, various and sundry classes, clusters, clumps, throngs or confluences of pupils were supposed to get together informally in odd corners, niches or nooks in order to be educated. Inside walls, in other words, were taboo. Everyone practiced togetherness, and nobody had any privacy.

The sound engineers found that "in spite of 'interaction, cross-fertilization, shared learning experiences' and similar rationalizations for open-plan buildings, it is apparent that lack of acoustical privacy far outweighs any potential or hoped-for advantages of open classroom spaces." (In other words, no one can hear himself think.)

(It is) a "stupid, rattle-brained, dunderheaded, multi-million-dollar mess."

IV. THE SIZE OF CLASSES

Back to Mark Hopkins. Even when President Garfield was praising the Williams College President, he must have known that no nation can afford a teacher for every student. As we have seen the ratio inching downward, now about 19 per teacher in Pennsylvania, for example, we wonder how long we can afford it and whether it really improves the learning process that much.

The former Secretary of Education, John Pittenger, placed an unexpected weapon in our hands several years ago when he mentioned to the Senate Appropriations committee that reliable studies indicated there was no provable relationship between the size of the class and the amount of learning which entered the child's head. The Coleman and other studies seem to confirm this. Teachers' organizations notwithstanding, it seems to me the burden is on those who assert we must have smaller classes.

For one thing, an increase in the average class size by one pupil in our state would mean a saving of $60 million. You can see how attractive that is to a legislature.

We are further fortified in the position by the progress made in removing from the typical classroom the pupils who do not fit the general pattern, whether by reason of handicap, genius, preference for vo-tech, or whatever. The best counter-argument is the individual attention each pupil can receive in a smaller class, but give me the proof he or she actually receives it, and I will, like Galileo, recant.

V. THE SUBSTANCE OF LEARNING

We come to a more substantive point: What are the schools and colleges teaching? If we are abandoning "basics" are we substituting spun sugar candy for ham-and-eggs on the academic menu? Some of it sounds pretty nebulous.

Here again the parochial schools seem to be ahead of the publics. Perhaps it is sometimes their press which is better, but three New Jersey parochial systems which were subject to scrutiny had better scores by 17 points, and attributed it to more basics and less fluff.

Language study never seemed to thrive in America as it does in Europe, and here there is an invasion of ersatz learning. At the annual convention of the Modern Language Association of America, there were seminars and workshops on such subjects as "Marxist Literary Theory," "Lesbians and Literature," "Radical Caucus Workshop" and "Literature and Philosophy of the 20th Century: Lying."

What of the end product of college learning? "Before and after" tests yielded the odd results of a *less* enlightened graduate, measured by certain concepts of economics. Incoming freshmen estimated the percentage of profits in industry more accurately than seniors. Nor am I reassured by a Harris poll last November that showed "75 percent of faculty members were *not* biased against business." What of the 25 percent who presumably *were* biased?

Higher education had better get to the bottom of this kind of thing. We are tired of hearing about Assistant Professor Leftwing, his salary paid from the productivity of industry, agriculture and other enterprise, making snide remarks to gullible young non-producers, and warping their malleable impulses into attitudes which cause them to choose vocations they otherwise would eschew.

The academic community disliked the advice of former Treasury Secretary William E. Simon who urged that corporate gifts be limited to those institutions which help to fight "to maintain our freedoms." But what is the matter with that? Why should one finance one's own destruction? Simon said: "No other society in my memory has reached such heights of prosperity for its people and yet has raised an entire new class of men and women who are hostile to the very institutions that make that progress possible."

To come back to the secondary level, Frank Armbruster, author of a recent book on this subject, attributes the decline in learning in part to the changed curriculum, abandoning the basics and offering too many selective junk courses. Couple this with "innovative" teaching, gimmickry, and permissiveness, and you have declining production. As Andy Jackson said: "Elevate them guns a little lower." Unless something changes, you'll be putting your objectives even lower to accommodate the falling accomplishments.

VI. QUANTITY OF LEARNING

Are we getting our money's worth in higher education? This state spends about a half billion on its colleges and universities, including scholarship aid. The Pennsylvania Higher Educational Assistance Agency (called PHEAA), a model in my view, helps about 124,000 students attend the colleges of their choice, in this state or out of it, and thereby aids the pluralism which is so desirable.

The question legislators are entitled to ask is whether we are getting the most from our tax dollar. As many of you know, the appropriation bills for Penn State, Temple and Pitt require the faculty to furnish the number of hours they spend weekly in classroom instruction, preparation, research and related activities. Similar surveys have been made in Illinois.

This was asked because the teaching load measured in hours seemed to be constantly declining at the same time the demand for dollars was rising out of proportion to normal inflation. An increase of teaching load of one hour per week in the three universities named, for example, would save the state budget over $14 million.

University faculty members teach in a classroom approximately nine or ten hours a week; at the state owned colleges, it is 12 hours, by contract. Even allowing for preparation, advising of students, and the like, this seems low to a layman. A study of dentists showed they stand 31 hours a week, hovering over patients, fixing teeth. Faculty rebuttal usually emphasizes research. Fine. We applaud Salk vaccine and splendid on-going progress in many fields. But how much more research does Chaucer need, for example? And what do the language professors research? "Lesbians and Literature"?

Admittedly, this over-simplification does not win the debate. We do not discount the devoted academic people who do spend 50, 60 or more hours weekly in productive activity, either advancing the frontiers of knowledge or inspiring their students. But we are realists, too. Some of us know that in our own professions one wastes time unless there is exact, regular and rigorous time-keeping. It is awfully easy to become careless.

It is tempting to digress on this subject. Some of us are skeptical of softer subjects in the social sciences, especially when we hear what celebrities have been invited to lecture on campus and what they say when they get there. There is an unhealthy emphasis on the "classes" of society, for example. Patrick Moynihan has aptly said there are social science facts which had better "be left unsaid." In my own case, I am happy that no one told us in Lititz High School in the '20s that there were social classes in our community. It would have ruined many happy relationships.

The legislator, individually or collectively, has no practical way to get at such matters without seeming like a buttinsky, a bookburner, a censor, or a rapist of academic honor. Yet as Grandpa said in "You Can't Take It with You," a cat can look at a king. We wish the academic royalists would clean up the palace stables.

The nexus between education and government is, to put it crassly, money. Yet if standards are declining, to pour on more funds seems like the fool's solution for the fire in the haystack: "Heap on more hay." And to quote Moynihan again, "After a point expenditure does not seem to have any notable influence on school achievement."

Be assured that we do not begrudge members of the profession a rising and respectable income. For what society expects of its teachers, they should have it. For example, when *The Chronicles of Higher Education* publishes its annual analysis of salaries, we note with pride that the state colleges pay quite well by comparison with others.

But getting the *most* for our dollar is important, not only for the saving to the taxpayer but for the sake of the student. When we question class size or faculty hours of teaching, it is in the hope that more result may be had for the cash spent. We all gain by that.

VII. IMPLAUSIBLE IDEAS

There are some prevalent concepts which deserve knocking down:

(a) That reasonable supervision of a school or college newspaper by the faculty violates the First Amendment. James Kilpatrick nailed this one. To agree with this is to put responsibility in the hands of minors or young adults who are judgment-proof. Someone must take responsibility, and the administration had better assume it.

(b) To deny certain celebrities use of the college auditorium violates freedom of speech. Nonsense. You are just denying the prestige of the campus for their speech. Let them get a soapbox and go to a public park.

(c) That constructing the Kent State gym was a violation of martyrdom. The only reason the four students got such continuing attention was because they were convenient martyrs for a point of view. The same four deaths in an auto crash would have been long since forgotten.

(d) That cooperation with the CIA, FBI or the recruiting services violates some sort of academic integrity. This rests on the mistaken notion that this nation can exist in a vacuum. It can't, and a college cannot either. Face reality and help those entities which are helping free education survive.

(e) That eccentricity in a professor connotes wisdom. This is palpably false, but students seem infatuated by it. The best interests of students would be served by frequent changes in the faculty, to improve it—as industry does with its personnel. However, whenever a replacement is made, the students rally to defend the dismissed professor.

I mention these only because fuzzy thinking seems prevalent on campuses—precisely where objective and precise logic should prevail.

VIII. SHOULD WE HAVE MORE FEDERAL CONTROL?

President Carter made a campaign promise to establish a Department of Education. He is expected to urge it upon Congress. Knowing that this is among the easier promises to comply with, we may expect a law to do it, a pleasant ceremony in the White House rose garden, distribution of pens to the sponsors of the bill (smiling and in a line to the rear of the President) and the appointment of the first Secretary of Education. Incidentally, your current issue of *Kappan* advocates this in an editorial.

What will be gained? Will it be any different than now, when we have a *Commissioner* of Education in Washington? Positions like these are filled, as Max Rafferty has written, by "birds of passage"—bland administrators lifted from the dull grey group unknown to the general public, and measured usually by how much money they can persuade Congress to appropriate to education. There have been 13 commissioners in the last 12 years.

A dilemma arises here. Would the new prestige of education actually bring more federal dollars, or would separating it from the Health, Education and Welfare package (where it is now) simply make education more vulnerable to attack? If the latter, you lose rather than gain funds.

We ought to be worried, too, about the situation if it *does* bring more federal funds. More controls follow, of course. More uniformity. More likelihood of nationwide blunders. Fewer pilot efforts by the states.

Let us not forget the blessings of the federal system of sovereign states. The right to do it our own way, right or wrong, and to profit by the attempts of sister states. The growth of our economy and its incredible blessing for all was due to the absence of national control and direction—not by reason of Federal regulation, Heaven forbid.

We should be wise enough to remember our limitations when it comes to national planning. Even the best minds are mistaken at times. Back in 1905 the President of Princeton spoke out against automobiles as showing "the arrogance of wealth." He said they would promote socialism by dividing the nation into haves and have-nots—those who could afford cars and those who would be denied them. What would he say today, when we have enough cars in America to put every man, woman and child in an automobile with enough back seat room for all the people of Canada, Mexico, and Central America? The name of the President of Princeton in 1905 is known to you. He was Woodrow Wilson, later President of the United States.

To make education a federal rather than a state and local function risks more big government which, as Churchill said, "up with which we will not put." The central government does some things well: collect taxes, run our army and navy, handle foreign relations. Remember that it does some poorly: spending on social projects, especially. You can better control the destiny of your profession yourselves if you avoid national direction.

What to do about the foregoing problems?

It is surprising how little influence the individual lawmaker exercises on public educational policy. As legislation comes up in the Education Committee, it gets voted up or down. In this goldfish bowl, legislators discuss it in guarded, self-conscious tones, quite aware that in the spectators' chairs sit the lobbyists or other representatives of the teachers, school directors, administrators, and the Department itself.

At the annual appropriation hearings, the Secretary of Education, flanked by deputies, tells what she feels is needed to keep a famished department from starvation. On another day, the 14 presidents of the state colleges appear, anxious to keep their buildings from collapsing into rubble and their campuses fresh and green, at least until commencement.

So many learned men in one room at one time is impressive. Henry Kissinger might say it is the most inspiring assemblage of brains since he dined alone in the Hall of Mirrors.

At any rate, these sessions are not overly significant for substance. The legislators give vent to their peeves: "Why wasn't my neighbor's daughter admitted to college?" for example. As far as the college presidents are concerned, they reply warily, aware more of the presence of their 13 peers, I suspect, and glad when the hearing is over for another year.

Consequently, whatever the reason for our sea of troubles—anarchy, dropping scores, rising costs, sagging standards—no legislature or Congress is likely to solve it. Nor will a Federal Department of Education, if it is created.

The baby is on our doorstep, just as it has been all along. But, if the educational fraternity is going to improve that log of Mark Hopkins, this layman/legislator believes you would do better yourselves. Give short shrift to those who have led us down so many blind alleys, whoever they are.

There's an old couplet:

Be not the first by whom the new is tried
Nor yet the last to lay the old aside.

We see no objection to a scattering of *pilot projects* on consolidation, new math, open classrooms, insipid elective courses, and open admissions. Trying new ideas is always appropriate. What works, let us use. What fails, forget. Any plausible idea should be tried, but on a limited scale. The trouble has been we have blanketed the whole countryside with such experiments and they have been what the French say is "worse than a crime—a blunder."

The old saloons had a sign: "Do not shoot the piano-player." We will do well not to shoot the educators or the classroom teachers. They must find the remedies, and there are enough of them with the good judgment to do it.

Further, the remedies will be found in places like Millersville, Grand Rapids, South Bend and Des Moines. They will *not* be found in legislative halls. Nor should we look to the trendy big centers. Let us remember that New York is home for six of the nation's seven biggest banks, and has trouble keeping its own city government out of bankruptcy, and that Washington, capital of the world's most powerful nation (as of now) cannot keep its streets safe at night. Our strength is out in the provinces, and we had better remember it.

Mayor Daley of Chicago once said: "We should all rise to higher platitudes together." What he wanted to say was a great truth. We can rise. Lift high the banners. But let it be the right flags: Order, loyalty, dedication, scholarship, truth.

Emerson's self-reliance. Tom Edison's patient experimentation. A bit of H. L. Mencken's skepticism. Robert E. Lee's military orderliness. Washington's strength of character. Shake all this together and you have an all-American concoction that will remedy our education ills and cure other national shortcomings as well.

The educators must lead the way. The rest of us will follow, gladly. God bless you and good luck.

DISCUSSION QUESTIONS

1. In his talk, the author quotes from President Garfield, H. G. Wells, George Bernard Shaw, Alexander Pope, Rebecca West, Dean Erwin Griswold, Max Rafferty, William E. Simon, Andrew Jackson, Patrick Moynihan, Woodrow Wilson, Winston Churchill, and Mayor Daley. What effect does this have on his argument?
2. Evaluate these examples of semantic argument:
   a. Blackboard jungles
   b. this Spock-marked generation
   c. a mini-nuthouse
   d. a sacramental duty (referring to keeping discipline)
   e. cognitive moral development
   f. loyalty
   g. this bill of goods
   h. a stupid, rattle-brained, dunderheaded, multi-million-dollar mess
   i. spun sugar candy . . . on the academic menu
   j. ersatz learning
   k. a rapist of academic honor
   l. fuzzy thinking
3. The author describes those who would favor removing religion from the schools: "So, with the cackling of an atheist or two, joined by a henhouse of

way-out liberals anxious for a cause, fortified by those who would seize on anything to make trouble, you immobilize the greatest inspirational force known to man." Whom is the author referring to here?
4. The author affirms traditional professors: " 'the scholars' were well-behaved, acquired a practical use of the English language, knew some math, some historical dates, and so forth." Does this seem an adequate ideal?
5. Quoting Pope's view that "order is heaven's first law," the author submits that this would hold true "for a hospital operation room, an automobile assembly line, or a schoolroom." Are the purposes and values of these three areas really comparable?
6. "We are tired of hearing about Assistant Professor Leftwing, his salary paid from the productivity of industry, agriculture and other enterprise, making snide remarks to gullible young non-producers, and warping their malleable impulses into attitudes which cause them to choose vocations they otherwise would eschew." How realistic is this complaint?
7. "But how much more research does Chaucer need, for example? And what do the language professors research? 'Lesbians and Literature'?" Is this a reasonable argument for increasing the hourly workload of professors?
8. What is the difference between the "moral education" the author affirms and the programs in "values clarification" and "cognitive moral devleopment" that he deplores?
9. Concluding, the author says, "Lift high the banners. But let it be the right flags: Order, loyalty, dedication, scholarship, truth." What assumptions underlie his championing these values?

James Council

THE CASE FOR TOBACCO

Good morning.

I am pleased to be here to speak to you today. I want to thank your president, Tom Robinson, and your program-director, Louis Gardipee, for their invitation and their hospitality. They have told me of the fine work your club has done in sponsoring the oratorical contests and in promoting the Boys' Ranch. I am impressed.

I am here as a spokesman for tobacco. I am also, in my other roles, an English professor, a Bible scholar, a long-distance runner, and an author who writes books about argument and evidence.

I am not here to urge anyone to smoke cigarettes. You all should make up your own mind about that. But I do want to talk to you for a few minutes about the tobacco industry and the health question and government regulation. I hope I can put a number of issues in perspective.

I could begin, of course, by spelling out many good things about tobacco. I could mention the genuine pleasure and social relaxation and personal reinforcement which I and some of you get from smoking. Many of you know what I mean. I could discuss the role of tobacco in sustaining the agricultural health of the nation and in maintaining those "rural virtues" which have contributed so much to our history. I could mention the important effect on the American economy of an industry which employs some 60,000 people and provides a payroll of hundreds of millions of dollars. And I would *have* to mention the value to all of us in the almost $6,000,000,000 which tobacco generates in federal, state, and local taxes every year. (That number, gentlemen, is six *billion* dollars.)

But all this, however impressive, would seem to some of you to be special pleading—and more-or-less irrelevant. The tobacco industry has had unfortunate publicity. Health-hazard claims come repeatedly from Secretary Califano of the Department of Health, Education, and Welfare; from private health agencies; and from columnists and spokesmen who sometimes seem personally offended by smokers and smoking. Consequently, anyone speaking for tobacco must first take up the large questions: (1) Is tobacco smoking a genuine health hazard? And (2) does smoking cigarettes cause cancer?

The answer is, of course, that no one knows what causes cancer. Your own doctor will tell you that.

But I want you just for a moment to look at an odd situation. If you asked the ordinary, informed man-on-the-street what causes bone cancer, he'd say he doesn't know, that nobody knows. If you asked him what causes brain cancer or breast cancer or leukemia, he'd say the same thing. But if you asked him what causes lung cancer, he might—because of all the claims he's read—he might say it's caused by smoking cigarettes. That's what bothers those of us who support tobacco. It is obvious the issue just isn't that simple.

Let me assure you of something. If it were really demonstrated that cigarettes are *the* cause of cancerous growths, the tobacco industry would join the rest of the world in rejoicing that the cause of cancer had at last been identified. It would celebrate the medical breakthrough which would bring protection and new hope to everyone, including tobacco people. It would be most happy to stop cigarette production and diversify into new areas. (If you stop to think about it, it would be a good time to buy up a few insurance companies.)

Regrettably, the issue is not that simple. Several medical studies *have* shown what seems to be a statistical relationship between cigarette smoking and the occurrence of certain diseases. But, as any number of authorities will admit, a statistical relationship is a far cry from a causal relationship. It does not demonstrate that one thing causes another.

Let me make this distinction clear by considering one of the most extensive—and most quoted—studies in the area.

In 1963, the American Cancer Society presented the results of a program of research that had been going on for four years. From an overall sample of more than a million men and women, researchers selected the records of 422,000 men between the ages of 40 and 70. (It is between 40 and 70 that certain diseases are more likely to occur.) From these records, they used a computer to isolate 36,975 (let's round that off to 37,000)—to isolate 37,000 pairs of individuals, pairs of men. The men in each pair were chosen to be alike in many features—in age, weight, race, religion, marital status, drinking habits, exercise, and medical history, etc. The only difference seemed to be that, in each pair, one member smoked at least a pack of cigarettes a day, and the other member didn't smoke at all. (The researchers were, as you see, trying to isolate the effects of cigarette smoking.)

Over the period of the test, what happened? A higher proportion of smokers than nonsmokers did die of lung cancer and of coronary artery disease. That is the fact.

And it sounds terribly implicating until you see the whole picture. Of the 37,000 smokers—all over forty, all men who presumably had been lighting up a pack a day for twenty or more years—of these, only 3/10 of 1 percent died of lung cancer. And about 1½ percent died of heart disease. And—get this—over the same period, a significant number of men in the nonsmoking control group also died of lung cancer and of coronary artery disease. So you see what I mean when I submit that the survey does not begin to prove that cigarette smoking is *the cause* of heart disease or of lung cancer.

Look at it this way. There are, say, sixty people in this room. Suppose I went around to those of you in this half of the room and punched each of you in the shoulder (like this)—and nobody fell down. (I use this example because I have a teenage son, Nicholas, and he and I punch shoulders a lot.)

Now imagine some incredible circumstance which keeps us all in this room for ten years. And every day of those ten years, I punch the same half of you (the ones over here) ten or fifteen times on the shoulder—and nobody falls down.

Then suppose that one day at the end of these ten years, I punch the same half on the shoulder—and three of you fall down. Two from the group I've been punching and one from the group I haven't been punching. What at that point have we proven with respect to my punching people and people falling down? Clearly not much.

Now it is certainly possible that my ten years of punching had some kind of effect on particular people—who knows? But since an overwhelming majority of you are still solidly erect despite my punches, it is reasonable to assume that the three who fell had some singular characteristic. They had some predisposition, some vulnerability, some falling-down tendency. And if you were investigating the overall situation, you would scrutinize that feature.

So you see, by our standards, the complete returns are not in yet. The various studies which claim to have identified cigarette smoking as a health hazard still have not answered three questions. (And these are reasonable questions.)

1. If smoking causes cancer, why do the vast majority of smokers not develop it?
2. If cigarette smoking causes lung cancer, heart disease, and emphysema, why do large numbers of nonsmokers develop these diseases?
3. What effect do genetic endowment and occupational exposures have on these ailments?

Like you, those of us in tobacco hope that answers to such questions will emerge soon. And, in pursuit of those answers, the tobacco industry has spent tens of millions of dollars supporting independent research in medical schools, hospitals, and other scientific institutions here and abroad.

Let me move on to a different area.

Despite the fact that the case against cigarette smoking has by no means been proven, the tobacco industry has in recent years suffered a notable degree of harassment: It has stopped advertising cigarettes on television. It has had to print on its packs the flat assertion that smoking "is dangerous" to one's health. We have seen effective and often very creative anti-smoking ads. Some magazines won't accept cigarette advertising. Some periodicals won't publish articles which tend to exonerate tobacco. Aboard commercial airlines and on interstate trains and buses, it is not only permissible to segregate smokers; it is federally mandated. (Smokers usually have to sit in the back of the plane where there is more engine noise and more chance of being served a cold meal.) Recent lawsuits have sought to ban smoking in the New Orleans Superdome and to limit it in federal office buildings. And sales and excise taxes, particularly at state and local levels, have climbed to the sumptuary point in many places.

Tobacco people don't want to seem paranoid, but there *is* a fair amount of flack being hurled our way.

Now we really do not protest individual or even group efforts to protect nonsmokers who may be offended by tobacco smoke. We like to think that such problems can best be solved by courtesy, tolerance, and the kind of understanding good-will that is essential in a society which is both crowded and democratic.

I am prepared to be understanding even of an organization which calls itself "SHAME"—that's S-H-A-M-E. Translated the acronym means "Society to Humiliate, Aggravate, Mortify, and Embarrass Smokers." I must tell you, in all honesty, that I do not think I would choose to invite any member of SHAME into my family-room to share my bottle of Wild Turkey. Yet I do respect the individual rights of these citizens.

What I and the people in tobacco do worry about is governmental and court actions which work against smoking and smokers. Here we are back at the old Prohibition-type effort to legislate personal morality. It has never worked. And in this case it is particularly unfair.

Think about it, gentlemen. In fairness, any legal effort to curtail cigarette smoking on the ground that it *may* be a health hazard, should also work against other possible health hazards: There should be no television advertisements for wine or beer. Every bottle of whiskey and of cough syrup should bear a health warning. T-bone steaks should carry a printed brand warning of cholesterol. It should be illegal for a restaurant to serve pecan pie to anyone who is twenty pounds overweight. To avoid danger to health, no one should be allowed to buy a gun—or a football—or a king-size bottle of aspirin. Clearly, very heavy regulations should govern the sale of something as deadly as an automobile. No one should be permitted to sunbathe on the beach or to shop in high-crime areas.

And if our government is to help people avoid dangerous, high-stress situations, I believe that some restriction on marriage wouldn't be unreasonable. Imagine the scene. At a key point in the marriage ceremony, the minister asks, "Can anyone here give just cause why these two should not be wed?" And in the back of the church, a bureaucrat from H.E.W. rises to announce, "Warning: The Surgeon-General has determined. . . ." Do you see the parallel?

The fact is, of course, that where there is no demonstrated, inevitable danger to a person using a product, and where there is no broad public danger, the only democratic solution is to give the individual all possible facts about the situation, and then leave him to make up his own mind. A man might well and reasonably welcome a certain degree of risk in the interest of eating a steak or smoking a cigarette or marrying a blond young lady.

And if today there is to be enforced segregation of so-called "offensive" smokers, we are working from a principle which can reasonably be applied to rambunctious children, epileptics, crippled old people, and citizens who eat bermuda onions or wear cheap perfume. By my standards, this is an objectionable principle.

Let me conclude.

What I and other tobacco people recommend is this: (1) That research on smoking and cancer and emphysema and genes and pollution and heart disease be carried on vigorously. (2) That all findings—even preliminary ones—be made public so that citizens can make informed decisions. (3) That—in health areas not involving broad public danger—no laws be enacted to legislate morality and curtail personal choice. And

(4) that social difficulties—like nonsmokers being bothered by tobacco smoke—be handled by the kind of courtesy and goodwill that are essential in a free society. These are our recommendations.

I appreciate your listening to me today. Thank you.

Tom tells me we have time for a few questions. Is there anything you care to ask me? Fine. Let me repeat your question so everyone can hear it.

Doesn't the existence and merchandizing of low-tar, low-nicotine cigarettes really amount to an admission of the harmfulness of regular cigarettes?

That's a reasonable question, Tony, but the answer is no.

The tobacco industry does not believe that any cigarette has been proven unsafe—for reasons I've already given. However, many smokers have understandably been troubled by all the health-hazard publicity, and they have wanted cigarettes with lower levels of tar and nicotine. As good businessmen, the industry has answered that demand. It rejects any implication that these are "safer" cigarettes.

Next question.

The gentleman wants to know how many cigarettes a day I smoke, and what brand?

I smoke anywhere from no cigarettes a day to ten or fifteen. When I'm writing, when I'm sitting at the typewriter and the words aren't coming, I regard a cigarette as a friend, and I welcome a few. On days when I'm not writing and there is no convivial social occasion, I may not smoke at all. I would say I average six to ten cigarettes a day. I try to keep the number down because I'm a runner, and I want to maintain my wind.

I smoke Viceroy. I do this because they remind me of a girl named Patricia. I haven't seen her in twenty-six years.

Next question.

Are there any situations when I think individuals shouldn't smoke?

Of course. One should always honor the specific recommendation of his doctor. We've all been told at times that we have a particular condition and should forego alcohol or sex or coffee or cigarettes. No one should smoke if his physician warns it will aggravate a particular condition.

Also, I don't think anyone should light up if he thinks someone else in the area might be bothered by tobacco smoke. Speaking as an Alabamian, I would say that such smoking is not the act of a Southern gentleman.

Next question.

Have I ever seen anyone die of lung cancer?

Un-hunh. May I ask your name, sir. Thank you. That is a formidable question, Mr. Ryan, and I respect you for asking it. You are concerned about a tragically sad issue. I suspect you have already faced it. I value that concern. My answer is that I have seen someone die of lung cancer, and that it is—like other cancers—a vastly unpleasant way to die. Anyone experiencing cancer, even at second hand, has my compassion and my prayers.

In fairness, I have to add that I reject the implication of your question, the assumption that smoking routinely causes cancer. This is a fallacy which I and others who write textbooks on logic call "begging the question"—assuming what it is one's burden to prove. It's like asking someone "Have you given up cocaine?"

Next question please.

No, wait a minute. Since you asked me a particularly emotional question, Mr. Ryan, I am not above giving you a somewhat emotional answer. The person I saw die of lung-cancer was my mother. She was a lovely lady, and she never smoked a cigarette in her life.

We have time for one last question.

Is the tobacco industry gearing up for marijuana?

No, it is not. The industry does not believe that marijuana is going to be legalized for ten or twenty years, if then. And it feels it has enough legal hassles with plain tobacco. It would rather not welcome any more. Therefore the industry is not now giving any particular attention to marijuana.

That's all the time we have. Let me thank you again for listening to me. I've enjoyed being here.

DISCUSSION QUESTIONS

1. Though he has a factual argument as well, the author employs a particularly persuasive style. What do these features say about him, and what do they contribute to his case?
   a. praising the charitable work of the club
   b. mentioning members of the audience by name
   c. giving his own description as professor, Bible scholar, runner, and author of logic books
   d. speaking directly to the audience: "Many of you know what I mean,"

"Your own doctor will tell you that," "Let me assure you of something," and so on

e. using short sentences as well as sentences that emphasize his concern for clarity: "Let me make this distinction clear . . .," "Over the period of the test, what happened?" "Look at it this way," and so on

f. referring to his son, his mother, his girl friend of twenty-six years ago, his family room, his bottle of Wild Turkey, and so on

g. seeking legal "fairness" for the tobacco industry

h. defending the rights of epileptics, crippled old people, and citizens who eat bermuda onions

i. repeatedly using "gentlemen," "please," and "thank you"

2. The author mentions health-hazard claims that come from Secretary Califano, from private health agencies, and from columnists and spokesmen. What isn't he more specific here?

3. The author suggests that if cigarette packages have to carry a warning, some comparable warning should be given about marriage. Is he being at all serious here? Think about it.

4. Does his reference to his mother's having died of lung cancer help or weaken his case?

PSYCHO-COMMAND POWER

Money ... love ... power .... friends ... everything you want! The amazing miracle of *Psycho-Command Power* can automatically bring you the things you most desire.

Find out how!

Scott Reed—Master Researcher—has just made what may well be one of the most exciting revelations in the history of Psychic Research. For the first time anywhere, he reveals an amazing materialization method ... in a thrilling new book called *The Miracle of Psycho-Command Power: The New Way to Riches, Love, and Happiness.*

The Discovery that Could Change Your Life

Scott Reed says, "For years I dreamed of an automatic way to do things, that would make life a heaven on earth. I spent all my time in scientific and occult libraries, searching for the secret ... until one day it hap-

Advertisement reprinted from *Baer's Agricultural Alamanac for the Year 1975* (Lancaster, Pa.: John Baer's Sons, 1974). The ellipsis marks are those of the author.

pened! I discovered THE SUPREME COMMAND FOR SUMMONING DESIRES OUT OF THIN AIR . . . and I found that I could actually materialize desires and make things happen automatically! Everything I asked for I received, with this secret . . . a new home . . . a new car . . . thousands of dollars, and more! All problems seemed to dissolve. I felt a mysterious aura around me . . . a feeling of power!"

The Words of the SUPREME COMMAND:

"I B------ I- M----- A-- T-- H----- P---- T--- R------- M--- I- M-
M--- A-- I- T-- M--- O- T- E------ O-- A----"

"Into those blanks fit the opening words of THE SUPREME COMMAND, as I discovered it," says Scott Reed—and he gives you the words, in this new book. Then, Reed says, "you'll have a secret that is *guaranteed* to bring about any event or condition you desire, *starting immediately. Anything* is within the realm of possibility!"

Scott Reed Gives Startling Proof!

"On nearly every page of this book," Reed says, "I show you how ordinary men and women from all walks of life—no better, no smarter, no luckier or harder working than you—got what they wanted, easily and automatically, with the Miracle of Psycho-Command Power. It worked for them—it will work for you, too!"

Reed tells of Phillip O., who—desperate for money—sent up THE SUPREME COMMAND with Psycho-Command Power! A short while later, staring at the kitchen table, empty moments before, he noticed an envelope with a thick bulge in it. It contained $600, the exact amount he needed!

And he tells of Bradford D., who achieved love and companionship with THE SUPREME COMMAND . . . of Bill N., who found a steady stream of money . . . Jill H., who made her boyfriend say "Yes!" instead of no . . . Gloria D., who brought her mate to her without asking.

Find Out for Yourself How to Gain This Power!
Accept Our 10-Day, No-Risk Offer

Put to work in your own life THE MIRACLE OF PSYCHO-COMMAND POWER. Just fill out and return the coupon below, and we'll send you a copy of Scott Reed's amazing book, for ten days at no risk or obligation. This is the book that will enable you to ask for anything and expect to receive it. This is the book that will change your life—instantly.

Don't waste another minute. You have nothing to lose and everything to gain! Fill out the coupon and mail it right now!

No Risk, Mail Coupon Today

PSYCHO-COMMAND POWERS, Dept. B-75
380 Madison Ave., New York., N.Y. 10017

Yes! send me a copy of Scott Reed's *The Miracle of Psycho-Command Power* for 10 days' no-risk trial. I enclose $7.95 as payment in full. If after ten days I am not delighted with this book, I will simply return it for a complete refund.

Name _____

Address _____

City _____ State _____ Zip _____

YOU RISK NOTHING! Send $7.95 with coupon—publisher pays all tax, postage, shipping and handling charges for you! Refund guaranteed if you decide to return book.

DISCUSSION QUESTIONS

1. The discoverer of Psycho-Command Power is Scott Reed. Would the discovery be equally credible if it were made by
   a. Irving Reed
   b. Nancy Reed
   c. Maharisha Krishna
   d. Bruno Kinkade
   e. Ashley Poindexter III
   f. Donald Sniegowski
   Would the addition of "Dr." or "Professor" or "Major" or "Rev." to these names make them more worthy of belief?
2. What is a "Master Researcher"? What (or perhaps where) are "scientific and occult libraries"?
3. Discuss the denotative and connotative meaning of these terms:
   a. amazing miracle
   b. Psycho-Command Power
   c. automatically
   d. an amazing materialization method
   e. the secret
4. How persuasive are the experiences of Phillip O., Bradford D., Jill H., and

Gloria D.? Would the argument be more impressive if it included their last names and the cities they live in?

5. "I B------ I- M----- A-- T-- H----- ..." Why are such "words" effective as persuasion?

6. The book is sold as a "10-Day, No-Risk Trial Offer." Why the 10-day feature?

7. Is it possible the book might be of useful benefit to a number of people?

Fallacies

The flowers that bloom in the spring, tra la, Have nothing
to do with the case.

—William S. Gilbert, *The Mikado*

Certain forms of misleading argument occur so commonly that they have
been specifically labeled. Though most could be analyzed as faulty induction, deduction, and so on, they are treated separately here because
the terms describing them are ones you should know. You will meet them
often; they are part of the language of argument.

FALSE ANALOGY

To argue by analogy is to compare two things known to be alike in one or
more features and to suggest they will be alike in other features as well.
This method constitutes reasonable argument if the compared features
are genuinely similar. (Josh Woodward is an *outstanding player-coach;*
he will make a fine *manager.*) It is fallacious if the features are essentially
different. (You have *fruit* for breakfast; why not try *Jell-O* for breakfast?)

You test an analogy by asking whether the comparison statement (if
there is one) is true and whether the elements compared in the argument
are sufficiently alike. A comparison statement is particularly questionable if it is simply an adage. Reelection campaigns regularly submit, for
example, that "You wouldn't change horses in the middle of a stream."
But even the smallest consideration will remind you of situations in
which you would be eager to change horses. Equally vulnerable are arguments insisting, "You can lead a horse to water but you can't make him
drink" (meaning some people are unteachable) and "Where there's
smoke, there's fire" (meaning some gossip is true). Hearing these analo-

gies, you might want to point out that scientists can, with brain probes, make a horse drink itself sick—and that where there's smoke, there could be dry ice.

More often, you challenge an analogy by showing a fundamental difference between the things compared. A common argument insists, "We have Pure Food and Drug Laws, why can't we have comparable laws to keep movie makers from giving us filth?" Here you must examine the definitions relating to "pure" and "filth." Food is called *impure* when the person eating it gets physically sick. Because the individual who devours x-rated moves does not get sick, there is no comparable definition of pornographic *filth.* Thus the analogy fails. Similarly, facing the argument "We should no more teach communism in the schools than we should teach safe-cracking"—you can respond that knowing a thing is not practicing it and that, unlike safe-cracking, being a communist is not a crime.

Some analogies are more complex. An instance is this argument, which has appeared in many temperance campaigns: "There are 10,000 deaths from alcohol poisoning to 1 from mad-dog bites in this country. In spite of this, we license liquor but shoot the dogs." Since it is desirable to get rid of any dogs or any liquor that proves deadly, this analogy seems reasonable. But the argument hinges on the implicit recommendation that *all* liquor be outlawed. And this action is reasonable only if you are willing to pursue the comparison and get rid of certain diseased animals by shooting all dogs. Similarly, you should scrutinize popular arguments that compare independent nations with dominoes, and federal deficit spending with a family budget.

In writing persuasive essays, you will find analogies useful for illustrating a point or speculating on an event. But keep them simple and direct. Elaborate comparisons are rarely effective as argument.

PRESUMED CAUSE-EFFECT

Relating an event to its cause can lead to three different fallacies.

Argument in a Circle

Circular argument occurs when a spokesman offers a restatement of his assertion as a reason for accepting it. He makes a claim, adds "because," then repeats the claim in different words. ("Smoking is injurious because it harms the human body." Or, "One phone is not enough in the modern home because modern homes have plenty of phones.")

Sometimes the expression is more oblique, with the "because" implied rather than stated. (William Jennings Bryan once declared, "There is only one argument that can be made to one who rejects the authority of the Bible, namely, that the Bible is true.") It is pointless to argue that a thing is true because it is true. Repetition is not evidence.

Post Hoc Ergo Propter Hoc

The *post hoc* fallacy ("After this, therefore because of this") occurs when someone cites two past events and insists that because one happened first, it necessarily caused the second. On such evidence, he can argue that Martin Luther left the Catholic priesthood in order to get married, that President Hoover caused the Depression, and that young people rioted during the 1960s because they were brought up under the permissive theories of Dr. Spock. Such logic can make much of trivial events: In 1964 an anti-Jewish newspaper found sinister implications in the fact that President Johnson had breakfast with Supreme Court Justice Arthur Goldberg shortly before he announced Hubert Humphrey as his running mate.

Post hoc reasoning is fallacious because it ignores more complex factors that contribute to an event. A Smith-Corona advertisement proclaims that, "Students Who Type Usually Receive Better Grades," and suggests that buying one's child a typewriter will improve his grades. The fallacy here is the implication that simply owning a typewriter makes the difference. Other factors seem more likely to account for the higher grades: the parents who would buy their child a typewriter were those concerned about his education, those who took pains to see he studied, those who could afford to provide other cultural advantages as well. The typewriter alone gave no one higher grades.

Recognizing the post hoc fallacy will keep you from jumping to unwarranted conclusions. No one can doubt, for example, that there exist people wearing copper bracelets who no longer suffer arthritis pain; patients treated with L-DOPA who have experienced aphrodisiac effects; individuals related to John Kennedy's assassination who have died in a variety of ways; and heroin addicts who have been shown to have significantly fewer accidents than other drivers. Nevertheless, the cases do not justify sensational cause-effect conclusions. A post hoc judgment ignores the range of other factors involved.

Non Sequitur

Non sequitur means, "It does not follow." This fallacy occurs when a spokesman submits that one fact has led or must inevitably lead to a particular consequence. He can take a present fact (Senator Tom Eagleton underwent shock treatments to relieve mental fatigue) and project a conclusion (he would make a poor Vice President). Or he can take an anticipated fact ("If the Equal Rights Amendment becomes law") and spell out the consequences ("American family life is doomed"). The reasonable objection, of course, is that the conclusion does not necessarily follow from the given cause.

The term "non sequitur" is widely used. And it lends itself to describe a multiple-cause argument ("The more you know—the more you do—the more you tax your nerves—the more important it is to relax tired nerves. Try safe, non-habit-forming Sedquilin") or an argument so extreme that it falls outside the usual categories ("Of course the Jehovah Witnesses are communists; otherwise there wouldn't be so many of them"). But the term is of little value in defining general argument; almost any kind of fallacious reasoning is a non sequitur.

BEGGING THE QUESTION

One begs the question by assuming what it is his responsibility to prove; he builds his argument on an undemonstrated claim. Generally it takes the form of a question. ("Have you stopped beating your wife?" Or, "Is it true blondes have more fun?") But it can appear as a declaration. ("Busing is no more the law of the land than is any other communist doctrine.")

Another form of begging the question is to make a charge and then insist that someone else disprove it. ("How do you know that flying saucers haven't been visiting the Earth for centuries?" Or "How can you explain the many miraculous cures produced by Edgar Cayce?") In all argument, the burden of proof is on the individual making the assertion. Never try to disprove a claim that was never proved in the first place.

IGNORING THE QUESTION

One can ignore the question in two ways: he can leave the subject to attack his opponent or he can leave the subject to discuss a different topic.

Argumentum ad Hominem

An *ad hominem* argument attacks the opposing arguer rather than the question at issue. ("You favor resumption of the draft because you're too old to have to serve" or "District Attorney Phillips wants to become famous prosecuting my client so he can run for governor.") The speaker says nothing of the main issue; he ignores the question by attacking his adversary.

To avoid confusion it should be added that an argument about a particular individual—a candidate, a defendant—is probably not *ad hominem* argument. In such a case the person *is* the issue.

In your writing, try to avoid *ad hominem* argument. Attacking your opponent is almost an admission that your case is weak. If you have a substantial argument and want people to know it, it is good policy to flatter your adversary.

Extension

The fallacy of extension has the same effect. Here one "extends" the question until he is arguing a different subject altogether. (Invoking Senator Kennedy and Chappaquiddick, pro-Nixon bumper stickers proclaimed, "Nobody Drowned at the Watergate!") Invariably the new subject is one the speaker finds easier to discuss. Regularly, opponents of gun registration begin their argument, "If guns are *outlawed.* . . ."

Either-Or

The either-or fallacy is a form of extension. Here a spokesman distorts the issue by insisting that only two alternatives exist, his recommendation and something much worse. He will describe a temperance election as a choice between Christianity and debauchery. He will depict abortion as a choice between American family life and murder. Should you question America's involvement in a foreign war, he can challenge, "Which side are you on, anyway?"

To all such examples of ignoring the question, the reasonable response is "Let's get back to the issue."

FALLACIES IN OTHER FORMS

Most of the fallacies mentioned can be analyzed as examples of induction, deduction, semantic argument, and so on. Any false analogy, for example, is a deduction with invalid form. Any post-hoc error is induction with an insufficient sample. And any kind of bad argument can be called a non sequitur. But special terms do exist for these fallacies, and it is perhaps valuable to have two different ways of looking at them.

Unless you are championing a particularly weak cause, keep these fallacies out of your writing.

EXERCISES

Identify the fallacies in these arguments.

1. Senator Baker would make a poor President; his wife once had a drinking problem. Governor Reagan would be worse; he's divorced. And Governor Brown would be worst of all; he's been involved with Linda Ronstadt.
2. Major Claude Eatherly must be honored as a man of upright conscience.

After partaking in the atomic raid on Hiroshima, he left the Air Force and suffered a mental breakdown.
3. All the speakers at the women's liberation rally were ugly as sin. No wonder they hate men.
4. Black Power vs. White Power! The war against the white race has already begun. Which side are you on?
5. I pay for my college education just the way I pay for my groceries in a supermarket. Why does the administration think it can tell me what courses I have to take?
6. Arguing from the principle that a person is sick "when he fails to function in his appropriate gender identification," Dr. Charles Socarides, a New York psychoanalyst, concludes that homosexuality is a form of emotional illness.
7. If evolution is true, why has it stopped?
8. Senator Thurmond favors resumption of the draft because he's too old to have to serve.
9. No one in his right mind would give a baby a loaded machine gun to play with. Why then do so many people keep urging academic freedom on campuses?
10. Of course, alcoholics lack willpower. That's why they're alcoholics.
11. A professor who would teach Eliot's *Wasteland* to college freshmen is like a doctor doing intricate brain surgery on an appendicitis patient. It's a case of almost criminal irresponsibility.
12. I don't like the idea of abortion either, but I think it's better than having some poor woman kill herself trying to raise eleven or twelve children.
13. Over the years since his conviction on spying charges, Alger Hiss has repeated one response to the claims and evidence produced by Whittaker Chambers: Chambers was a homosexual.

ESSAY ASSIGNMENTS

Write an essay either affirming or opposing one of these statements. The arguments you encounter in your background reading may well include logical fallacies. Your essay should have none.

1. We should never have deserted our allies in Viet Nam.
2. A massive conspiracy led to the assassination of President Kennedy.
3. Prostitution should not be considered a crime; there is no victim.
4. Daylight-savings time is unnatural.
5. Morality resides in a natural law.
6. America's space program was a waste of money.
7. X causes crime. (Fill in the X.)

The essays in this section either illustrate
or respond to particular fallacies.

Christopher P. Andersen

You Are What
You're Named

> One classes someone else when that person's name is given
> to him. Every Christian name has a conscious or subcon-
> scious cultural association which parades the images others
> form of its bearer, and has an influence on shaping the
> personality in a positive or negative way.
>
> —Claude Lévi-Strauss

Your name is the most important thing you will ever possess. What's in a
name? We now know that names are so important that they figure in
every human relationship. You must never enter into a business deal, fall
in love, get married, have an affair, hire, fire, promote or go to work for
someone else without first considering the implications of the other person's name.

What's in a name? Among other things, the difference between success or failure in the business world, or between social acceptability and
an emotional, educational, even sexual handicap. Names are far more
than mere identity tags. They are charged with hidden meanings and

unspoken overtones that profoundly help or hinder you in your relationships and your life.

A rose by any other name may smell as sweet, but many people by another name would undoubtedly be better off. Some names trigger a positive response when we hear them; we tend to associate others with negative qualities. And if after reading this book you discover that you are a victim of your name, there *is* something you can do to make your name work for you.

Onomatology—the study of names—has been confined over the years to examining the etymology (linguistic origins) of names. But a handful of psychologists and other students of human behavior, so few that they scarcely number a dozen, have uncovered a startling new aspect to the science of onomatology. They have discovered that we are all affected in our business, family, social and sexual relationships by the connotations our names carry.

The scientific data are growing steadily. Three separate studies—among Harvard graduates in 1948, among child inmates of a New Jersey psychiatric institute and among mental patients in a Chicago institution—indicated that behavior problems occur much more frequently among those people with "peculiar" names. Not that a name need be bizarre to elicit a strong response from others. John may well inspire trust and confidence, while Benjamin is viewed with suspicion. Whatever the reactions of others, a name is unquestionably a vital part of each individual's psychological profile. For example: People with out-of-the-ordinary names are much more likely to commit crimes or suffer from some psychosis. Girls named Agatha are less popular and generally less attractive than girls named Susan. An Elmer is less likely to get good grades in school than a David. Barbaras tend to be aggressive—and successful. An Allen is generally regarded as serious, sincere and sensitive, and a Nancy as spiteful. Michaels are often perceived as winners, and Oscars as losers. People whose last names begin with the letters A through R generally live longer, healthier lives than do people in the S-Z group. The rich and the super-rich are, as we shall see, much more inclined to have strange names and use them to intimidate others. Learning about the power and influence of names can help you be a winner at—the Name Game.

In fact, you have been playing the Name Game all your life, whether you are aware of it or not. But even before you could start playing, your parents played, using you as a pawn. "There is no doubt that in many cases given names, short names and nicknames or whatever forename is bestowed or inflicted on the innocent newborn is a clear indicator of where his parents want him to go," contended psychiatrist Eric Berne, author of the bestselling *Games People Play* and originator of Transactional Analysis. "He will have to struggle against such influences, which will be continued in other forms as well, if he is to break away.

This is something parents have control over and should be able to foresee." The sorry fact is that parents choose not to recognize the power that they possess. Instead, they show roughly the same degree of care in naming their children as they do in naming their pets, and sometimes less.

Soon enough, it was your turn to play the Game. As a child, you were influenced by your playmates' names, and you picked friends and enemies accordingly. In school, you either benefited or suffered from your name. Teachers viewed you, it has now been scientifically established, in a certain way in large part because of your name. These associations were to be reinforced over the years.

When you enrolled in college, or applied for your first job, you may well have used your full formal name—first, middle and last—to lend weight to your application. Before getting engaged, you almost certainly toyed with your intended's name. Perhaps you scribbled it over and over again next to yours, or tried to imagine what your first name would look like once it was wedded to his surname on a marriage license.

On the job, you have been swayed by the impressive-sounding names of your superiors. But you have also felt superior to some of your co-workers because their names conveyed the unarticulated message that they are losers. If you have ever hired someone, you avoided applications with names that for some reason made you feel uncomfortable. At the same time, you were inclined to give the nod to those whose names, carrying positive connotations, spelled out success. And when your first child arrived, you dipped into your own deep well of prejudices and came up with a name that, as Eric Berne stated, was "a clear indicator of where you want him to go."

Thus the circle closed.

YOUR NAME IS YOUR FATE

Test your familiarity with the powerful influence names have on our lives by arranging the following men's and women's names according to what you perceive to be their general desirability. Which would *you* choose to name your son, your daughter?

Arlene	Barrett
Maureen	Kevin
Jennifer	Benjamin
Norma	Stephen
Shirley	Michael

Studies indicate that Jennifer should rate at the top of the girls' names, followed by Shirley, then Arlene, Norma and Maureen. Michael is the most positive of the boys' names. Close behind are Stephen and Kevin—two strong, easily accepted names—while Barrett and Benjamin trail at a considerable distance. To you, the differences may have been imperceptible. But they nonetheless would have had an unparalleled impact on your child throughout his life.

The proof that we are either the victims or beneficiaries of our names is all around us. Yet despite the substantial evidence, every year names are inflicted on an estimated 3 million newborn Americans whose parents give little or no thought to the broad implications. More and more parents are consulting astrology charts and numerologists, but the overriding concern in selecting a name (aside from paying homage to a relative) is still the same: How does it sound? Phonetic balance, as name authority Evelyn Wells pointed out as early as 1946, is a legitimate concern. "Science," she wrote, "tells us of the power of sounds and words to influence the mind." But science now tells us that the cadence and the melody of a name are not nearly so significant as the associations it carries.

One who understands all too well is *New York Times* columnist Russel Baker. "At this very moment," he lamented, "it is an almost certain bet that somewhere in America a mother is naming her newborn son Kenneth and thereby freighting him with heavy psychological luggage that he will carry with him to the grave. The difficulty with being a Kenneth is that Kenneths are expected to be lean and fibrous. A Sydney or a Wallace has a perfect right to be shaped like a rail or a balloon, and the Kenneths' knowledge that they are denied this freedom of contour must surely fill them with hostility." As for those poor fellows named Irving, Baker continued with tongue firmly planted in cheek, an Irving "knows that he is consigned to the intellectual life, doomed at worst to years with Nietzsche in the library stacks, at best to writing brilliantly denunciatory letters to the editors of elite magazines."

Humorous—and quite plausible. We tend to become what others expect us to become, to conform to society's expectations. That may even extend to one's physical appearance. A person whose name implies obesity—Bertha, for example—may subconsciously try to live up to that preconception. The name Irving *does* have a certain egghead quality; hence the proliferation of Irvings on the faculties of universities. And as Harveys became increasingly incensed over their lackluster image, thousands of them (including one closet Harvey, pianist Van Cliburn) banded together in 1970 to get people to stop thinking of Harveys as bumbling boobs—and thereby lessen every Harvey's chances of becoming one.

There is ample cross-cultural evidence that this phenomenon is by no means restricted to American society. The *British Journal of Psychology* reported that the Ashantis of Ghana name their children after the day of the week on which they were born. According to the old nursery rhyme, "Monday's child is fair of face/ Tuesday's child is full of grace/ Wednesday's child is full of woe/ Thursday's child has far to go/ Friday's child is loving and giving/ Saturday's child works hard for a living/ But the child that is born on the Sabbath Day/ Is bonny, and blithe, and good, and gay."

Monday's child, named Kwadwo, is expected to be quiet and peaceful. The grim forecast for Wednesday's child, named Kwaku, is apparently shared by the Ashanti, who look upon Wednesday's child as aggressive and temperamental—a monumental headache. In accordance with this self-fulfilling prophecy, boys born on Wednesday were found among the Ashanti to have a significantly greater frequency of juvenile court arrests than boys bearing the names of other days of the week.

As author Muriel Beadle says, "For any child a name which interferes substantially with normal interaction is a handicap. The expectations of one's society shape behavior."

DISCUSSION QUESTIONS

1. The author mentions the "science of onomatology," the "scientific data [which] are growing steadily," the "ample cross-cultural evidence," and the "proof" that is "all around us." What substantial evidence does he give to show that Susans are attractive, Barbaras aggressive, and Nancys spiteful?
2. "People whose last names begin with the letters A through R generally live longer, healthier lives than do people in the S–Z group?" What evidence supports this? What evidence *could* support it?
3. If you met a person named Cabbage Mackeral Smith and discovered he had had a difficult, frustrated life, would you assume that his name contributed to his difficulty? What besides his name was probably a significant cause?
4. What common fallacy is illustrated when one says a person's name was the cause of his personal problems?
5. Consider your own first name. According to Dr. Berne, this is a "clear indicator" of where your parents wanted you to go? Where did your parents want you to go?
6. Have you ever chosen or rejected a friend on the basis of his or her first name? Is it possible you may have done it unconsciously?
7. How creditable is Russell Baker in a scientifically persuasive essay?
8. "The name Irving *does* have a certain egghead quality; hence the proliferation of Irvings on the faculties of universities." How many Irvings teach at your school?

Alan Stang

AIDING THE ENEMY

AIDING THE ENEMY

The Carter Administration recently decided to suspend—temporarily—
the sale of computer and petroleum technology to Communist-occupied
Russia. The reason given for the suspension is of course the Nazi-style
suppression of human rights in that unhappy country. And the suspension also dramatizes something else: the fact that the people who control
our American institutions have been helping the Soviets for many decades; not only since the beginning, but before the beginning. In fact, it is
fair to say that without that aid the Soviets would have collapsed long
ago.

For instance, in 1917, after the abdication of Tsar Nicholas, the Canadian government interned a boatload of Reds, including Leon Trotsky,
who were going back to Russia to help the Communists take over. But
the Wilson Administration forced the Canadians to release them, and the

Taken from *The Alan Stang Report,* a daily five-minute news commentary produced by
The John Birch Society. Tape 327, nos. 1–4, broadcast the week of August 21, 1978. Reprinted by permission of *The Alan Stang Reports,* Belmont, Massachusetts 02178.

Communists went back to Russia and did exactly that. In the early 1920s, the new Soviet government was about to collapse because of the famine engendered by the recent civil war. But the American Relief Administration sent in the necessary food, and the collapse was prevented.

In the early 1930s, under Stalin, the Soviets were about to collapse again. But again the United States saved them by means of the diplomatic recognition extended by the Roosevelt Administration. In 1941, Hitler attacked Stalin, who until that moment had been his partner by treaty. Even in 1941 Stalin had already murdered, by genocide, many more millions than Hitler, and the only difference between them was the difference between cancer and stroke. They were both Socialists. But our Socialist rulers in Washington decided to send about $12 billion of your property as Lend-Lease to Stalin—even though from the very beginning he had been doing everything he could to plot the destruction of our country. And again, in 1956, it was American influence that prevented the successful rebellion of the Captive Nations in Eastern Europe. Recently, we have been sending the Soviets our most advanced technology, so that they can build themselves into the threat we are supposed to need protection from. Regular listeners know that David Rockefeller built the largest truck factory in the world on the Kama River in Russia.

So you see, friends, it *is* perfectly reasonable to speculate that without American help, the Soviets not only would have collapsed many times but never would have even begun.

The Soviets claim their system is better than ours. Why not make them prove it? Why not *permanently* stop the delivery of our technology to them? Why keep building the enemy who for 60 years has boasted that he will destroy us? Be with me tomorrow when we'll take a further look.

PLANNING FOR WAR

Yesterday, as you will recall, we looked at the fact that the United States has kept the Soviets in power from the beginning. Recently, the Carter Administration suspended, at least temporarily, the shipment of still more American technology to the Reds, a decision we could applaud even more heartily if it were changed from a public relations gesture into a permanent policy. Indeed, there may be an ominous purpose behind the Administration's newfound, alleged anti-Communism.

Notice that while Washington appears to be getting more hostile to Communist-occupied Russia, it is at the very same time getting more friendly to Communist-occupied China. Indeed, Washington is going so far in that direction it is making us look stupid. For instance, Zbigniew Brzezinski recently was in Peking as a guest of the men who have murdered more than 45 million people, and he told his hosts that "our shared views outweigh our differences. We both oppose efforts by others to seek a monolithic world." This of course was a reference to the so-called Sino-Soviet split, in which China is supposed to be hostile to Russia. While in Peking, Brzezinski also made some derogatory remarks about the Soviets. He told his Red Chinese hosts that "our two countries are destined to grow closer together for our mutual benefit and for the benefit of all mankind."

As far as your reporter knows, Brzezinski did not explain why we should grow closer to a government that not only has murdered many millions of its own people, but has also been smuggling heroin into the United States to destroy millions of ours. Indeed, at a banquet in Peking, Brzezinski also said this: "Neither of us dispatches international marauders who masquerade as non-aligned to advance big-power ambitions in Africa. Neither of us seeks to enforce the political obedience of our neighbors through military force."

And the trouble with this is that Communist-occupied China is also active in southern Africa. Indeed, Peking is right now using military force to impose political obedience on its neighbor, Tibet. In short, American policy now apparently is to blurt any nonsense, no matter how fantastic, in order to line the United States up with Red China against Soviet Russia. It is amusing to note that Zbigniew Brzezinski, whom the Soviets are now denouncing, is a fervent admirer of Karl Marx.

Why is all this happening? Could the answer be that the millionaire, totalitarian Socialist conspirators who rule us, along with their Socialist partners in Moscow and Peking, are trying to use the so-called Sino-Soviet split to maneuver us into a war in which Chinese troops would be a Trojan horse?

CHINESE TROJAN HORSE

Yesterday, as you will recall, we saw that the Administration is talking blatant nonsense in order to convince us to become firm allies of the mass murderers who run Communist China. Why? Part of the answer no doubt is the impending betrayal of our genuine allies on Taiwan. But there is another even more ominous angle we should wonder about.

Through the years, our Socialist rulers have reversed themselves time after time, as it suited their purposes. For instance, when the Communists first grabbed Russia, Washington said they were bad guys. During the early thirties, according to Washington, the Soviets became *good* guys. A few years later, because of the purge trials, they were bad guys again. During World War Two, they again were good guys. Later, during the Cold War, they were bad guys. They were good guys again dur-

ing the years of détente. And now it appears they are becoming bad guys
again. Of course, during all these years nothing *basic* ever changed; from
the beginning, the Soviets have been plotting to destroy us. The so-called
changes were nothing but public relations gimmicks.

And the Red Chinese have received the same treatment. In the beginning, Washington said they were good guys, so-called agrarian re-
formers. Then they were bad guys. Not it appears they are becoming
so-called good guys again. Even though they have been flooding our
country with heroin to cripple our young people, we are supposed to join
up with them in order to stop the now-nasty Soviets. It's like a fancy
game of musical chairs. And along these lines, remember George Or-
well's speculation in *1984*, when he guessed there would be three com-
peting power blocks, always at war, always changing sides in order to
keep their respective populations under control.

So the question arises: Could it be that we are being prepared for a
war, or at least the threat and appearance of a war, with Soviet Russia,
which we have assiduously been *building* into a threat by delivering our
most advanced technology? And could it be that such a so-called war
would give our Socialist rulers the excuse to ask our so-called friends in
Red China to send millions of their soldiers into our country allegedly to
help in our defense? And suppose that later the sides changed again, so
that both the Soviets and the Red Chinese were now fighting us, with
Red Chinese troops already on our soil?

Of course, all of this is complete speculation, but the hair on the
back of your neck is standing up anyway, isn't it? We are constantly
being told that the Carter foreign policy is incomprehensible. Could the
scenario we looked at today be the real purpose of that superficially confusing policy?

FOREIGN AID

For the last few days, we have been talking about the sad fact that our
government for many years has been using your tax dollars to build up
the enemies who are trying to destroy our beloved nation. So today it
may be appropriate to take a look at foreign aid. Congressman Jim Collins, the great legislator from Texas, tells us that last year he sat down to
find out how much foreign aid has cost us since 1946. The answer turns
out to be that our total contribution—plus the net interest paid on what
we have borrowed to give away—came to almost $537 billion dollars.
That's right, friends, in order to give so much money away, we had to
borrow it, and we pay interest on what we borrowed. How much money
is $537 billion dollars? Well, for instance, it is more than 75 percent of
our current national debt.

Now let's take a look at who got your money. For instance, Congressman Collins reports that since 1946, we have given Communist-oc-

cupied Russia more than $1.2 billion. This of course is on top of the $12 billion or so that we gave the Soviets during World War II. And believe it or not, in this year's foreign aid budget, while the Soviets are conquering southern Africa by force, the United States is sending them $2 million more.

Then there is the Communist United Nations. During the next five years, the UN Development Fund is planning to give $30 million to Uganda, run by Idi Amin; $44 million to Vietnam, which killed and maimed many of your relatives; $13 million to Cuba, which is now fighting throughout Africa; $18 million to Communist Mozambique; and, $42 million to Communist Ethiopia. Needless to say friends, *you* will pick up most of the tab for this madness. Indeed, remember that the United States pays 25 percent of the United Nations budget, while 16 Communist nations put together pay less than that and still get one vote apiece. What it boils down to is that you are being forced to finance your own destruction.

Congressman Collins tells us of a study we saw recently which shows that for every dollar of foreign aid the government gives, only eight cents finally get to the people of the country receiving the aid. The rest is lost along the way in the pockets of the so-called humanitarians who run the show. And the problem is getting worse, not better.

So it's no wonder you're going broke. Americans can barely afford to buy groceries, they can't find mortgage money and are being kicked out of their homes for taxes, the dollar is collapsing daily, but our Socialist rulers in Washington are giving more of your money away than ever.

DISCUSSION QUESTIONS

1. What is implied in the author's references to "Communist-occupied Russia" and "Communist-occupied China"?
2. The first segment claims that the United States has kept the Russian communists in power by its continuing support. Specify and evaluate the varying forms of support.
3. What example follows the author's claim that America has been "sending the Soviets our most advanced technology"? Does this help his case?
4. The author defines the Chinese communist leaders as "the men who have murdered more than 45 million people." What is he referring to? How did he arrive at that figure?
5. Who are the "millionaire, totalitarian Socialist conspirators who rule us"?
6. The author speculates that these "conspirators" along with their partners in Moscow and Peking "are trying to use the so-called Sino-Soviet split to maneuver us into a war in which Chinese troops would be a Trojan horse." Analyze the Trojan horse metaphor. What is the author suggesting?
7. Obviously, all this makes sense only if one accepts a number of implicit assumptions. What fallacy is illustrated by the essay as a whole?

Evelle J. Younger

CAPITAL PUNISHMENT:
THE PEOPLE'S MANDATE

I think people feel strongly about capital punishment. I rarely meet someone who says, "I don't know how I feel about capital punishment." I usually meet someone whose mind is made up for one reason or another. In that connection, I think people are for or against capital punishment for different reasons, some are valid, some are not. I'd like to explore some of those reasons, particularly some of those I suggest are invalid. I don't mind people disagreeing with me on this position. I do mind people disagreeing with me for improper reason.

For example, the old question—punishment of "an eye for an eye." That attitude in support of capital punishment has generally fallen into disrepute. If you believe that just punishing someone is good enough reason for capital punishment, you don't go around in polite circles saying so. The fact is that I've known a few people willing to admit that's their motivation.

Address of the California Attorney General to the Commonwealth Club of California, San Francisco, July 15, 1977. Reprinted from *Vital Speeches of the Day*, September 1, 1977, pp. 682–685.

Often a person's attitude about capital punishment has something to do with their own personal experience. The Bible can be used to support either position you want to take. You can find just about as many quotations to support opposition to capital punishment as you can to support an attitude in favor of capital punishment.

So far as I'm concerned, I'm human enough to think my position in support of capital punishment is the valid one and, simply stated, has to do with cost. For a million years, we've been trying to control human behavior by applying a certain formula. Every human institution, whether you're talking about a government of 22 million people as we have in California, or a high school football team, or a Sunday school class, or whatever. Whatever you're operating, if you're trying to control behavior, you do it by, number one, establishing ground rules; number two, setting up a procedure to determine when someone violates a ground rule. In other words, try them—are they guilty or innocent, and if they're guilty, if they've violated the ground rules, punishing them. That's the way you raise children. That's the way we try to handle dangerous violent criminals. But there has to be some logical connection between the offense and the cost.

A few years ago, I strongly supported an amendment to the law making the sale of heroin a mandatory prison sentence, because absent that mandatory prison sentence, 80 percent of those who sold heroin were getting probation. And it's a little hard being Attorney General charged with the responsibility of enforcing laws relating to the sale of heroin, if those violating the law get probation in four out of five cases. The price isn't high enough in other words to discourage someone who wants to go into the business of selling heroin.

Ditto absent capital punishment, the price for killing someone under certain circumstances isn't high enough. For example, absent capital punishment, there is no reason for a rapist to leave his victim alive. Because a rape calls for life imprisonment, absent capital punishment, murder calls for the penalty of life imprisonment. So the rapist can murder his victim and eliminate a witness, and increase his chances of avoiding successful prosecution, all secure in the knowledge that if he is caught and punished, he hasn't increased the price of his crime one whit.

Ditto a person who holds up a filling station, and binds and gags the attendant. Absent capital punishment, there's no reason for the gunman to not execute the attendant. I'd like to give the gunman a reason for leaving the attendant bound, gagged and alive on the floor of the filling station.

That's my rationalization. That's my reason for strongly supporting capital punishment. I don't believe the death penalty will deter all murders. It won't even deter most murders. It will deter, in my firm opinion, some murders. And, when you're talking about deterring the murder of innocent people, I don't think you have to deal in thousands before you can justify what I believe to be a very realistic penalty.

And I'm also aware that 75 percent of the people in California believe the death penalty is a protection which they need and are entitled to. Now, this question is not subject to any scientific analysis; not something one person knows a great deal about and another person knows nothing about. You can't come up with a right answer by using a slide rule. Everyone in this room, and most of the citizens in this state are just as well qualified to arrive at a correct conclusion in this as I am, or as is Professor Amsterdam, or as is Governor Brown. This is not something that's subject to expert testimony. I think every citizen has a stake in this and the fact 75 percent of our citizens support the reenactment of the death penalty is significant. Also, statistics are relevant, not conclusive, but relevant. The courts abolished capital punishment in California in 1963. There's been one execution since then. Since then, the murder rate has tripled in California. From 1954 to 1963, the murder rate was three to four per one hundred thousand. It skyrocketed to over 10.4 per one hundred thousand in the last couple years.

In 1975, 2196 willful homicides occurred, as compared to 666 in 1963.

Those who oppose capital punishment will say, "so what, crime has gone up during this same period." That's true. And I think the reason is precisely the same. We were just as unrealistic dealing with rapists and robbers as we were in dealing with murderers.

In the 60s and early 70s it was every man to his own supreme court. We went through a period here where young people, if they wanted to improve the educational system they were attending, they would try to burn down the administration building. We rationalized an awful lot of weird conduct during the 60s and this was the period when we made it financially attractive for local authorities to put people on probation.

We did a lot of foolish things, like amending the law in 1965 to remove all restrictions on the grant of probation. It was a turbulent period, and the fact crime generally went up proves to me we weren't dealing with crime very realistically.

As I've indicated, I want to identify some of those reasons for opposing capital punishment that I regard as unsupportable. I just think the arguments are not valid. For example, one of the favorite arguments for anyone who opposes capital punishment is that it really doesn't have public support. If people were asked a question by someone taking a poll, they'll say "I'm for capital punishment," but if they're put on a jury where they have to act on it as a juror or a private citizen, they don't really support the concept.

That argument is absolutely and completely untrue. It's rather remarkable that the argument was stated so forcefully by our own state

Supreme Court in 1972. They said in an attempt to rationalize their legislatively abolishing the death penalty in California, that although death penalty statutes remain on the books of many jurisdictions, the frequency of its application suggests that among persons called upon to carry out the death penalty, it's being repudiated with ever increasing frequency.

Well, that decision is certainly an interesting piece of social legislation, but as a legal document it falls far short of the usual high standards set by our Supreme Court.

Capital punishment has been infrequently applied because Appellate Courts have repeatedly interfered. In 1972, when the California Supreme Court struck down this state's death penalty, 107 persons whom judges or juries had sentenced to death, including Charles Manson and Sirhan Sirhan, were spared. In that same year, the United States Supreme Court invalidated the as then applied death penalty laws nationwide, and approximately 600 persons under sentence of death could not be executed.

Before the California Supreme Court again struck down this last law in December of 1976, approximately 69 additional persons had been condemned to die. Therefore, it's hard to see how anybody could conclude the death penalty lacks public support.

We pointed out in our brief before the California Supreme Court in 1972, accepting for the purpose of argument that the Court's explanation that the delay in execution rendered the death penalty unconstitutional as cruel punishment, can it be assumed that had this court not permitted and caused excessive delay, the death penalty would therefore be constitutional? If so, it's not society's standards of decency that transform capital punishment from constitutional to unconstitutional. It's the procrastination that this court has built into our system of criminal justice.

Another false concept that's been foisted on substantial portions of our population relates to the concept that only the poor and friendless get the death penalty. Of course, the argument that juries are likely to inflict the death penalty on the indigent rather than the wealthy is just not valid.

Under California's death penalty law struck down last December, the death penalty was possible only for those first degree murderers in which aggravating special circumstances occurred, such as hired killings, killing more than one person, killing while committing rape, child molesting, kidnapping, robbery or burglary, killing a witness to prevent his testimony, or killing a peace officer in line of duty where proved beyond a reasonable doubt.

Seven of the inmates on death row were there because they agreed to pay others to commit murders. The occupations of the 69 persons on death row at that time were seven owners of businesses, one housewife, 35 skilled workers, eleven laborers, 12 unemployed and three unknown.

Makes it pretty clear that California's judges and juries haven't been concerned just with the occupation or economic status of the killer in applying the death penalty.

They've really concentrated on the aggravated nature of the murder instead. I think it's also significant that of those 69 on death row, when the decision commuted their sentences to life imprisonment, 24 were on death row because they had killed a witness to avoid prosecution for some other crime. It's true they're not many millionaires on death row. That's true but not valid, because millionares do not commit crimes that rate a position on death row. Millionaires do not hold up filling stations and execute the attendant.

Those who think someone like Dr. Finch and Carol Tregoff escaped the death penalty because of their financial and social position overlook the fact that no matter how poor an individual, nobody in that kind of triangular emotional sort of thing goes to death row. Nobody makes it to death row by killing a wife or husband or sweetheart, unless they do it for pay.

Only in the Soviet Union, among the major countries today, is an economical crime punishable by death, and even there, while they have such a law on the books, they have not applied the law for many years.

Another argument, a favorite of those who oppose the death penalty, is that we can accomplish the same thing by life imprisonment without possibility of parole. There's several things wrong with that. There is no such thing in our nation or in our state as true life imprisonment, nor should there be.

The governor has, and always should have, the power to commute. In any civilized system, the chief executive has to have the power to pardon. That's the safety valve that will work when everything else fails. So I wouldn't be in favor of, if we could, and it would be impossible, to try and take away the governor's power to commute. Given that power to commute, there's no such thing as life imprisonment. You simply substitute the governor's clemency hearing for a parole hearing now.

But eventually a person who goes into prison for a sentence other than the death penalty will likely get out.

If you're the victim of an individual once sentenced to death and later paroled, you're not concerned with large numbers, you're just concerned with the outrageousness that a person who has demonstrated the willingness to commit cold blooded murder could be treated with unrealistic kindness.

Also, another argument for not having in your system the concept of life imprisonment without parole, is that there is always the possibility of escape. Now those who favor life imprisonment without possibility of parole minimize that.

There's one other reason why life without possibility of parole is not a realistic alternative, and that is that you cannot run a prison without giving those in prison some hope of eventual release. Heavens knows it's bad enough in prison now. If everyone in San Quentin knows that someday he's going to get out, and yet they still cut each other up and do terrible things over there, can you imagine what life imprisonment would be like if no one there had any hope of release? If everyone in prison, or even a substantial portion, were there literally for life, there'd be no way you could maintain any degree of order.

The one thing that makes most prison communities manageable now is the fact that the vast majority of prisoners are on good behavior looking forward to that day when someone says, "O.K., we're going to put you on parole."

Of course, there are arguments to the effect that mistakes are always possible, and if a person is executed there is no way to correct the mistake. Well, maybe. But as a practical matter, under our system in California today, it's impossible, inconceivable that an innocent person would ever be executed.

The system tilts heavily, and properly so, in favor of a person accused of crimes. We have so many checks and protections now that didn't exist 20 years ago. The problem today is not that we are going to convict an innocent person of murder, the problem is how do you convict those that are admittedly guilty? The Supreme Court in its landmark cases for the past 25 years has virtually no concern for guilt or innocence. It's been referred to sneeringly as the irrelevance of guilt when talking about the American system. The fact is, I selected 25 landmark cases of the Supreme Court in the last 25 years, and only in two cases did the court express any doubt as to the guilt of the defendants. In the other 23 cases where they reversed the trial court's convictions, they did so because of procedural matters. They assumed the guilt acknowledged the guilt of the defendant. So, I say, as a practical matter, the possibility of an innocent person being executed for murder is completely unrealistic and unsupportable by any facts.

One thing I might mention with the question of capital punishment: in case the governor's veto stands, I along with most of the heads of statewide law enforcement organizations, along with a number of distinguished lawmakers, will take a leadership role in getting the initiative on the ballot to give you and the other citizens of the state the chance to again express your support of the death penalty. I hope that isn't necessary. I hope that we can override the governor's veto, in which case the death penalty will be restored immediately. And I think it should be.

The death penalty is not the kind of thing you play political games with. I believe the death penalty is a protection people need. I believe the death penalty will save lives, so I'd like to have it restored as soon as possible. If we cannot override the governor's veto, it's going to be November of 1978 before we can get it on the ballot and the death penalty can be restored.

Now, in the meantime, there are going to be some innocent people killed, and some of those innocent people could have conceivably been spared, given the fact the death penalty might have been in effect at that time.

DISCUSSION QUESTIONS

1. "I want to identify some of those reasons for opposing capital punishment that I regard as unsupportable." Why this negative approach to the subject?
2. Does the author support the Biblical "eye for an eye" concept?
3. The author submits that "absent capital punishment, the price for killing someone isn't high enough." This commercial metaphor is the fundamental basis of his argument. Is it a reasonable metaphor?
4. "Absent capital punishment, there's no reason for the gunman not to execute the [filling station] attendant." During the years that capital punishment was illegal in this country, hundreds of filling station attendants were robbed and not killed. How can one account for this?
5. "The courts abolished capital punishment in California in 1963. . . . Since then, the murder rate has tripled in California." What common fallacy is illustrated by this argument?
6. "This is not something that's subject to expert testimony, I think every citizen has a stake in this and the fact 75 percent of our citizens support the reenactment of the death penalty is significant." What features of the capital punishment issue *are* subject to expert testimony?
7. Responding to the argument that the death penalty is unjust because it punishes only "poor and friendless" people, the author responds that this could not happen under California's particular law. Does this answer the fundamental argument?
8. Is it a real indictment of the Supreme Court that in twenty-five cases selected by the author, it reversed trial-court convictions solely on procedural grounds, that it did not involve itself in questions of guilt or innocence?
9. What is implicit in the author's final judgment "I believe the death penalty will save lives"?

Ron Caylor
Gordon Gregor

DEADLY KING TUT CURSE
STRIKES AGAIN

A horrifying chain of death and suffering has struck a British Royal Air Force flight crew who defied the legendary curse of King Tut's tomb.

The 3,000-year-old curse damns anyone who disturbs the Pharaoh —and all seven members of the RAF crew have been stalked by tragedy since transporting Tutankhamen's death mask and other priceless relics to London for a 1972 exhibition.

Here's what has happened to the seven, according to crew members and their families.

- The pilot and flight engineer have died of heart attacks—although military physical exams had showed them to be in perfect health.
- A crew member who playfully kicked the crate containing Tut's mask later shattered the very same foot in 18 places.
- The flight steward has been plagued by ill health and tragedies within his family.

Reprinted from the NATIONAL ENQUIRER, October 17, 1978, p. 37.

- The navigator's home was gutted by fire.
- The co-pilot narrowly escaped being crushed in an accident, and his marriage has broken up.
- The only female member of the crew has had to undergo a serious head operation.

"Tutankhamen's curse killed my husband—I'm convinced of that!" declared Mrs. Dolores Laurie, the widow of pilot Rick Laurie. "And there is no telling who will be next.

"Make no mistake, this curse is very real. It is not a legend. It is horrifying—a deadly, diabolic curse that is not to be played with."

The world first learned of the curse in 1922 when archaeologists discovered King Tut's tomb near Cairo, Egypt, according to writer Philipp Vandenberg, author of "The Curse of the Pharaohs."

He said a hieroglyphic-laden clay tablet found in the tomb read: "Death will slay with his wings whoever disturbs the peace of the Pharaoh."

Since then the curse has claimed the lives of more than 30 people, among them scientists, archaeologists and scholars, said Vandenberg.

Surviving members of the RAF flight crew admit they knew about the curse when they flew to Cairo in 1972 to transport Tut's artifacts—valued at hundreds of millions of dollars—back to the British Museum.

"But we didn't take it seriously," recalled flight steward Brian Rounsfull. "In fact, we took turns sitting on the box containing the death mask, and we laughed and joked about it. We weren't being disrespectful—it was just a bit of fun."

And on the flight returning to England, the crewmen even played cards on top of the crates containing Tut's sacred objects—and ground engineer Ian Landsdowne once even playfully kicked the case containing the death mask, joking that he was kicking the most valuable thing in the world.

Recalled co-pilot John Tate: "We joshed each other about being the first to go (die), but none of us took it seriously. I didn't believe a word. I just didn't accept that a curse could work." But then things began happening—and suddenly the curse was no longer a joke.

In December 1972 a mysterious fire struck the home of navigator Jim Webb in Oxfordshire, England, and destroyed nearly everything the family owned.

"It wasn't like an ordinary house fire—it was just a mass of flames which consumed everything," said Dolores Laurie, who watched the blaze. "It was frightening."

Then, in May of 1974, Mrs. Laurie's husband Rick, 40, suddenly keeled over dead—the victim of a heart attack.

"It was mind-numbing," said the widow. "Rich had never spent a day in the hospital in 17 years we were married, and he'd passed all his annual medical checkups to insure his fitness for flying. He was in the best of health. I believe the curse of King Tut is to blame. It is a very powerful curse."

Shortly after Laurie's death, while flying the very same route the ill-fated flight crew had taken three years before, flight engineer Ken Parkinson suffered a heart attack and had to be hospitalized.

Three more attacks followed—and the last one killed him.

"The doctors were totally unable to find anything wrong with his heart," remembered Parkinson's puzzled widow, Ida. "They couldn't understand why he'd had an attack."

Meanwhile, catastrophe also was striking the other members of that ill-fated crew.

Crewman Landsdowne, who had kicked the crate containing Tut's golden death mask, fell 15 feet off a ladder in September of 1975 and broke his left foot in 18 places. "It wasn't until three weeks later that someone reminded me of the curse," he said. "It was then I remembered I'd kicked the case with this very same foot!"

Then, said co-pilot Tate, came the news that the crew's only female member, Pat Horne, "had an operation on her head."

Multiple tragedies hit flight steward Rounsfull. Twice severe chest pains sent him into a hospital's intensive care unit. Next, his brother-in-law died of a heart attack. Then his father-in-law fell down a flight of stairs and fractured his skull.

"Since the King Tutankhamen flight I've suffered a period of very bad luck," admitted Rounsfull. "I thought I was too sensible to believe in legends, but I do believe it could be the curse which has affected my life and those of other people."

For Tate, tragedy came in the form of a shattering breakup with his wife. He said he also was almost crushed recently when he raised a heavy garage door and it jumped its tracks, narrowly missing him.

"I'd like to believe that there isn't really anything to it (the curse), but it's difficult," he told The ENQUIRER.

Tate is convinced even worse things are in store for him.

"I'm the last one, so I've got to be the next victim," he said.

"I know I'm a marked man."

DISCUSSION QUESTIONS

1. King Tut's curse reads, "Death will slay with his wings whoever disturbs the peace of the Pharaoh." How many of the seven members of the RAF crew died? How many will die in the future?
2. Since the world learned of the curse in 1922, "more than 30 people, among them scientists, archaeologists and scholars" have died. Can these deaths be explained in any other way than as the result of the curse?

3. Is it more than an impressive coincidence that Ian Landsdowne later broke the "very same foot" he had used to kick the crate bearing Tut's mask? How many other feet might he have broken?
4. How amazing is it that over a period of six years, a crew of seven people have experienced heart attacks, a fire, accidents, near accidents, injuries to relatives, divorce, and surgery?
5. Pat Horne had a "serious head operation." Why the vagueness here, especially after the vivid description of Landsdowne's broken foot? What might a "serious head operation" refer to?
6. Is there any reason to question the reliability of Dolores Laurie and of John Tate when they gave the *National Enquirer* dramatic statements about Tut's curse?
7. What common fallacy is illustrated by this essay?

Statistics

There are three kinds of lies: lies, damn lies, and statistics.
—attributed to Benjamin Disraeli

There are a number of ways in which statistics can be used to distort argument. A spokesman can cite impressive averages, irrelevant totals, and homemade figures. He can present his numbers in a context that make them appear larger or smaller, according to his wish.

AVERAGES

A common fallacy involves the use of "average" figures: average income, average price, average audience size, and so on. It is easy to argue from such statistics because the word "average" can mean three things.

What, for example, is the average if a group of fifteen housewives, responding to a poll question, say that they watch television 48, 40, 30, 26, 22, 18, 12, 10, 9, 8, 5, 5, 5, 1, and 0 hours a week? From this, it can be said that the group watches television an average of 15.933 hours a week, or 10 hours a week, or 5 hours a week. The 15.933 figure is the *mean* (the total number of hours watched divided by the number of viewers); the 10 figure is the *median* (the middle number in the series); and the 5 figure is the *mode* (the number that appears most frequently.)

Each kind of average has its value, according to the kind of material being measured. But all three are available to the spokesman seeking to manipulate an argument.

Questionable Figures

Vague statistics can produce impressive averages. Numbers derived from memory, guesswork, and exaggeration can be averaged with exquisite precision. (In the preceding paragraph, the 15.933 average has computed after fifteen housewives made rough guesses of their television viewing time.) Dr. Kinsey interviewed American men and reported that those without a high school education averaged 3.21 sex experiences a week. The annual FBI report *Crime in the United States,* compiling material from police departments across the country, showed that Baltimore in one year had suffered a crime increase of 71 percent. But police departments report crimes differently and with different degrees of accuracy; the sensational Baltimore figure derived not from a huge increase in crime, but from more accurate police reporting in the second year.

Similarly, amazing claims can be drawn from a small or partial sample. Some years ago a survey reported that 33 1/3 percent of all coeds at Johns Hopkins University had married faculty members. Johns Hopkins had three women students at the time. Advocates of extrasensory perception thrive on partial samples. They like to report cases where a gifted individual (Hubert Pearce, Basil Shakleton, or another) have produced laboratory results in which the odds were 10,000,000 to 1 against chance as the explanation. Commonly, it is discovered that such cases were *part* of a longer series of tests and that the results of the entire experiment were not given.

IRRELEVANT NUMBERS

An argument can be bulwarked with irrelevant statistics. Some years ago cigarette companies responded to evidence that smoking may cause cancer by counting filter traps. Viceroy boasted 20,000 filters ("twice as many as the other two largest-selling brands") until Parliament began claiming 30,000, and Hit Parade overwhelmed both with 400,000. These are impressive figures but totally pointless. There was no evidence that *any* filter protected one from the dangerous effects of smoking. And no one had defined "filter trap." This practice of putting large numbers to undefined elements has been particularly notable in those given to counting communist-front citations, UFO's, and angels.

Even when counting clearly defined entities, a spokesman can offer irrelevant numbers. In a period of high unemployment, he can proclaim that more Americans are working than ever before. Responding to the demonstrated statistical relationship between cigarettes and lung cancer, he can observe that the vast majority of smokers do not get cancer. As violent crimes increase, he can oppose gun-control legislation by computing that only 34/10,000 of 1 percent of American handguns are involved in homicides.

There is also a kind of irrelevance in statistics derived from a singular example. Hollywood Bread, for instance, advertised that it had fewer calories per slice than other breads; this occurred because its slices were cut thinner. Carlton cigarettes boasts it has regularly been tested as lowest in "tar" of all filter kings; one reason is that it has a longer filter than other cigarettes of the same length and therefore contains less tobacco. Television personality Hugh Downs announced that he got 28.3 miles per gallon driving a Mustang II from Phoenix to Los Angeles; the trip is largely downhill.

HOMEMADE STATISTICS

The preceding examples indicate that one does not have to make up statistics to create a misleading argument. But, of course, one can make up statistics if he or she wants to. For example, the temperance spokesperson who built an analogy on the claim that there were 10,000 deaths from alcohol poisoning to 1 from mad-dog bites, was using figures that exist nowhere else.

Homemade statistics usually relate to events that have not been measured or are impossible to measure. Authorities can be suspiciously precise about events too trivial to have been counted. (Dr. Joyce Brothers reported that the "American girl kisses an average of seventy-nine men before getting married." And a Lane cedar chest advertisement warned that moths destroy $400,000,000 worth of goods each year.) They can be glibly confident about obscure facts. (A *Nation* article said there were 9,000,000 rats in New York City. And the 1979 Surgeon General's Report declared that cigarette smoking costs this country $27,000,000,-000 in "medical care, absenteeism, decreased work productivity, and accidents.")

Imaginary numbers like these usually relate to areas in which it is impossible to get real figures. To make an impressive argument a spokesman may want to specify the number of homosexuals in America today—or the number of pot smokers or adulterous husbands. He may want to report how much money was spent on pornography last year— or on welfare cheats or illegal abortions. The writer can find some information in these areas, but—because final exact counts remain unavailable—he faces a strong temptation to produce a statistic that supports the case he is trying to make. Many succumb. Remember this the next time you see headlines declaring that a rail strike in Chicago is costing the city $60,000,000 a day.

Even in instances where a measure of scientific computation has occurred, resulting statistics often seem singularly creative. Recent news stories have announced that 17 percent of babies born to near-affluent parents are unwanted; that 5 percent of Americans dream in color; that heroin addicts in New York City steal $2 billion to $5 billion worth of goods a year; and that men aged 35 to 50 average one sexual thought every twenty-five minutes. With a little practice, one can identify home-made statistics with the naked eye.

ENHANCING A STATISTIC

By careful presentation a spokesman can make any statistic seem bigger or smaller, as his argument requires. For example, many newspapers reported the 1968 Oberlin College poll revealing that 40 percent of the unmarried coeds had engaged in sex, that one in thirteen of these became pregnant, and that 80 percent of the pregnancies were terminated by abortion. The "80 percent" figure seems startling until you ask "80 percent of what?"

Relatively modest statistics appear sensational when given as percentages of percentages of percentages.

More commonly, one changes the character of a statistic by simple comparison. He relates it to a smaller number to make it seem large, or to a larger number to make it seem small. The contrasting number need have no relevance aside from offering an advantageous comparison.

In 1972 when Senator George McGovern was running in state Presidential primaries, for example, his spokespeople regularly pointed out that the contest was not in his strongest state, that official duties had limited his public appearances, and that—all in all—the Senator would be lucky to win 15 percent of the vote. Then when he won 22 percent, they announced, "He did well. His vote far exceeded expectations." (Columnist Russell Baker called this technique "poormouthmanship.") One reverses the process to dwarf a statistic. In the same primaries, when George Wallace—the law and order candidate—had to face the fact that Alabama had the highest murder rate of any state in the nation (11.4 per 100,000), it was explained that this figure was not nearly as high as that of Detroit, Los Angeles, and other major cities.

In a summary statement on statistical manipulation, Darrell Huff (*How to Lie with Statistics,* 1954) counseled the business community:

> There are often many ways of expressing any figure. You can, for instance, express exactly the same fact by calling it a one percent return on sales, a

fifteen percent return on investment, a ten-million-dollar profit, an increase of profits of forty percent (compared with 1935–39 average), and a decrease of sixty percent from last year. The method is to choose the one that sounds best for the purpose at hand and trust that few who read it will recognize how imperfectly it reflects the situation.

In a society subject to political controversy, social argument, and Madison Avenue rhetoric, such argument is common.

You should recognize examples of distorted statistics and, of course, avoid them as much as possible in your writing.

Even when numbers favor your case, do not use them too extensively. A mass audience is rarely persuaded by a body of statistics. (This explains why they are used so infrequently in the antismoking campaigns of the American Cancer Society and the American Heart Association.)

You should remember, finally, that a number by itself means little or nothing. If in a particular year Montreal leads the major leagues with 179 double-plays, what does that mean? That it has a fine second baseman? That it has poor pitchers? That its home park has an Astro-turf infield? Who knows? What can you conclude about a $16,000 annual salary, a 150-word poem, a $7.95 meal? Not much. An important quality of statistical argument was expressed in a scene in *Annie Hall:* The lovers played by Diane Keaton and Woody Allen are asked by their psychiatrists how often they have sex. She responds, "All the time. Three times a week." And he says, "Hardly at all. Three times a week."

EXERCISES

How reliable are these statistical arguments?

1. If you begin having your hair styled, are people going to think you've gone soft. Half the Los Angeles Rams' line has theirs styled. If you want to laugh at them, go ahead. We don't.
2. Listerine Antiseptic stops bad breath four times better than tooth paste.
3. We need more federal aid to local schools. There are still 1,400,000 illiterates in the United States.
4. When Presidential candidate George Wallace toured Chicago in 1968, the crowd on the street was estimated at "20,000 to 30,000" (by liberal students), at "50,000" (by Chicago police), and at "2 million" (by Mr. Wallace).
5. Read *One in Twenty* by Bryan Magee—an adult, plainly written study of male and female homosexuality.
6. Antismoking advertisements announce that cigarette smoking, on the average, reduces a smoker's life by 8.3 years and that every cigarette he smokes takes one minute from his life.
7. Leo Guild's book *What Are the Odds?* reports that a young person with a

   broken engagement behind him is "75 percent as happy" as one who was
   never engaged.
8. Wartime statistics: Last week the Viet Cong lost 1231 men. American and
   Vietnamese losses were moderate.
9. In 1933–34 Hubert Pearce and J. G. Pratt performed ESP experiments at
   Duke University with great success. The odds against their overall result
   occurring by chance are greater than 10,000,000,000,000,000,000,000,000 to 1.
   This is conclusive evidence that ESP exists.
10. Responding to complaints about increased gas prices, Mobil Oil published
    a statement showing that, on all its products, it averaged only 1½ cents
    profit per gallon in 1972, and that, in 1973, it would make only about 2
    cents a gallon.

ESSAY ASSIGNMENTS

Write an essay either affirming or opposing one of these statements. The material you encounter in your background reading will include statistical argument; so should your essay.

1. American industry *is* fighting pollution.
2. We need gun-control laws to curtail crime.
3. Sex education leads to promiscuity, pregnancy, and disease.
4. It's proved: cigarette smoking causes lung cancer.
5. IQ tests do not prove anything.
6. American income-tax laws should be revised.
7. Statistics demonstrate that X is a mistake. (Fill in the X.)

R. F. Shaw

WHY NUCLEAR ENERGY!

We live in a world of fragmentation and confrontation. Great minds and small have learned to exploit human emotions to gain their ends. So it is with nuclear energy.

But the decisions we make should be based on thoughtful assessment and, as far as we are able, on common sense judgment.

Mankind's toughest environmental problem is an exploding population.

We are already four point three billion souls on this earth and increasing at two percent each year toward a doubling—that's 8.6 billion in thirty years.

We can feed that many and more if we are organized to do so—but we already have trouble organizing to feed our 4.3 billion.

For sure there are already so many of us that we cannot achieve an adequate standard of living by "returning to nature" and living off the land.

Address delivered at a Rotary Club District Meeting, Sherbrooke, Quebec, Canada, June 17, 1977. Reprinted from *Vital Speeches of the Day,* August 15, 1977, pp. 648–651.

Therefore, we must mass produce for survival.

And mass production means using energy slaves, not human or animal slaves.

We no longer pull the plow over our shoulder!

We must find sources of energy, new and old, to meet the demand and at the same time design our way out of the resulting environmental problems.

Here in Canada we must find energy for our twenty-three million, plus enough to deliver an appropriate part of our huge surplus wealth to a world, three quarters of which is suffering from a very inferior standard of living—

Canada's current energy resources are water power, oil, gas, coal and uranium.

Waiting in the wings are solar energy, wind power, tidal power, biomass energy, geothermal energy and others.

We must use all of them and we must in addition implement vigorous conservation measures if we are to do our duty to Canadians and the world which depends on our surpluses.

In my view the salvation of our energy problems in the next thirty to forty years depends on coal and on nuclear energy—both of them.

The key is nuclear energy.

Let us, therefore, consider four questions:

1. Do we need nuclear energy?
2. Are there viable alternatives?
3. Is nuclear energy economical?
4. Is it environmentally safe?

First: Do we need nuclear energy?

Canada is already importing oil and coal. The U.S.A. imports oil, gas and uranium. In both countries the total value of energy resources imports will increase year by year for decades.

And this in a world which is today about 98 percent dependent on fossil energy.

The restraints likely to be imposed by a continued dependence on fossil fuels become clearer when viewed in world perspective. It took nature 600 million years to lay down the world's resources of fossil energy. Of this, about one-fiftieth is thought to be recoverable by man, mostly as coal (about 90 percent). If these resources were exploited in the normal pattern of production growth, it would be impossible to elevate the present world population of 4.3 billion to current North American living standards. In fact, less than 60 percent of this standard might be achieved for only a brief moment in history. If we take into account the current growth in world population and recognize that more energy per capita will be needed to recover leaner resources, and for recycling and for the control of the environment, it is unlikely that the world could aspire to a standard of living approaching one-fifth that which we in Canada enjoy today—and that for only a few decades.

Yes in considering our already established energy sources, it is obvious that we do need nuclear energy.

Second: Are there viable alternatives?

a. If we were to wave a magic wand and immediately achieve the 40 percent savings of energy through conservation as claimed by enthusiasts, we would gain maybe 9 years of respite in our search for new energy. Without that magic wand, we can save maybe 2 or 3 years. After that we must continue to find new sources of energy at about the same rate of annual increase as before, if we are to meet our obligations at home and abroad.

b. We have used up most of our accessible hydro-electric sites.

c. Solar electricity is expensive and the technology has a long way to go. To produce the current electric requirements for Montreal would require about 120 square miles of solar collectors. Because of its inherent intermittent nature, solar heating requires either standby capacity or a large thermal storage capacity to look after nights, clouds and seasonal variation in sunshine. Solar heating can make a worthwhile contribution but it will take time to make a significant impact and it cannot solve the whole energy problem.

d. It would take about thirty thousand windmills of 190′ diameter to generate the power now produced from the Pickering nuclear plant.

e. Tidal power is viable but it has an environmental impact on fisheries and tides. Besides there is very little of it and at best it can only solve regional problems.

f. Biomass to fuel an energy plant the size of Pickering would require a forest of many thousands of acres to supply the wood.

g. Geothermal energy can make a small regional contribution if we control the tough environmental problems of air and water pollution. All of these renewable resources must be used wherever feasible and research must continue. But they are at least 25 years away from making important contributions to the solving of our energy problems.

h. Coal is a good prospect, although it presents some very tough environmental problems.

Transport from the huge mines in Canada's west is the big problem. The railroads can now deliver one million tons annually from Alberta and B.C. to Ontario. They plan to increase this to 12 million tons but Ontario will need 42 million tons a year by 1995 and if it stops its nuclear energy program Ontario will need 93 million tons of coal per year by 1995. Except for a small amount from the Maritimes and Northern Ontario the rest must come from the U.S.A. which expects to double its own demand on its coal mines by 1985. It's not a very secure prospect.

Canada's Candu nuclear energy plant is probably the world's most efficient in uranium utilization.

Now uranium supplies are dwindling in some areas. As a result there is work being done on the development of a new generation of nuclear energy units known as "fast breeding reactors" which are designed to manufacture as much fuel as they consume. There are, however, still some real tough unsolved problems with these breeders. *This* is the program that President Carter opposes—NOT the whole nuclear energy program, as sometimes reported.

We don't need fast breeders in Canada because we can introduce a thorium-uranium cycle in the existing Candu reactor for an almost equivalent result—and we have lots of thorium. We have lots of uranium too—provided we combine it with thorium soon enough.

It all boils down to this. There is currently no known viable alternative to our nuclear energy program.

Third: Is nuclear energy economical?

Already it is cheaper than thermal energy from fossil fuel plants.

And a doubling of the cost of fuel won't hit your electric bills much if you are tied into a nuclear plant because

—One pound of coal produces 1.5 kwh of energy
—One pound of oil produces 2.0 kwh of energy
—One pound of gas produces 2.2 kwh of energy
—One pound of uranium produces 29,000 kwh of energy.

Don't buy that rumour that it takes more electricity to build a nuclear plant than the plant will ever produce.

Pickering paid off its total energy debt in fifteen months.

Fourth: Is nuclear energy environmentally safe?

No! But it's safer than its competitors.

Nuclear energy came to us from the most terrible weapon of warfare.

It is mysterious to you—and me.

An overdose of radiation can cause death, illness and maybe sterility or hereditary disease and malformation.

Warfare, mystery, death, sex—what a combination!

No wonder so many react emotionally against it.

I can only wish that we could as vividly recognize the other equal or greater threats to the human environment from coal or asbestos or the 5 billion tons of the products of combustion that mankind adds to the environment each year.

Take coal mining for example:

95 lives are lost in coal mining for each life lost in uranium mining.
50 coal miners die of black lung disease for each death by cancer due to the increased radiation encountered in uranium mining.

100 die in the transportation of coal for a near zero in transporting uranium.

However, let us accept our blessings.

We are so emotional about pollution from the peaceful use of the atom that the people who control it are the most effective anti-pollutionists in industry.

There has not been one single fatal radiation accident in a British, American or Canadian nuclear power plant. There has never been a lost time accident due to radiation in a Canadian plant. Nevertheless, we must understand and control the risks of radiation if we are to obtain the benefits from nuclear reactors, x-rays, cobalt 60, cancer therapy, sophisticated research equipment, industrial radiography, micro-waves, lasers, television, luminous devices and the use of radiation to trace the path of pollutants through the biosphere.

Radiation is measured in millirems—a unit related to the biological effect of an x-ray.

Does everyone receive the same amount from Mother Nature? No!

There is a considerable range between the highest and the lowest dose-rates. The average background is about 125 mR per year; levels of 1000 mR occur in India and Brazil due to the radium and thorium in the soil. Some individuals in these regions receive as much as 5000 mR per year.

As we go up to higher altitudes we get less atmospheric protection from the sun and, therefore, a higher dose. People living in Calgary receive a background dose two or three times higher than ours in Montreal, but research has not yet found a medical link related to variations in the natural background of radiation.

But let us not relax on that account.

The experts agree that man-made radiation exposures should not go much beyond the natural exposures.

The recommended maximum doses are extremely conservative. The permissible dose established by the International Commission on Radiological Protection (ICRP) is 500 millirems per year, which is much lower than people get from the natural background in those regions of the world that I mentioned earlier.

How are we doing in nuclear energy?

As a matter of policy, Canadian nuclear power plants design to 1 percent of the ICRP allowable dose and achieve monitoring results at the power plant boundary which are indistinguishable from the background. Let us take a look at all of the radiation which is around us. Here again the experts give slightly different figures but the message is clear.

—From the sun, the air and the ground you receive a background radiation of about 90 mREMS/YR

—And from your house, office, factory and street about 35 mREMS/YR

Total about 125 mREMS/YR

—Now if you eat to stay alive add 25 mREMS/YR
—And if you undergo the average amount of x-ray and other medical radiation add 72 mREMS/YR
—Or fly once from coast to coast add 2 mREMS/YR
—For Chinese atomic bomb tests add 4 mREMS/YR
—And for your T.V., wrist watch and other miscellaneous exposures add 3 mREMS/YR
—Now if you live beside the fence of a nuclear power plant add 2 mREMS/YR
—And if you drink the effluent water and eat the fish from it add 2 more

It all adds up to 235 mREMS/YR

As compared to the ICRP allowable dose of 500 mREMS/YR

The nice fellow who monitors at Pickering told me that an Ontario fossil fuel plant can put more radioactivity (in the fly ash) up the stack than is "leaked" by Pickering. He also told me that he had been obliged to conduct a survey which located 12 cows within a ten mile radius—and thereafter he had been required to sample and monitor the milk every two months.

"I wonder" he said plaintively "if it wouldn't be cheaper to buy the cows."

Finally, you should know that because we eat we are all radioactive and, therefore, irradiate each other—so if you go to an anti-nuclear meeting—or this one—you will receive more radiation than you will receive at the fenceline of a nuclear plant. If you kiss your wife once a day then to the above tabulated total add . . . something. And if you sleep with her, the radiations can be even more noticeable. (Sleeping with two women is postively dangerous.) 85,000 Canadians develop cancer or genetic diseases each year. If you were to increase the radiation dose all over Canada by 2 mR for a whole year, you would add about 20 people to that total.

In the U.K. from 1962 to 1975 there were four fatal accidents in the nuclear energy program—two falls, one asphixiation and one electrocution. There were three injuries due to radiation burns, one of which required significant medical attention. During the same period 66 off duty employees were killed in traffic accidents.

As the figures quoted earlier indicate, from mine to electricity, thermal energy from coal is many times more dangerous than nuclear energy.

I wonder how many more deaths result from the air pollution going up the stacks of coal fired plants. Nuclear plants have no stacks.

Don't buy the claim that hydro-electric developments are the safest energy producers. Since 1928, 2980 persons have been killed by dam failures. Although there have so far been no radiation deaths in the USA from reactor accidents, nevertheless the U.S. reactor safety report worked out the following probabilities of accidents per year to 15 million people living within 25 miles of 100 nuclear energy plants.

ACCIDENT	FATALITIES
Automobile	4,200
Accidental falls	1,500
Fires	560
Electrocution	90
Lightning	8
Reactor accidents	2

In simpler terms—your chances of being killed by a reactor accident are about the same as your chances of being struck by a meteor.

Let us look at those two deaths resulting from reactor accidents. If all the automatic and manual fail-safe devices plus the safety devices watching the safety devices were to fail and if as a result the reactor were to lose its coolant and melt down through the structure into the ground then find some water, develop steam and blow a hole to the surface thus releasing radioactivity to the atmosphere—and if at the same time there was to be a temperature inversion and a gentle wind to blow the radioactivity toward a populated area then people might die.

But in 1966 you read an article in the *Reader's Digest* entitled "We Almost Lost Detroit." A beautiful example of scare reporting. What happened at a nearby nuclear energy plant was that a metal plate came adrift and blocked the coolant to two out of 100 fuel assemblies. They melted and triggered the safety devices which operated as designed. Repairs were made and the plant resumed operation. It happened also that the plant was brand new and had not yet produced enough material to make much of a melt possible anyway. Not even a fly in Detroit was threatened.

The risk of mass death from air pollution was far greater in January 1973 when two oil tankers and some storage tanks burned in Bayonne, New Jersey, and again only 3 years later when 3 oil storage tanks burned in South Brooklyn. Fortunately there was no temperature inversion on either occasion and nobody wrote a headline saying "We Almost Lost New York." London was not so fortunate in December 1952 when a temperature inversion trapped all of the city's air pollution, killing 3900 in one week. But the shouting and the writing goes on:

An editorial in the *Montreal Gazette* of June 14, 1977 entitled "Nuclear Lobby vs The Media" says:

> Dr. Morton Shulman, a maverick member of the Ontario legislature, drove to the Pickering nuclear generating station—through an unguarded entrance—he breezed into a storage area for lethal radioactive material. Press coverage given that visit—and to his charge that with six sticks of dynamite he could have released enough radioactivity to wipe out Toronto—has resulted in extra guards and in a new alarm system. . . .

Six sticks of dynamite (invented by Nobel for peaceful purposes) would have thrown up a lot of water in the spent fuel storage area but there is no way that a single soul in Toronto could have been wiped out. But I too would have increased the security against the Shulmans of this world.

Nuclear bombs are, of course, a real threat and hundreds of "organizations" must be able to make them. For our survival we must control warfare and terrorism, be it conventional or nuclear—and for our survival we *must* have energy.

A Candu energy plant cannot explode. The fuel and waste are too "dirty." A gang of saboteurs would have a huge, tough job to release dangerous amounts of radiation even if they were undetected.

Until recently we have not been as careful with the uranium mine as we have been with the energy plant. However, you have no doubt read in the press of the major cleanup of mine wastes now in hand in Ontario. There is another tough problem—the management of radioactive wastes from all nuclear uses. In particular we must deal with spent fuel effectively and soon enough to be ready when the amounts build up in the next—say—25 or 30 years.

First, the radioactivity must be contained and it must be contained for a very long period of time, for example, plutonium-239 has a half life of 24,000 years so it would need at least 800,000 years to decay completely or 250,000 years to decay to a harmless level.

The second factor that must be considered is decay heat. When a spent fuel bundle is first stored under water in the fuel bay, it is generating about 6000 watts of heat. This decays rapidly and after one year in storage it is giving off about 85 watts. When the heat has decayed sufficiently, the spent fuel can be placed in a more permanent storage. However, the quantities are very small. A 1000 MW thermal plant requires 38,000 rail cars per year of that great polluter coal, whereas a 1000 MW nuclear plant needs only 6 truck loads of nuclear fuel. The total spent fuel storage for Canada if we realize present plans to the year 2000 could be stored in a building the size of a football field and 3 stories high.

Serious consideration is being given to permanent disposal in salt mines (where obviously no ground water has ever penetrated) or in deep rock which has been stable for a billion years and, therefore, probably won't move much in the next 800,000 years. In both cases the waste products would be cast in glass or some other leach resistant matrix. We are also looking at above ground storage for shorter term storage.

—First, because we do not know what use man may wish to make of his deep down geology
—Second, because reactor design is being improved to the point that spent fuel will be re-processed and reused
—Third, we have enough faith in man's ability to believe he will make as much progress in the use of the atom in the next 50 years as he has in the last 50 years. Waste fuel should, therefore, be kept in a location where it will be easily recoverable.

In all this discussion, I have said:

—We need nuclear energy
—There is no viable alternative in sight at this moment
—Nuclear energy is economical
—It is the safest environmentally of the currently available sources of energy.

So I say to you: be thoughtful—not emotional about nuclear energy. For the well being of our species, we will need to apply the utmost reaches of wisdom when considering our energy future.

DISCUSSION QUESTIONS

1. "Great minds and small have learned to exploit human emotions to gain their ends. So it is with nuclear energy." What minds is the author referring to?
2. The author asks (a) Do we need nuclear energy? (b) Are there viable alternatives? (c) Is nuclear energy economical? And (d) is it environmentally safe? If the first two questions are answered, respectively, "yes" and "no," how important do the third and fourth questions become?
3. Do these statistical statements invite inquiry?
   a. "It is unlikely [with continued reliance on fossil fuels] that the world could aspire to a standard of living approaching one-fifth that which we in Canada enjoy today—and that for only a few decades."
   b. "If we were to wave a magic wand and immediately achieve the 40 percent savings of energy through conservation as claimed by enthusiasts, we would gain maybe 9 years of respite in our search for new energy."
   c. "The railroads . . . plan to increase this [transportation of coal] to 12 million tons but Ontario will need 42 million tons a year by 1995 and if it stops its nuclear energy program Ontario will need 93 million tons of coal per year by 1995."
   d. "From the sun, the air and the ground you receive a background radiation of about 90 mREMS/YR. And from your house, office, factory

and street about 35 mREMS/YR. Total about 125 mREMS/YR. Now if you eat to stay alive add 25 mREMS/YR. . . . It all adds up to 235 mREMS/YR. As compared to the ICRP allowable dose of 500 mREMS/YR."

e. "85,000 Canadians develop cancer or genetic diseases each year. If you were to increase the radiation dose all over Canada by 2mR for a whole year, you would add about 20 people to that total."

f. "In simpler terms—your chances of being killed by a reactor accident are about the same as your chances of being struck by a meteor."

4. Observing that in the United Kingdom from 1962 to 1975 there were three injuries due to radiation burns, one of which required significant medical attention, the author adds, "During the same period 66 off-duty employees were killed in traffic accidents." How relevant is this statistic?

5. "The total spent fuel storage for Canada if we realize present plans to the year 2000 could be stored in a building the size of a football field and 3 stories high." Considering what the essay says about nuclear wastes, does this seem a reassuring prospect?

6. Do you feel the essay says all there is to say about the dangers of nuclear energy?

ASTOUNDING NEW DISCOVERIES ABOUT THE BIBLE

What are the amazing facts which have been discovered beneath the very surface of the original Bible text? What are these facts which *scientifically prove* that the Bible could not possibly have been written by mere human beings alone, but that it is a supernatural, God-inspired, God-given book?

It has been stated that the facts have been mysteriously hidden beneath the very surface of the *original Bible text*. In order to understand what these facts are, it will be necessary to know—

THE MEANING OF THE TERM "ORIGINAL BIBLE TEXT"

Most persons are acquainted with the fact that the Bible contains two main divisions—the Old Testament and the New Testament. Strange as it may seem, these two main divisions of the Bible were originally written in different languages. The Old Testament was originally written in

Reprinted from *Astounding New Discoveries*, a pamphlet distributed by Southwest Radio Church of the Air, Oklahoma City, Oklahoma, pp. 6–10, 16, 17, 21–22.

Hebrew while the New Testament was written in Greek. By the term "original Bible text" is meant the Hebrew and Greek text of the Bible—the words of the writers in the *original languages, not their words translated into some other language.* The facts, then, have been discovered beneath the surface of the *Hebrew* Old Testament text and the *Greek* New Testament text.

Now the reader's attention is called to something very important. We wish to point out a *certain number*—a number which occurs in Scripture more times than any other. It is the number *"seven."* From the first book of the Bible through the last book, *"seven"* is by far the outstanding number. For example, the Sabbath was the seventh day. In Egypt there were seven years of plenty and seven years of famine. When the city of Jericho was captured, the people and seven priests who had seven trumpets marched around the city seven times. Every seventh year the land of the Israelites was not to be cultivated or planted. Solomon was seven years building the temple. After its completion he held the feast for seven days. Naaman washed seven times in the river.

In the book of Revelation, the last book of the Bible, this number is especially outstanding. Seven churches, seven lampstands, seven seals, seven trumpets, seven vials, seven stars, seven spirits, etc., are mentioned. In all the number seven occurs in the book of Revelation more than *fifty* times!

It has long been known that the number seven occurs in the Bible in this particular manner more frequently than any other number. However, only recently it has been discovered that this *same number* also occurs in a mysterious and peculiar manner *beneath the very surface* of the Hebrew Old Testament text and the Greek New Testament text.

When it is stated that the *"sevens"* occur in a peculiar manner *"beneath the surface"* of the original Bible text, we mean that they occur in such a way that they are not noticed or discovered by merely reading the *surface,* or words. The *sevens* are strangely out of the sight of ordinary Hebrew and Greek readers. They are mysteriously hidden. Thousands who have read and studied the original Hebrew and Greek text of the Bible have passed by these strange occurrences of the number seven without even noticing their presence. These sevens are so deeply concealed that special searching and investigation and special counting are necessary in order to find them. Thus, they are said to occur *"beneath the surface"* of the text because they are beyond the observation and view of ordinary Hebrew and Greek readers.

It has been discovered that *thousands* of these *sevens* are mysteriously hidden in the structure of the text. They are strangely and remarkably concealed in every conceivable manner in the Hebrew and Greek *letters, words, sentences, paragraphs, and passages!*

What are the newly discovered facts? The *"sevens"*—the *"sevens"* which occur beneath the surface of the original Hebrew and Greek text of the Bible—are the amazing newly discovered facts. The "Astounding New Discoveries" are *numerical discoveries*—discoveries having to do with numbers. These recently revealed numerical facts or "sevens," in a most extraordinary way, enable us to see before our very eyes an actual scientific demonstration of the divine verbal inspiration of the Bible.

The reader is given *examples* of these newly discovered numerical facts before he learns *how* they scientifically prove that the Bible is a supernatural, God-breathed book.

The following are examples of facts or "sevens" which have been discovered beneath the surface of the *Hebrew text* of the first verse in the Old Testament—the very first verse in the Bible.

BOOK OF GENESIS, CHAPTER ONE, VERSE 1

It is indeed strange to note that the number of Hebrew words in this verse is not 6, not 8, but exactly 7. Here the number seven is discovered by counting the *words*.

Now if a person counts the Hebrew *letters* in these seven words, he will discover that the number of letters divides perfectly by seven—is an exact multiple of seven. The number of *letters* in the seven words is not 27, not 29, but exactly 28, or 4 7's.

(These seven Hebrew words and their 28 letters are displayed in the complete, unabridged, 167-page edition of "Astounding New Discoveries.")

Each numerical "fact" or "seven" which occurs in the structure of the text is called a "feature"—a "numeric feature." The first two have already been mentioned.

Feature one. The number of Hebrew words in this verse is exactly 7.

Feature two. The number of letters in the seven words is exactly 28, or 4 7's. Now let us continue.

Feature three. The first three of these seven Hebrew words contain the subject and predicate of the sentence. These three words are translated—"In the beginning God created." The number of *letters* in these first three Hebrew words is exactly 14, or 2 7's. The last four of these seven words contain the object of the sentence. These four words are translated—"the heavens and the earth." The number of *letters* in these last four Hebrew words is 14, or 2 7's.

Feature four. These last four Hebrew words consist of two objects. The first is "the heavens," and the second is "and the earth." The number of letters in the first object is exactly 7. The number of letters in the second object is 7.

Feature five. The three leading words in this verse of seven words are "God"—the subject—and "heavens" and "earth"—the objects. The number of letters in these three Hebrew words is exactly 14, or 2 7's. The number of letters in the other four words of the verse is 14, or 2 7's.

Feature six. The shortest word is in the middle. The number of letters in this word and the word to its left is exactly 7.

Feature seven. The number of letters in the middle word and the word to its right is exactly 7.

These sevens—these numeric features or facts—are indeed strangely hidden "beneath the surface." They are truly beyond the view of ordinary readers of the Hebrew text and are discovered only by special investigation and counting.

The above are only a few examples of the many amazing numeric facts which have been discovered in the structure of this first verse of only seven Hebrew words. Literally dozens of other phenomenal numeric features strangely underlie the structure of this verse. (Additional features are given in the complete, 167-page edition of "Astounding New Discoveries.")

Examples of these newly discovered facts or numerical features should be pointed out from other passages before the reader learns *how* the facts *scientifically prove* that the Bible could not possibly have been written by mere human beings alone, but that it is a supernatural, God-inspired, God-given book.

The following are examples of the newly discovered fact or "sevens" which occur in a peculiar manner beneath the surface of the *Greek text* of the first verses in the New Testament.

BOOK OF MATTHEW, CHAPTER ONE, VERSES 1–17:

The Account of Christ's Genealogy

The first seventeen verses in the book of Matthew form a natural, logical division by themselves, for they deal with one particular subject, namely, the genealogy of Christ.

These first seventeen verses of the Greek New Testament consist of two main sections. (I) Verses 1–11. (II) Verses 12–17. Each section contains amazing numeric features in the structure of its text.

The following are a few examples of the facts or "sevens" which have been discovered beneath the surface of the first main section, verses 1–11.

Feature one. The number of Greek vocabulary words used in the first eleven verses is not 48, not 50, but exactly 49, or 7 7's.

It must be remembered that the number of *vocabulary words* in a passage is usually different from the *total number of words* in a passage. The vocabulary words are the *different* words used. For instance, the word "and" is one word in the vocabulary, but it may be repeated many times in the passage itself. A man may have a vocabulary of only five hundred words. With these five hundred different words he may write an essay of four thousand words. Some of the words, such as "and," "for." "by," etc., may be used over and over again. The number of vocabulary words, or the number of different words used in a passage, is thus not the same as the total number of words used. (We mentioned that the number of vocabulary words in the first eleven verses of Matthew is exactly 49, or 7 7's. Now let us continue.)

Feature two.　The number of letters in these 49 words is exactly 266, or 38 7's.

Feature three.　Of these 266 letters of the vocabulary words, the number of vowels is exactly 140, or 20 7's. Of these 266 letters of the vocabulary, the number of consonants is 126, or 18 7's.

Feature four.　Of these 49 words, the number which begin with a vowel is exactly 28, or 4 7's. The number of words which begin with a consonant is 21, or 3　7's.

Feature five.　Of the 49 Greek vocabulary words, the number which are nouns is exactly 42, or 6 7's. The number which are not nouns is 7.

Feature six.　Of the 42 nouns in the first eleven verses, the number which are proper nouns is exactly 35, or 5 7's. The number which are common nouns is 7.

Feature seven.　The number of Greek letters in these 7 common nouns is exactly 49, or 7 7's. It is amazing to note that in these 7 common nouns alone, there are more than 20 numeric features.

Feature eight.　The number of times the 35 proper names occur is exactly 63, or 9 7's.

Feature nine.　Of the 35 proper names in the vocabulary of the first eleven verses of Matthew, the number of male names is exactly 28, or 4 7's. The number which are not male names is 7.

Feature ten.　The number of times these 28 male names occur is exactly 56, or 8 7's.

Feature eleven.　In these first 11 verses, three women are mentioned—Tamar, Rahab, and Ruth. The number of Greek letters in these three names is exactly 14, or 2 7's.

Feature twelve.　Just one city is named in this passage, namely, Babylon. The number of Greek letters in this word is exactly 7.

Feature thirteen.　Of these 49 Greek vocabulary words in the first eleven verses, the number of words which occur more than once is exactly 35, or 5 7's. The number of words which occur only once is 14, or 2 7's.

Feature fourteen.   Of these 49 Greek vocabulary words, the number which appear in only one form is exactly 42, or 6 7's. The number which appear in more than one form is 7.

These numeric facts or sevens *are* indeed beyond the view of mere "readers" of the Greek text. They are truly mysteriously hidden beneath the surface and can be discovered only by special searching and calculations.

No doubt some are of the opinion that these features occurred accidentally—that they occurred in this peculiar manner merely by sheer chance. Therefore, let us suppose that there are twenty-four numerical features or facts in the structure of a certain passage. *What chances are there that these 24 features would occur together in one passage accidentally?* This is easily calculated, for there is a standard, recognized, scientific method of calculating chances—there is an established law of chances.

Only one number in seven is a multiple of seven. The other six numbers which are not multiples of seven have as good a chance to occur accidentally as the one that is a multiple of seven. Therefore,

According to the law of chances, for any *1 number* to be a multiple of 7 accidentally, there is only 1 chance in 7

According to the law of chances, for any *2 numbers* to be multiples of 7 accidentally, there is only 1 chance in 7 × 7, or only 1 chance in 49

According to the law of chances, for any *3 numbers* to be multiples of 7 accidentally there is only 1 chance in 7 × 49, or only 1 chance in 343

(The calculation continues on the same basis)

Thus, according to the law of chances, for any *1 feature or numeric fact to occur accidentally*, there is only 1 chance in 7

For 2 features* 1 chance in... 49

For 3 features* 1 chance in...343

For 4 features* 1 chance in...2,401

For 23 features* 1 chance in 27,368,747,340,080,916,343

For 24 features* 1 chance in 191,581,231,380,566,414,401

Thus, according to the law of chance, for 24 features to occur in a passage accidentally, there is only 1 chance in 191,581,231,380,566,414,-401—only 1 chance in one hundred ninety-one quintillion, five hundred

* "to occur accidentally, there is only"

eighty-one quadrillion, two hundred thirty-one trillion, three hundred eighty billion, five hundred sixty-six million, four hundred fourteen tousand, four hundred one. (The nomenclature herein used is the American, not the British.)

Many brief Bible passages have as many as seventy or a hundred or more amazing numeric features in the very structure of their text. If there is only one chance in quintillions that 24 features could occur together accidentally, what would the chance be for 70 features to occur accidentally?

When there is only one chance in *thousands* for something to happen accidentally, it is already considered highly improbable that it will occur at all. When there is only one chance in *hundreds of thousands*, it is considered practically impossible. But here there is one chance in not only *millions*, but *billions*, and *trillions*, and *quadrillions*, and *quintillions*, that merely 24 features could occur together in a passage accidentally.

The argument and demonstration is convincing enough. The amazing numerical features of even one small passage, to say nothing of the thousands in the entire Bible, could not possibly have occurred by accident—by sheer chance. All this evidence simply cannot be explained by the doctrine of chances. If these features did not occur accidentally, then there is only one conclusion, one alternative. They were purposely designed or arranged—their occurrence in such a marvelous and mysterious manner was intended or planned. The point can be illustrated as follows:

Suppose for example, someone were carrying a bag   O O O O
which contained 24 oranges. Suppose that suddenly the   O O O O
bag broke and the 24 oranges fell to the floor. What   O O O O
chance would there be that the oranges would fall into   O O O O
four perfect rows with six in each row, each orange   O O O O
being exactly opposite the other? Such self arrangement O O O O
would be considered impossible!

Suppose on the other hand you came into the room and found the oranges arranged in the manner described. You would come to only one conclusion, namely, that they were purposely designed or arranged in that unusual manner. No one would risk being called insane by insisting that such a thing occurred accidentally!

Likewise, these profound numeric features found in the very structure of the original Bible text are not there by sheer chance or accident, but by design. They are arranged according to definite plan; they form thousands of perfect and uniform designs.

It has been conclusively shown that there are amazing numerical features in the very structure of the Bible—their presence cannot be denied, but is a truth which everyone must accept. It has also been proved that these features could not possibly have occurred by sheer chance or accident, but that they were arranged or designed. This is a second truth which everyone must accept.

If human logic is worth anything at all we are simply driven to the conclusion that the thousands of amazing numeric designs in the very structure of the original Bible text could not possibly have been planned by the men who wrote the books of the Bible—they could never have been produced by mere human minds.

It is evident that the Bible is not the work of many minds, but the work of One Mind. The designs furnish clear proof that the whole Bible has but one Author. All the books of both the Old and New Testaments were planned and produced by the same Mind.

Every candid, logical minded individual is simply compelled to admit that the intelligence which planned and designed the Bible must have been Superhuman, Divine. That one Designer was a Supernatural, Master Designer. Only the Supreme, Omniscient, Omnipotent God could have caused such phenomenal numeric designs to occur beneath the surface of the Bible text. Only God could have constructed the Bible in the amazing manner in which it is constructed. The Eternal, Omnipotent Author designed, superintended, worked, and carried out His Own infinite plans. There is no escape from his conclusion.

DISCUSSION QUESTIONS

1. Prior to his mathematical demonstration, the author has to prove that 7 is a number of special importance in the Bible. Does he do this?
2. This selection shows the mathematical system operating in two Scriptural passages. Is there any reason to doubt an equally significant collection of sevens could be found in many other passages as well?
3. The author says his numeric features "can be discovered only by special searching and calculations." In the genealogy from Matthew, for example, he counts the number of male names (28). Since the number of female names (3) does not fit his system, he counts letters. Since the number of letters in individual names do not fit, he counts the cumulative letters in the three names (14) and records another "amazing" feature. How amazing is it?
4. How does such analysis of his features affect his elaborate calculations concerning probability?
5. Bergen Evans once said, "The odds against anything's having happened just the way it did can be shown to be enormous." For example, the chance of being dealt a poker hand containing the ten, jack, queen, king, and ace of hearts is 1 in 2,598,960. (That's $5/52 \times 4/51 \times 3/50 \times 2/49 \times 1/48$.) What is the chance of being dealt any specific ordinary hand you can name?
6. Turn to page 66 of this book and consider the sixth complete sentence on

the page. See how many sixes you can find in that sentence. If you cannot find any, what does that prove?
7. Granting the author's assumptions and his conclusion that God put the hidden sevens in Scriptural texts, speculate why He might have done it.

George DeLeon

THE BALDNESS EXPERIMENT

The winos who hung around my Brooklyn neighborhood in 1950 were not funny. With their handout hands, reeking breaths, and weird, ugly injuries, they were so self-rejecting that you could bark them away even while you shoved them a nickel. My friends and I didn't think they were funny, but we observed one thing that always busted us up. Almost without exception, they had all their hair.

Seriously: we never saw a bald bum. Have you? When was the last time you remember a street alky stumbler with nothing on top?

Black, white, old, young, short, tall, all of them had a full mop. And hair that wouldn't quit. It leaped up as if it were electrified, or shagged down in complete asocial indifference, or zoomed back absurdly neat, gray-black and glued. Inexplicably, it seemed that boozing burned out the guts but grew hair.

Fifteen years later, I offered this observation to my undergraduate classes in the psychology of personality. Then, one semester, I decided to

Reprinted from *Psychology Today Magazine*, October 1977, pp. 62, 66. Copyright © 1978 Ziff-Davis Publishing Company.

get past the laugh, integrate my present self with my past self, and actually test the hypothesis that booze grows hair.

I conceived a simple investigation, with the class participating as co-researchers. In the project, we'd get some real data on the density, or rather the incidence, of baldness in a random sample of rummies. The tactic was to beachhead ourselves on the Bowery in New York City, fan out in teams of two, and gradually move up from somewhere around Prince Street to 14st Street, the end of the bum region.

On two successive Saturday mornings, the whole research outfit—me, four men, and two women—met on the corner of Bowery and Houston to carry out the plan. Every other derelict who was not unconscious was approached, talked to, and looked at. Since no one usually walks up to a rummy except cops and other rummies, something seemed to happen when two pretty young students of mine would say, "Sir, I'd like to ask you a few questions." The winos would rock a bit and—no kidding—you could almost see a little ego emerging.

In planning the research, I decided that we should gather as much information as we could that might be relevant to the experiment. We decided to mark down answers to questions about age, race, ethnicity, marital staus, family baldness, drinking life, etc. We even asked our subjects where they usually slept (in or out of doors), figuring that, too, might influence their hair growth.

While one team member interrogated, the other circled around the subject, studying the head, raised and lowered, to observe the pate. Subjects were evaluated on a four-point baldness scale as hairy, receding, bald pate, or totally bald.

Interesting problems developed from the beginning; what appeared to be simple was really complex. When do you call a guy bald? What does "receding" mean? (We dispensed with the use of rulers or vernier calipers, assuming that, bombed or not, the derelict would shuffle off as soon as we pulled out any kind of hardware. We felt grateful that he tolerated the paper, pencils, and questions.) So there was no quantification, no precision. We simply had to make quick judgments.

Our teams interviewed over 60 Bowery subjects, paying them a quarter a pop, all of which came out of my pocket. Back at the school, the data were tallied and, sure enough, the results confirmed my intuition. Only about 25 percent could be called receding or totally bald, with the remainder being pated or hirsute. I had been right all along, and we reported the results to the class.

But it turns out that the skepticism of annoyed youth may actually be the quintessence of good scientific research. After I enjoyed the laughs and took a few bows, a number of students, not on the teams, were quick to raise some sharp objections.

First, and most obvious, was that we needed to study baldness in a group of nonderelicts in order to make proper conclusions. Second, wasn't it possible that the teams had been influenced by my colorful classroom predictions about hairy bums and had tended to judge the subjects as nonbalding?

The criticism was first rate. I knew that because it threw me into an immediate depression. I hated the students who offered it. I also knew that we'd have to do the whole study again with new teams and new derelicts. This time, nonderelicts would have to be included, too, and I would offer no advance hypothesis that might bias, in my favor, the way kids looked at heads.

I waited a whole academic year, got a new personality class, and this time took no chances. During the lectures, it was necessary to arouse the interest of the class in the broad issue of bums and baldness. So I suggested that derelicts were a special group of people who seemed to lose their hair sooner and more completely than other men. In short, I lied. Morality aside, it was a tough one to tell because I feared that it would shape the kids' perception the other way. They might actually see receding hairlines and shiny heads where there really was only hair. But I had to take the risk of betting against myself to make the win more sure.

Out on the turf again a new and larger research squad of six men and six women worked over five straight Saturdays. They did the Bowery in pairs, interviewing about 80 derelicts.

We also went after a comparison group. Any man walking in or out of Bloomingdale's or cruising along 5th Avenue in the 50s was operationally defined as a nonderelict. These fine fellows we decided to call "sterlings." "Sterling" male shoppers in tweeds were stopped on a random basis in front of Bloomingdale's revolving doors. They were put through the whole routine of questions about drinking, age, etc., and their heads were carefully checked out. One difference was that we were too embarrassed to hand them quarters, so we didn't. Then, about a month later, to extend our control group, I sent five squads into a faculty meeting at Wagner College and got the same information on 49 college professors in one sweep.

Happily, the new set of derelict data turned out the same as the old, and the results of the three comparison groups were more striking than expected. When the information was presented simply as nonbald versus balding (which combined receding plus pated plus total), we found that 71 percent of the college professors were balding, 53 percent of the sterlings, and, of the derelicts (both years), only 36 percent (see Figure 1).

There were no ethnic or racial differences, nor were the other factors in the questionnaire very important. Still, age must matter, and it does.

Under age 25, we found 17 (21 percent) sterlings, but only one derelict and no professors. In fact, the average age of the sterlings was 37.5,

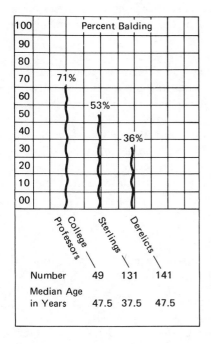

Figure 1

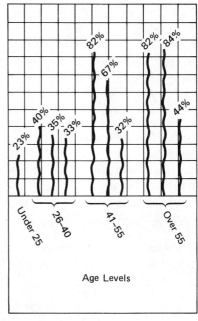

Figure 2

while it was 47.5 for the other two groups. This makes sense, since it takes a lot of years to become either a derelict or a college professor.

Figure 2 shows the percentage of balding across several age levels. Naturally, the older men in all groups contain a greater proportion of hair losers. But after age 40, the differences among the groups are fascinating. The sterlings and professors reveal similar rising percentages, with the profs leading. The derelicts, however, in the years 41 to 55, actually show a slight decrease, and of the 50 guys on the Bowery past age 55, only 44 percent showed signs of balding as compared with about 80 percent of the oldies in the other groups. So the stereotype of the balding egghead professor is not contradicted by these data. For the Bowery bum, there's no doubt that he simply keeps his hair.

Now comes the hard part: what does it all mean? Though it did not show up in our data, I'm sure that genetics is relevant. Even so, what is the likelihood that only the bums have fewer bald daddies? Not much.

These results also rule out ethnic and racial factors. Hair and air didn't go together, since the derelicts who said they usually slept out were no less bald than those who snoozed in the dorms of the flophouse hotels.

Are the bums breezier and more carefree? Calm or numbed so that they don't feel the stress that most of us do? Is it the food they eat, or don't eat?

No. We concluded that it must be the alcohol and some resulting biochemical activity. It happens, since completing the study, that I've learned that medical literature does point to some interaction between liver damage, alcohol metabolism, the female hormone estrogen, hair growth and retention. Seems reasonable to me.

If so, I'm elated that our finds are valid. But, in a way, it doesn't matter. The whole trip started for me back in Brooklyn, as a joke. Later, my students and I really observed, recorded what we saw, and attempted to draw conclusions. Seeking the truth is always an adventure; the scientist is in all of us.

DISCUSSION QUESTIONS

1. The author reports three separate readings of the derelict-baldness issue: his observations as a youth, the first study he and his class made, and the final study. Since they all came to the same conclusion, why is the final study more significant than the others?
2. Why did the teams ask questions about age, race, ethnicity, marital status, family baldness, drinking habits, sleeping place, and so on? Why didn't they just check hair?
3. Explain the following:
   a. why the first research team interviewed only every other derelict
   b. why they made no precise measurements of the derelicts' hair
   c. why the author lied to the second research team about what he expected to prove
   d. why the derelicts were compared to men around Bloomingdale's and to professors
   e. why the author offered an age analysis at the end
4. "Black, white, old, young, short, tall, all of them had a full mop. And hair that wouldn't quit." What is the tone of this essay? Does the tone add to the author's case?
5. Baldness is usually considered a genetic factor. How does the author explain this away? Is he persuasive?
6. What is amusing about defining male Bloomingdale shoppers as "non-derelict"?
7. "Now comes the hard part: what does it all mean?" What does this sentence tell you about statistics?

Bernard Gittelson

BIORHYTHM:
A PERSONAL SCIENCE

On the evening of November 11, 1960, a retired Swiss importer named George Thommen was interviewed on the "Long John Nebel Show," a radio talkathon based in New York City. What Thommen had to say sounded surprising to most people and incredible to some. However, the strangest thing Thommen said was in the form of a warning. He cautioned that Clark Gable, who was then in the hospital recovering from a heart attack suffered six days before while filming *The Misfits* with Marilyn Monroe, would have to be very careful on November 16. On that date, explained Thommen, Gable's "physical rhythm" would be "critical." As a result, his condition would be unstable, putting him in danger of a fatal relapse.

Few listeners took Thommen's warning seriously; Gable and his doctors were probably unaware of it. On Wednesday, November 16, 1960, Clark Gable suffered an unexpected second heart attack and died. His doctor later admitted that the actor's life might have been saved if

Reprinted from *Biorhythm: A Personal Science* (New York: Warner Books, 1977), pp. 12–20, 144–146, 148–149.

223

the needed medical equipment had been in place beside his bed when he was stricken a second time.

Pure coincidence? Maybe. But George Thommen's advice was neither a random prediction nor an occult speculation. He was not speaking off the top of his head, gazing into a crystal ball, plotting the influences of the stars, or claiming psychic powers. Instead, as a leading student of the emerging science of biorhythm, Thommen had made detailed calculations showing that for Gable, one of the three general biological rhythms that characterize human life would be changing from a high to a low phase on November 16. For healthy people, this kind of shift need not be dangerous; even for a man recuperating in the hospital, it was not necessarily a matter of life and death. However, the rhythm shift did indicate that Gable would be more than usually susceptible that day, and that the hospital should take appropriate precautions just in case something happened. If only Gable's doctors had known of biorhythm and its implications for their famous patient, that second heart attack might not have proved fatal.

"If only . . . ." There are few more common or poignant phrases. We speak those words when we have accidents, miss opportunities, witness disasters, or whenever we are regretfully surprised by events in our own lives or in those of others. We would speak them much less often if we had a deeper understanding of the roots of human behavior and the causes of human frailty; some way to increase our knowledge of what people are likely to do and what may happen to them. It is exactly this kind of knowledge and understanding that biorhythm offers.

The basics of biorhythm are easy to understand. In its simplest form, the theory states that from birth to death each of us in influenced by three internal cycles—the physical, the emotional, and the intellectual. The physical cycle takes 23 days to complete, and it affects a broad range of physical factors, including resistance to disease, strength, coordination, speed, physiology, other basic body functions, and the sensation of physical well-being. The emotional cycle governs creativity, sensitivity, mental health, mood perceptions of the world and of ourselves, and, to some degree, the sex of children conceived during different phases of the cycle. It takes 28 days to come full circle. Finally, the intellectual cycle, which takes place over a 33-day period, regulates memory, alertness, receptivity to knowledge, and the logical or analytical functions of the mind.

On the day of birth, each of the cycles starts at a neutral baseline or zero point. From there, it begins to rise in a positive phase, during which the energies and abilities associated with each cycle are high. Gradually declining, the cycles cross the zero point midway through their complete periods—11½ days from the point of origin for the 23-day physical cycle, 14 days for the 28-day emotional cycle, and 16½ days for the 33-day intellectual cycle. For the balance of the period each rhythm is in a negative phase in which energies are recharged and our physical, emotional, and intellectual capabilities are low, or at least somewhat diminished. We pick up increasing amounts of energy as the negative phase continues until, at the end of each cycle, the zero point is recrossed into the positive phase, and the whole process begins again. (See Figure 1—Biorhythmic Cycles in the First Month of Life.)

Since the three cycles last for different numbers of days, they very rarely coincide and cross the baseline at exactly the same time (only at birth and every 58 years plus 67 or 68 days thereafter). Therefore, we are usually influenced by mixed rhythms. Some will be high while others are low; some will cross the neutral point while others have many days to go until they reach the same level; to make an even finer distinction, one rhythm may be in a stronger part of the positive phase (or a weaker part of the negative phase) than others that are going through the same phase. The result is that our behavior—from physical endurance to creativity to performance on academic examinations—is a composite of these differing rhythms. We seldom have absolutely wonderful or absolutely terrible days. We have up days, down days, and a good many in-between days, but every day can be understood in terms of a particular and almost unique combination of the three basic cycles.

Biorhythms seem to affect behavior in a peculiar way. Our weakest and most vulnerable moments are not those of the negative phases, as you might suspect. Rather, they occur when each cycle crosses the base line, switching from positive to negative or *vice versa*, and it is at these times that we can expect ourselves to be in the most danger. It appears that at these points the rhythms that guide our lives—and on whose regularity we depend as much as on the steady pulse of the heart—become unstable. They seem temporarily out of step, as though uncertain of their true direction and movement or unsettled by the ebb and flow of energy. These days of cross-over from one phase to another are called *critical days*. Students of biorhythm often compare them to the moments at which we switch a lightbulb on or off, since it is then that the bulb is most likely to burn out, not when the switch is in one of its two positions or phases.

As the Clark Gable case shows, critical days can be very important. On physically critical days, we are most likely to have accidents, catch colds, and suffer all types of bodily harm, including death. Quarrels, fights, depressions, and senseless frustration are typical of emotionally critical days. When the intellectual rhythm is at the critical point, we can expect bad judgment, difficulty in expressing things clearly, and a general resistance to learning anything new or remembering what we already know. The point is that by calculating and studying your biorhythms in advance, you can know what to expect and can do much to avoid the worst. For example, businessmen familiar with biorhythm make a point of refusing to sign crucial contracts on emotionally and (especially) intellectually critical days. Athletes in all sports are well-advised to play with extra care—or to avoid play altogether—on physically critical days, when they are very vulnerable to injury. All of us could avoid unnecessary arguments simply be exerting a little more self-control on emotionally critical days. Days when not one, but two or all three cycles are critical require special prudence—although probably not to the extent practiced by one follower of biorhythm, who swears that on triply critical days he stays in bed and tries not to move, feel, or think at all!

Planning for critical days may be the most significant application of biorhythm, since this can literally make the difference between life and death. But it is less than half the story, since critical days make up only 20% of the days of your life. The remaining 80% are mixed days, whose character is varied and ambiguous. You can do much to regulate your future by making plans that harmonize with your biorhythmic profile for non-critical days. It makes sense, for instance, to try to set records on days when all three cycles are near their peaks and you have as much energy and ability as possible. Conversely, knowing that all three cycles are near the bottom of their negative phases is a clear indication that you cannot count on turning in an outstanding performance. Other examples of how the study of biorhythm can improve your life are obvious, although more precise analysis of the implications of a particular biorhythmic profile is possible only with experience and a more complete knowledge of the theory.

TRUE OR FALSE?

At this point, skepticism about biorhythm and eyebrows raised in vigorous disbelief are normal. Although the theory is not supernatural and requires no "leap of faith" to accept, it *is* startling. Both its substance and its ramifications may seem outrageous—or at least foolish—when first discussed. The object of this book is to give you enough information to decide for yourself whether or not biorhythm makes sense. Along the way, there are some fascinating stories to be told.

Actually, the theory of biorhythm is little more than an extension and generalization of the enormous amount of research that scientists have already done on the many biological rhythms and cycles of life. From the migrations of swallows and the feeding patterns of oysters to the levels of hormones in human blood and the patterns of sleep, life can be defined as regulated time. Countless rhythms, most of them fairly predictable, can be found in even the simplest of our bodily functions. Even the smallest component of our bodies, the cell, follows several clearly defined cycles as it creates and uses up energy. As Gay Luce put it in her book, *Body Time,* "We must be constructed out of time as certainly as we are constructed of bones and flesh."

At this stage in its development, research on biorhythm is not at all comparable to the rigorous and painstaking studies that have been made of smaller biological cycles. This is partly because the length of biorhythm cycles is so much greater than the length of most biological rhythms. Phenomena like changes in blood chemistry and sleep patterns can be measured in minutes or hours, and this makes them easier to study than biorhythms which take tens of days to complete. Also, the physical, emotional, and intellectual cycles relate to such complex behavior—made up of hundreds and maybe thousands of subtle physical and psychological changes over time—that studying them with any degree of scientific rigor is extraordinarily difficult. Also, unlike other long-term cycles such as seasonal migrations, the three great biorhythms do not always produce a predictable result. They render humans *likely,* but not *sure,* to behave in particular ways, and scientists prefer to work with concrete, totally reliable phenomena.

However, there is nothing in the biorhythm theory that contradicts scientific knowledge. Biorhythm theory is totally consistent with the fundamental thesis of biology, which holds that all life consists of the discharge and creation of energy, or, in biorhythmic terms, an alternation of positive and negative phases. In addition, given that we are subject to a host of smaller but nonetheless finely regulated biological rhythms, it seems reasonable that larger, longer rhythms will also come into play. Those rhythms may depend on vast numbers of the most discrete cycles that science has already proven to exist; or they may depend in part on external cues, such as geomagnetism and light, many of which have been shown to influence the smaller cycles. But until we can perform strictly controlled studies of how and why biorhythm works, and until many other researchers have been able to replicate these studies,

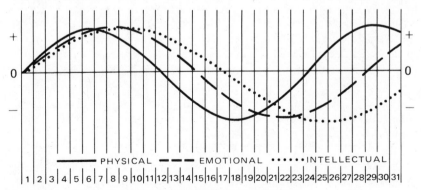

Figure 1   Biorhythmic cycles in the first month of life.

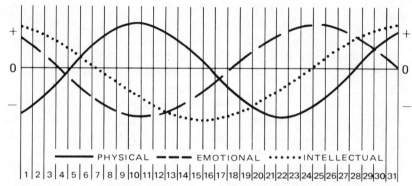

Figure 2   Clark Gable suffered a heart attack on November 5, 1960, when his physical rhythm was critical. He didn't die until November 16, when he suffered a second heart attack on his next physically critical day.

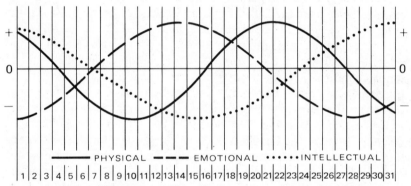

Figure 3   Marilyn Monroe was found dead of an overdose of sleeping pills on August 5, 1962, when she was physically critical and emotionally low.

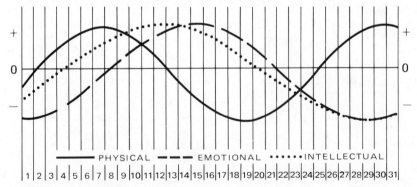

Figure 4   Judy Garland dies of a drug overdose on the night of June 21, 1969, when she was emotionally critical, with both physical and intellectual rhythms in low.

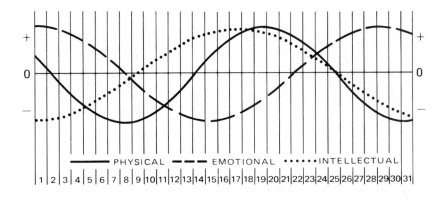

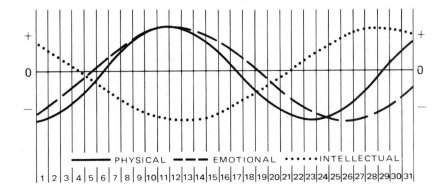

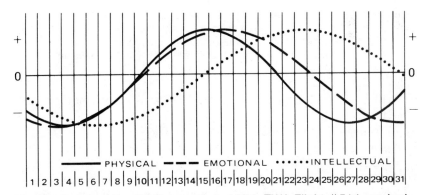

Figures 5, 6, and 7   On December 1, 1974, TWA Flight #514 crashed into a low mountain outside Dulles Airport in Washington D.C. Flight Controller Merle W. Dameron was physically critical on that day, which may have made him slow to warn the flight crew of its dangerous descent. Captain Richard Brock was physically and emotionally negative, while Co-Pilot Leonard Kreschek had just recovered from a double-critical and was low in all three rhythms.

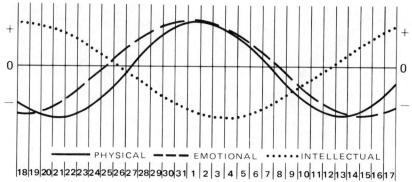

Figure 8   Mark Spitz won his record-breaking seven Olympic Gold Medals on days that were highly favorable in his physical and emotional rhythms.

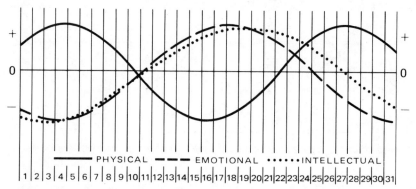

Figure 9   On December 10, 1972, Franco Harris of the Pittsburgh Steelers failed to gain 100 yards for the first time in seven weeks. He was suffering from a triple critical on that day. On December 23, less than two weeks later, he made the "Catch of the Century." On that day, he was in a triple positive phase.

we will have to base the case for biorhythm on purely empirical research.

Fortunately, there is a large and growing body of such research. The European scientists who discovered biorhythm during the early 1900's based their conclusions on literally thousands of individual cases. This kind of clinical work gives the theory a firm foundation. Since then, as understanding and application of biorhythm have spread throughout the world, much more evidence has been amassed. Doctors, government agencies, and corporations in many countries, particularly Switzerland and Japan, have applied biorhythm with great effectiveness to reduce the risk of death in operations, in automobile accidents, and from industrial hazards. In the United States, members of organizations such as the

National Safety Council, the Flight Safety Foundation, the U.S. Air Force, and N.A.S.A. have begun to consider the theory, and some of them have conducted research and issued reports that apparently confirm it. For obvious reasons, insurance companies have shown a special interest in biorhythm; available studies of their accident and death statistics in light of the victim's birth date and biorhythmic profile on the day of the mishap have done much to bolster the case for biorhythm. On a less convincing but still valuable level, thousands of individuals who use biorhythm to guide their lives have made reports that show its usefulness and have offered suggestions for fruitful types of new research.

Ultimately, however, the most convincing studies of biorhythm are those you can do yourself. By working out your own biorhythm chart and biorhythm profiles for particular days, and then comparing them with your experience of up and down days, of illness and health, of success and failure, you will be able to judge for yourself. Since the mathematics of biorhythmic computation can be difficult, we have provided in an appendix a simple method that you can use to plot your individual biorhythms accurately, from day to day and month to month. When you have learned more about the foundations, proofs, and applications of biorhythms, try out the theory in your own life. It could keep you from having to say, "If only . . . ."

DISCUSSION QUESTIONS

1. Granting the premise—that humans have physical, emotional, and intellectual cycles of unvarying length—is there any reason to question the calculations that produced the biorhythm charts?
2. What evidence is offered to support the initial premise?
3. Are such cycles any harder to believe than that women have menstrual cycles and that everyone has sleep patterns?
4. Why should an intellectual cycle take 33 days when a physical cycle takes only 23?
5. "The point is that by calculating and studying your biorhythms in advance, you can know what to expect and can do much to avoid the worst." Is it likely a believer would find that the events of his life do reflect his biorhythm pattern?
6. How reliable does this make the anecdotal evidence, the "literally thousands of individual cases" the author mentions?
7. One believer, it is said, does not even get out of bed on triply critical days. How often would a true triply-critical day occur?
8. How impressive is the authority of Swiss and Japanese doctors who have used biorhythm "with great effectiveness" to reduce the danger in operations?
9. How impressive is the opinion of the National Safety Council, the Flight Safety Foundation, the U.S. Air Force, and NASA concerning biorhythms?
10. Since one is vulnerable either in a low phase or at a "critical" transition,

and since most human problems involve physical, emotional, and intellectual elements, how difficult would it be to explain any misfortune in terms of biorhythms?

11. How persuasive is the evidence of the charts? (If Clark Gable had died any time in November prior to the 29th, would a biorhythm authority have had any trouble explaining the event?)

EXERCISES FOR REVIEW

How valid are these arguments? Identify examples of induction, deduction, expert testimony, semantic argument, analogy, argument in a circle, post hoc, begging the question, argumentum ad hominem, *extension, the either-or fallacy, and statistical manipulation.*

1. Of course you support federal aid to education. You're a teacher; you stand to profit on the deal.
2. "Ever wonder why kids instinctively go for soft drinks in bottles?"—Glass Container Manufacturers Institute
3. Register Communists, Not Guns!
4. Naval ROTC should be abolished; I'm learning nothing from it.
5. America's greatest threat is not from without but from the traitors within. Everyone knows that.
6. It's not safe to walk on the streets of New York City; I'm glad I live in St. Louis.
7. As you go to the polls to decide this temperance issue, ask yourself, "How does Jesus want me to vote?"
8. I disagree with Abby Van Buren when she says no woman should be forced to have a baby she does not want. A lot of people are forced to have parents they do not like, but we don't let them go around murdering their parents.
9. "There is no proof that sugar confectionary gives rise to dental cavities."—*Association Internationale des Fabricants de Confiserie*
10. In 1936 the *Literary Digest* chose 10 million names at random from telephone books and lists of registered automobile owners. The magazine sent preelection ballots to these persons and received over 2 million responses. The resulting prediction: Landon would defeat Roosevelt.
11. A *Saturday Review* article on the Middle East carried the subtitle: "Do the Arabs Have a Case?"
12. I never knew a University of Alabama varsity football player who could read or write beyond the eighth-grade level.
13. "Seven out of every ten Americans cheat on their income tax."—Professor R. Van Dyke Ellington
14. "Obscene material is material which deals with sex in a manner appealing to prurient interest."—Justice Brennan, delivering the opinion of the Supreme Court, *Roth* v. *United States*, June 24, 1957
15. Athletics teaches our young people good sportsmanship and how to play the game of life.
16. *The Husband* (a novel by Sol Stein). "The dilemma of countervailing demands on the sensual man of good will . . . rich and true . . . modulated with a respectful reserve . . . handled with hardly a false note."—*New York Times*
17. We scientists working with astrological data do not mind being criticized. We know that Newton and Einstein were ridiculed in the past.
18. All this effort to register and confiscate guns will not help us fight crime. Violence rises from the souls of men.

19. *Miss MacIntosh, My Darling* by Marguerite Young. "What we behold is a mammoth epic, a massive fable, a picaresque journey, a Faustian quest and a work of stunning magnitude and beauty . . . some of the richest, most expressive, most original and exhaustively revealing passages of prose that this writer has experienced in a long time. . . . It is a masterpiece."—William Goyen, *New York Times*

20. Homosexuality is no illness. It is a widespread practice, like vegetarianism. The homosexual has a sexual preference for members of the same sex; a vegetarian has an alimentary preference for noncarnivorous foods. In neither case is there any impairment of function or any disease.

21. Charlie's a gorgeous, sexy-young smell. (Concentrated!) And full of surprises. Just like you.

22. On a typical television poll, an early-evening newscaster poses a yes-or-no question, asking viewers to phone one number to vote "yes" and another to vote "no"; and a late-evening newscaster gives the results (e.g., 71 percent oppose socialized medicine).

23. If your name is Makay, Malloy, or Murray, beware of drink. According to John Gary, director of the Council for Alcoholism in Glasgow, Scotland, people whose surname begins with the letter "M" may be eight times more prone to alcoholism than others.

24. What I want to know is who masterminded the plan to get President Nixon impeached?

25. *Miss MacIntosh, My Darling* by Marguerite Young. "In fact, this is an outrageously bad book, written by an author with very little of interest to say, and very little skill in saying it . . . wholly unreadable."—*Time*

26. A clever magician can always perform his tricks; but a genuine mystic can sometimes produce paranormal effects and sometimes not. Uri Geller produced no effects at all when he appeared on the *Tonight Show*. He is a true psychic.

27. "To find her [Lizzy Borden] guilty, you must believe she is a fiend. Gentlemen, does she look it?"

28. Murder in Oklahoma jumped 93 percent in the first six weeks after the Supreme Court ruling abolishing the death penalty. I guess that proves something.

29. The United States Supreme Court Has Ruled That "Carnal Knowledge" is *Not Obscene*. See it Now!

30. *Hitler's Daughter* by Gary Goss. "A brilliant academic satire"—Dennis Renault, *Sacramento Bee;* "A hilarious time"—Harry Cargas, *Buffalo Spree;* "Raunchy and unfair"—Otto Tumiel, *The Reading Intelligencer*

31. *The Power of Prayer on Plants* by Rev. Franklin Loehr. "In 700 experiments conducted by 150 persons, using 27,000 seeds and comprising 100,000 measurements, prayer consistently made a difference, in some cases showing as much as 52.71% growth advantage for prayer seedlings. . . . I doubt if anyone who reads this book and sees the photographs of actual experiments can ever be complacent about prayer again."—Ruth Sheldon Knowles, *Tulsa World*

32. "I think the polls are a lot of rot. I think they make these things up in the back room."—Senator George McGovern

PART II
Effective Writing

Eight Rules for Good Writing

> What matters is that we get done what we have to do and
> get said what we have to say.
> —Donald J. Lloyd, "Our National Mania for
> Correctness"

The following pages will show you how to write clear, straight-forward prose. This is the language you would use in explaining a situation or arguing an issue. It expresses itself in a direct, informal style.

There are other styles of writing. For an inaugural address or a theological essay, you will want a more formal, balanced presentation. For an emotional appeal or an angry condemnation, you may want a more colloquial or slangy style. But such occasions are rare. The informal style recommended here will serve you in almost all writing situations.

The eight rules that follow should make you a better writer. They include material you need to know, and they omit areas you do not need to worry about. The intent is practical: not to tell you about "good writing," but to show you how to achieve it.

These rules will be sufficient for most people on most writing occasions. The weak student who cannot recognize a sentence and does not know that a period goes at the end of it will need additional help. So will the refined writer who seeks a singular style. Nevertheless, the rules can help most people become fluent, correct, and effective writers.

RULE 1: CHOOSE A SUBJECT YOU CAN WORK WITH

Choosing a subject is one of the hardest parts of writing, and perhaps the most important. In most writing situations, of course, you do not have to choose a topic. You want to write the power company protesting the latest rate hike. You have to write a thank-you letter to your aunt. Your boss asks you to prepare a marketing report. In these cases the subject is there, and you have to tell a particular audience about it.

Still there are occasions when you do select a topic for an essay or speech. And there are times when you might be given a general subject ("The American Way" or "Tomorrow's Promise"), but you can approach it in a number of different ways. You should recognize the problems in making a choice.

To produce a good essay, you should choose a topic that will interest your audience, that lends itself to detail, and that can be covered in a prescribed number of words. (The point here will be clearer if you recall the last dull sermon you heard.)

If you were assigned to write a 500-word theme for a general audience (think of the people you see around you in class or at a movie), how good would these topics be?

1. "DEATH AWAITS ALL MEN"

Unless you are going to write of something unusual— an exploding sun, the bloody prophecies of Revelation, or the mathematics of entropy— this will be a boring subject. When you write of "all men," you tend to say what everyone knows.

2. "MY BROTHER, THE PRACTICAL JOKER"

This topic concerns an individual person, rather than all men. But the experience is pretty close to that of all men. Most people have met practical jokers. Unless your brother's jokes are particularly brilliant or outrageous, you would do better with another subject.

3. "I AM SURE I HAVE PIERCED EARS"

This subject does not lend itself to detail. What can you write after the first sentence? Who would be interested?

4. "THE SUN ALSO RISES—HEMINGWAY'S MASTERPIECE"

This topic is interesting and rich with detail, but it is more suitable to a 300-page book than a 500-word theme. If you wish to write on a novel, you must restrict yourself to one feature of it. Here you could limit yourself to one character ("Robert Cohn—The Outsider") or to one fairly defined theme ("Fishing in Spain—A Symbolic Quest").

Remember that, almost invariably, your tendency will be to choose a subject that's too broad rather than one too narrow.

5. "HANK AARON WAS A BETTER HITTER THAN BABE RUTH"

This could be a good choice. The subject would interest many readers. It provides a lot of detail—comparison of number of times at bat, number of hits, quality of opposing pitchers, the kinds of baseballs used, sizes of stadiums, and so on. The theme—if you keep the focus on batting and avoid discussions of personality, fielding, and baserunning—can be finished in 500 words.

Another element which makes this a good subject is that it presents a minority view, something which always adds interest. "Cleanliness Is Important" is a vague truism, but "Cleanliness Is Dangerous" could make a fascinating theme.

6. "HOW TO CLEAN A BASSOON"

This subject lends itself to detail; it can be covered in 500 words; and it is beyond the experience of "all men." But, for whatever reason, it would have little appeal for a general audience.

Of course, a knowledgeable and creative writer can make any subject interesting. And one can imagine particular individuals who would respond to any topic. But these exceptions do not change the situation for you. You must try to choose a subject that will keep the interest of a fairly general audience.

EXERCISES

Which of these subjects would be more likely to produce an acceptable 500-word theme? Why?

1. The Virtue of Thrift
2. Space Travel Will Have a Drastic Effect on Contemporary Art
3. A Sure Way to Pick Winners at the Dog Track
4. The Importance of a College Education
5. Richard Nixon and the Watergate Tragedy
6. Who Needs College?
7. Dogs Are Better than Cats
8. Drag-racing Cars Perform Mathematically Impossible Feats
9. Ethnic Humor
10. Aspirin, Bufferin, Anacin—Somebody's Lying
11. The World Is Ending: Prophecy, Weaponry, and Ecology

RULE 2: GET YOUR FACTS

An interesting theme has to be specific. No one can write a compelling essay on entropy or Hank Aaron or space-age architecture or much else without seeking out a body of factual information. Writing involves research.

Unless you are writing from personal experience, you will probably want to build your theme around people you can quote and facts you can bring forward. You obtain such material from a number of sources.

Visit the Library

Large stores of information can be unearthed by using the card catalog and the *Reader's Guide*. The card catalog lists author, title, and subject for every book in the library. The *Reader's Guide*, under subject headings, lists magazine articles printed over the years. (You can find the magazines in the periodicals section or on microfilm.)

These titles illustrate the range of sources available to you.

Bartlett's Familiar Quotations
Black's Law Dictionary
Book Review Digest
The Congressional Directory
Crime in the United States (the FBI report)
Encyclopaedia Britannica—and annuals
Facts on File Yearbook
Fishbein's *Popular Medical Encyclopedia*
Griffith's *The Movies*
Keller's *Dictionary of Dates*
Larousse Encyclopedia of Mythology
McGraw-Hill Encyclopedia of Science and Technology
Menke's *Encyclopedia of Sport*
The New York Times Index
Oxford Companion to Music
Universal Jewish Encyclopedia
Vital Statistics of the United States
Webster's Biographical Dictionary
Webster's New International Dictionary of the English Language,
   3rd Ed.
Who Was Who
Who's Who
World Almanac

You will need such books to provide facts for your essay.

Don't be afraid to ask for help in the library. Most librarians are nice people.

Use Your Telephone

Libraries employ reference people who spend a good part of each day answering questions over the phone. If you need to know Babe Ruth's batting average in 1928, you can either find the answer in a baseball almanac or phone your local reference librarian, who will look up the information and call you back.

You can phone others too. If you have a brief legal question, call a lawyer or a law professor. If you need to know the current price for wastepaper, phone your junkyard. For specific information, don't hesitate to call your priest or banker or congressman or newsman or sheriff or insurance agent. Most of these people are willing to help you, and many will be happy to do so.

Write for Facts You Need

Many sources are available to you. United States government agencies will send you documents on a range of subjects. Organizations with a message will send you stacks of literature. (Both the American Cancer Society and the Tobacco Institute have pamphlets on smoking and health.) You can base your theme on materials from Liberty Lobby, Common Cause, the National Rifle Association, the Confraternity of Christian Doctrine, the U.S. Chamber of Commerce, the Non-Sectarian Committee for Life, and many comparable sources.

If you make the effort, you will find plenty of information to give meaning and interest to your writing.

A warning: Get your facts right. And don't put another writer's exact words in your paper without adding quotation marks. (Unless a particular quote makes an impressive point for you, it is probably better to paraphrase it.) If your readers recognize errors of fact in your essay or if they see you have offered someone else's language as your own, they will tend to discredit your writing.

EXERCISES

Use your library and other resources to locate this information.

1. What was the front-page headline and the sports-page headline in the *New York Times* on the day you were born?
2. Name all the presidents of the NAACP from the beginning up to now.
3. Give the source of these lines: (a) "the uncertain glory of an April day" and (b) "Letters are the soul of trade."
4. What did Wallace Stevens mean by the line "The only emperor is the emperor of ice cream"?
5. Distinguish between *Green Pastures*, white noise, the Scarlet Pimpernell, the Black and Tans, and the Gray Panthers.
6. Identify as many of these as you can:

Andrew Aguecheek	Jay Gould
Angelo Bertelli	Bruno Hauptmann
Jussi Bjoerling	Edward Hyde
Peaches Browning	Pope Joan
Chang and Eng	Leadbelly
Dick Deadeye	Ken Maynard

Threecard Monte	Olympia Spalanzani
Panini	Count Turf
John Peel	Michael Ventris
Bobby Shaftoe	Whizzer White
Sam Spade	Lester Young

RULE 3: LIMIT YOUR TOPIC TO MANAGEABLE SIZE

Most writing is subject to space and time limitations. You are preparing a magazine advertisement or a campaign document (one page). You are writing an editorial or a letter to the editor (under 1000 words). You are preparing a sermon or an after-dinner speech (twenty minutes or less). Rarely will you have an opportunity that will permit, or an audience that will tolerate, a discussion of all aspects of an issue.

Therefore you must limit your topic. Do not, for example, write about "Dieting." Even "Crash Dieting" is too broad a subject. You can maintain, however, that "Crash Dieting Is Dangerous." Similarly, do not speculate about "America's Unjust Drug Laws"; write "Alabama's Marijuana Laws Violate the Fifth Amendment." This topic narrowing is particularly important when you write argument. A dull essay is rarely persuasive.

Try to avoid writing an "about" theme—that is, a general theme about fishing, about communism, about heart disease, or about love and death. These aren't helped by vague titles like "The Joys of Fishing" or "The Truth About Communism." Such unfocused subjects lend themselves to vague generalizations. They produce themes that lack unity, coherence, and interest.

A limited topic demands specific detail. You will need specific facts if you want to keep your reader awake.

EXERCISES

Limit each of these topics—that is, isolate parts that you could express in a 500-word theme.

1. Improving American Education
2. LSD—A Blessing or a Curse?
3. The Energy Crisis
4. Women in Politics
5. God in Everyday Life
6. Watergate
7. Raising Houseplants
8. Travel Is Educational
9. Current Slang
10. Extrasensory Perception

11. Situational Ethics
12. Animals Can Talk
13. The Tobacco Issue

RULE 4: ORGANIZE YOUR MATERIAL

Most essays—and indeed most reports and business letters—are made up of an *introduction,* a *body,* and a *conclusion.* The introduction says, "I am going to write about X." The body discusses X in some organized way. And the conclusion says, "That's what I have to say about X." A good writer will keep this pattern from being too obvious, but this is the pattern he will use.

The Introduction

Most topics can be divided into parts. Your essay praising Johnny Bench might discuss his catching, his baserunning, and his hitting. Your argument against abortion might describe the growth of the fetus month by month. Your analysis of a physical or social problem (lung cancer, skyjacking, etc.) might first describe the effect, then indicate some probable causes.

Along with material you may include to catch the reader's attention, your first paragraph should have a *thesis statement* that announces the main idea and purpose of the essay. And it may include another sentence that indicates the kind of breakdown the subject will take. Here are some effective introductions.

There can be no doubt that extrasensory perception exists. How else can one explain the results of the Spranches-Malone experiment conducted at UCLA in 1975?

(The theme will discuss the experiment.)

Legal abortion is necessary. Otherwise we will be back with vast numbers of women getting amateur surgery in bloody abortion mills.

(The theme will discuss earlier years: [1] vast numbers of women and [2] bloody surgery.)

The only way to stop inflation is to raise taxes and impose wage and price controls, but I don't think the President has the courage to support these measures.

(The theme will cover [1] anti-inflation measures: [a] a tax raise and [b] wage-and-price controls; and [2] Presidential courage.)

Sometimes you can use a witty introduction to win the reader's at-

244 Effective Writing

tention. But if you are not confident about the quality of your wit, it is probably wiser to rely on a straight-forward opening.

Keep your introductions short.

The Body

The introduction and conclusion are little more than a frame surrounding what you have to say. The paragraphs of the body *are* your essay.

Each paragraph presents a unit of your message. This does not mean that each division of your topic, as announced in the introduction, must be covered in one paragraph. In the anti-inflation theme just introduced, your discussion of wage-price controls might take two, three, or six paragraphs.

Just as the introduction has a thesis statement announcing what the whole theme is about, each paragraph has a *topic sentence* telling what it will cover. Usually this is the first sentence. Because they show exactly what the rest of the paragraph will be about, these are effective topic sentences:

> These gun laws haven't reduced the level of crime in Cleveland.
> Why did the price of electricity go up in July?
> Consider what the fetus can do in the third month of its growth.
> Secretary Vance was equally unsuccessful in getting concessions from the Syrians.

Your paragraph should not bring in material beyond the scope of the topic sentence. In the paragraph about gun laws in Cleveland, for example, you should not discuss other crime-fighting measures in Cleveland, nor should you mention crime in Detroit.

Topic sentences are effective in linking paragraphs. In the examples given, the references to *"These* gun laws" and to Secretary Vance's being *"equally* unsuccessful" show a relation to material in previous paragraphs. Words like "therefore," "however," "such," "second," and "similarly" achieve the same effect.

Within each paragraph, try to give the sentences the same grammatical subject. (In the paragraph on Secretary Vance, the subject of most of the sentences should be "he" or "Vance" or "the Secretary.") If you vary the kinds of sentences, as in the following example, the practice should not seem monotonous.

> One frequently hears statements that simply lack evidence. *Advertisements* announce that "Ban is preferred by seven out of ten American women," that "four out of five movie stars use Lustre-Creme Shampoo." *Rumor* whispers that Viceroy filters are made of harmful fiber glass and that drinking fluoridated water can

cause brain damage. Such *claims* can safely be ignored until evidence is offered to support them.

A variation popular with sensational writers is to make an extravagant claim and point to concrete evidence—which happens to be unavailable. *They* charge that Warren Harding was murdered by his wife and that Franklin Roosevelt was poisoned by the Russians at Teheran—then regret that evidence is lost in the past. *They* affirm the existence of abominable snowmen, Atlantis, and the Loch Ness monster—then lament that proof remains out of reach. *They* know that UFO's are extraterrestrial spaceships and that a massive conspiracy led to the assassinations of John and Robert Kennedy—then insist that government agencies are withholding evidence. These too are inductions with an absent sample.

Remember that the grammatical subject is not necessarily the first word of a sentence. It may follow an introductory phrase ("After the dance, *he* . . .") or clause ("When Kathy remembered the accident, *she* . . .").

In some paragraphs, keeping the same subject will prevent you from saying what you want. Or it will make your writing seem stilted and artificial. In such cases, don't do it.

The Conclusion

The last paragraph of your essay echoes the introduction. It summarizes and generalizes about the subject discussed.

Unless your paper is long or particularly complicated, you do not need to restate the structural outline ("In this theme, I have discussed first the language of Mark's gospel, then its historical qualities, and finally its theology.") Instead, just give a sentence or two expressing the main point. Here are some acceptable concluding paragraphs:

> Mark's gospel is more like a sermon than like a biography. It is a work of profound faith and impressive artistry.
> No one favors abortion. But we have to admit that, in many cases, it is the only humane alternative.
> The Spranches-Malone experiment proves conclusively that ESP exists. Now we have to figure out what we can do with it.

Keep your conclusions short.

EXERCISE

Discuss the strengths and weaknesses of this essay. Consider the thesis statement, the topic sentences, transitions between paragraphs, keeping the same subject within a paragraph, unity of a paragraph, and so on.

Poetry

All my life I have hated poetry. I hated it in high school, in grade school, and in the sophomore poetry course I've just completed here at South Alabama. Why we serious students have to study jingled nonsense, I will never know.

I live in Reedsburg, a community of farmers, tradesmen, and practical people. Nevertheless, the Reedsburg Grade School subjected me to all sorts of frivolous and impractical poetry. From the first grade on, my class endured semester after semester of cute rhyme. We read teddy-bear poems from *Winnie the Pooh*. We read Mother Goose rhymes about Simple Simon and Robert Louis Stevenson poems about a "friendly cow all red and white." We read jingles telling us to drink our milk. I always wonder why the poets didn't just *say* things instead of chanting and jingling them. It was silly.

I had some poetry in Reedsburg High School too. However, I escaped much of it by signing up for speech classes. In speech I studied more sensible subjects. I learned to speak in front of a group. I learned to think on my feet. I learned to make a talk interesting by referring to the audience and by adding humor. Most important, I learned to say things directly, without all the cute ornament of poetry.

The sophomore poetry class I've just finished at South Alabama has only made me dislike poems more. Mr. Remington, my instructor, was incompetent. The way he read them, all poems sounded just alike. When he wasn't mumbling about Shelley, we were taking impossible tests on Keats and nightingales. Either it was assumed we knew everything about epics or he was talking down to the class as though we had never heard of metaphor. The day before the final exam, he didn't even show up for class. The whole quarter was a waste of time.

In fact, all the poetry discussions I've had from grade school up to now, have been a waste of time. I just don't like poetry.

RULE 5: MAKE YOUR WRITING INTERESTING

Remember that no one *has* to read your essay. And if people have to hear your speech, they don't have to pay attention. The burden is on you to make your subject interesting.

This is not a huge burden. If you have a topic that you think is important and if you present it with clarity and specific detail, your reader or listener will probably be interested.

Generally, you maintain interest by avoiding certain practices that deaden language.

Truisms

Do not say what everybody knows. Your reader will not be thrilled to hear that third-degree burns are painful and that the President of the

United States bears great responsibilities. Don't write, "Every great man has moments of profound sorrow, but Thomas Eaton's life was genuinely tragic." Write, "Thomas Eaton's life was tragic."

Clichés

Some phrases have lost meaning through overuse. Your writing will lose emphasis and interest if you use tired language like this:

> first and foremost
> on the other hand
> in the final analysis
> last but not least
> old as the hills
> few and far between
> burning the midnight oil
> in a very real sense
> sadder but wiser

Many words and phrases from current slang ("bad," "get down," "make the scene," "heavy," etc.) are objectionable not because they are informal, but because they have been overused.

A good rule: if you suspect a particular phrase might be a cliché, it is. Write something else.

Remember that avoiding a cliché can produce a rich substitution. A CBS sports announcer once described Green Bay quarterback Bart Starr as (not "cool as a cucumber" but) "cool as the other side of the pillow."

Generalized Language

The point cannot be overemphasized: *To be interesting, you must be specific.* Write of real things. Use specific names, numbers, places, dates, and quotations. You can, for example, refer to the same man in a number of ways:

> an athlete
> a ballplayer
> a baseball player
> an infielder
> a third baseman
> a Philadelphia third baseman
> Pete Rose

Always choose the most specific word that serves the purposes of your essay. An effective composition uses proper names.

In many instances your writing will be more interesting if you avoid the words "good," "bad," and "said."

Substituted words are almost always more meaningful. Instead of "good," write "even-tempered," "inexpensive," "compassionate," or "crisp." Instead of "bad," write "moldy," "pretentious," "degenerate," or "incompetent." The word "said" is always acceptable, but you can add richness to your prose by substituting "whispered," "suggested," "boasted," "conceded," "protested," or "gasped." (Try never to use "stated.")

Similarly, try to avoid forms of the verb "to be," that is, the words "is," "are," "was," "were," "am," and forms with "been." Much of the time, of course, you have to use these words, but substitutions are invariably more detailed and effective. For example, "Harold Lord *was* injured" becomes "Harold Lord broke his left wrist." And "The weather *was* horrible" becomes "Eight inches of snow fell on Buffalo yesterday afternoon." (Some scholars have designated the English language without "to be" forms as "E-prime.")

Inflated Language

Except in rare cases, you will want your writing to be clear. You do this by keeping your language as simple and direct as possible. When addressing a general audience, try to avoid these kinds of expressions:

Foreign words—*bête noir, ne plus ultra, coup d'état*
Learned words—*penultimate, datum, symbiotic*
Poetic words—*repine, oft, betimes*
Technical words—*manic, input, persona*
Literary allusions—*Lot's wife, protean, the sword of Damocles*
Current in-words—*parameter, viable, ambiance*

Such words are more acceptable if you are writing for an educated or specialized audience. But a really fine writer wouldn't use them there either.

Write words you would say. Do not use "in view of the above" or "for the above reasons"; write "consequently" or "for these reasons." Try not to use "the addressee," "the executrix," "the former," or "the latter"; write "Robin Carpenter" (or "she" or "her"). Never refer to yourself as "the writer" (or "we"); say "I."

The next time you hear a dull speech or sermon, don't tune it out. Ask yourself why it is dull. Probably it is a collection of truisms, clichés, and vague or inflated phrases. You can learn from such examples.

EXERCISES

Rewrite these sentences. Make them more likely to sustain the interest of a general audience.

1. This insult was the last straw. I decided to leave Marcel, and I spent the next few hours preparing for the trip.
2. The Book of Jonah illustrates the ludicrous intractability of a particular mind set.
3. Scott Daniel was a fine basketball player. I believe that he was the best to play in the league in the last thirty years. He was really fine.
4. Vis-à-vis our tête-à-tête, I must say the rendezvous filled me with ennui.
5. We will never know everything about the atom, but some of the recent discoveries have been fascinating.
6. Driving the L.A. freeway is like crossing the river Styx.
7. In the following weeks at school, I worked frantically. Every day I became busier and busier.
8. As we entered the restaurant, David stated that the chicken there was good but the service was bad.
9. Anyone can suffer with a rotten tooth or a sprained ankle, but the man with kidney stones endures a superexcruciating kind of pain.
10. In the final analysis, there are few rugged individualists in this day and age who are really down to earth in expressing nothing but the truth about the seamy side of life. Perhaps in the near future. . . .
11. Salesmen should cultivate a charismatic emphasis to facilitate and implement contractual negotiations on an interpersonal basis.

RULE 6: MAKE YOUR WRITING EMPHATIC

Sometimes unnecesary words or particular word-forms detract from the point you want to make. These recommendations should help you emphasize the important ideas in your writing.

Avoid Wordiness

Unnecessary words may confuse, bore, or antagonize your reader. Say what you have to say as briefly as possible. Too often a series of words exists where one will do.

> due to the fact that = because
> the man with the dark complexion = the dark man
> people who are concerned only with themselves = selfish people
> I disagree with the conclusion offered by Professor Brennan = I disagree with Professor Brennan

And commonly one or more words appear where none is necessary:

> Becky ~~really~~ is a ~~very~~ beautiful girl.
> ~~Personally,~~ I agree with him.

I dislike his personality ~~and his temperament.~~
~~There were~~ several people at the party ~~who~~ saw the fight.

Don't worry about wordiness when you are putting together the first draft of your essay; just get down what you have to say. Succinct prose usually comes with rewriting.

Write in the Active Voice

In active-voice sentences, the grammatical subject is the acting agent. ("The *Brezinsky Commission* has attacked public apathy.") In passive-voice constructions, the subject receives the action of the verb. ("Public *apathy* has been attacked by the Brezinsky Commission.")

In sentences where the acting agent is obvious or irrelevant, you will need passive-voice constructions. ("The President was reelected.") But, whenever possible, avoid them.

As often as not, using the active voice means beginning your sentence (or beginning the main clause of your sentence) with acting agents: *we, she, Robert Huntley, the Brezinsky Commission,* and so on. Try to avoid forms that keep from doing this. Here are examples:

My intention was. . . .
It was soon evident that. . . .
There were. . . .
. . . was seen.
. . . could be heard.
His cruelty. . . .

If you are writing a personal essay, begin most sentences (or main clause) with *I.*

Express Your Main Idea in the Subject-Verb of Your Sentence

Make the subject-verb unit of your sentence express your main thought. Put less important information in modifying phrases and clauses.

Try not to express your main thought as a modifying phrase ("Harold Lord slipped in the outfield, *thus breaking his arm*") or as a *that* clause ("I learned *that Aunt Maude had been arrested for arson*"). Give your point subject-verb emphasis:

Harold Lord slipped in the outfield and broke his arm.
Helen told me the sad news: Aunt Maude had been arrested for arson.

Do Not Waste the Ends of Your Sentences

Because the end of your sentence is a position of emphasis you should not use it to express minor thoughts or casual information. Don't write, "Both singers will appear here in July, if we can believe the reports." (This is correct only if you want to stress the doubtfulness of the reports.) Notice how the emphasis trails away in a sentence like this: "Trapped in a drab life with a dull husband, Hedda Gabler shoots herself, partly too because she is threatened by Judge Brack."

Because the beginning of a sentence also conveys a degree of emphasis, you should not waste that position either. Try to put words in like "however," "therefore," and "nevertheless" in the middle of sentences. ("The postman, however, arrived at five o'clock.") Do not do this if it makes your sentence sound awkward.

Keep Your Sentences Relatively Short

To avoid a monotonous style, you should build your essay with sentences of different kinds and lengths. But using short sentences will help you avoid difficulties. When sentences go beyond fifteen or twenty words, punctuation—which can be a problem—becomes complicated; meaning gets diffuse; their pronouns are separated from the words they refer to; and the reader or listener finds it difficult to see the continuity and may lose interest. Short sentences are better.

EXERCISES

What changes would make the meaning of these sentences more emphatic?

1. I was born in the city of Chicago, Illinois.
2. Trapped in a drab life with a dull husband, Hedda Gabler shoots herself, partly too because she is threatened by Judge Brack.
3. The eagle suddenly loosed its grip, allowing the climber to escape.
4. Though I had more than several reasons to dislike and distrust Libby MacDuffee before the accident, I found still more when she tried to take me to court to pay for hospital costs and when she claimed I had had three martinis at the Red Oak Bar within an hour (or at the most two hours) before the wreck.
5. Wilson drove home from the cocktail lounge and discovered a burglar climbing out of his bedroom window.
6. Nevertheless, I must refuse your kind offer.
7. His hope was that he could conquer Paris by June.
8. Although Alana feared flying, she took the 9:02 flight from Milwaukee, being already two days late for the convention.
9. This book concerns itself with language intended to deceive.
10. It was greatly feared by the crowd that an honest decision would not come from the referee.

RULE 7: AVOID LANGUAGE THAT DRAWS ATTENTION TO ITSELF

You want your reader to follow your meaning, the ideas you're developing. Do not distract the reader by using words or phrases that catch the eye. Try to avoid these forms.

Repetition

Repeating a word for emphasis can be effective ("government of the people, by the people, and for the people"), but often it distracts attention. Avoid repetition of sentence forms ("I went to see the accident. Fifteen people were there. Each told a different story"); of particular words ("Going to school is not going to be easy. If the going gets tough . . ."); and even of sounds ("I'm sorry about the story, Laurie").

Dangling and Misplaced Modifiers

Make it clear what words your adjectives and adverbs are modifying. You do this by putting modifiers close to the words they refer to. Avoid examples like these:

> *When nine years old*, my grandmother took me to the circus.
> No judge would sentence a man to hard labor *unless he were irresponsible.*
> I *only* shot two deer.
> *By knowing what you want to say*, your essay will progress more easily.

Notice that these sentences are clear enough; in context, your reader would know what you mean. But such awkward and even humorous lines draw attention to themselves and away from your meaning.

Elaborate Figures of Speech

A mixed metaphor often produces irrelevant laughter ("Into this forest, the hand of man had never set foot"). But even a meaningful figure of speech can be distracting. You could write, "Nixon steered the ship of state over treacherous seas; he was a star-crossed President." But such a sentence stops the reader. Instead of following the rest of your ideas, he pauses to interpret the metaphor.

You will, of course, want to use some figures of speech in your prose. Just don't let them get too complicated.

Faulty Parallelism

You should express coordinate ideas in similar form. You do this mainly to avoid awkward and distracting sentences. Clearly, "I was *alone, uncertain,* and *possessed of a considerable degree of fear"* is less emphatic than "I was *alone, uncertain,* and *afraid."* Notice how the awkwardness of these sentences weakens their impact:

> The teachers were burdened with *large classes, poor textbooks,* and *the necessity to cope with an incompetent principal.*
> I love *seeing* my daughter and *to hear* her voice.
> For a settlement, I will accept *a new stove* or *having my old stove repaired.*

Some sentences cannot be made parallel. You cannot change "Ted was tall, charming, and wore a blue hat" to "Ted was tall, charming and blue-hatted." In such a case, write the first units so your reader doesn't expect the final one to be parallel. Write, "Ted was tall and charming; he always wore a blue hat."

Awkward Constructions

Try to give your sentences the sound of natural speech. Don't break the continuity of your meaning with intrusive passages:

> I promised to, if the expected raise came through, take her to the Grand Hotel.
> Her brother, if we can believe local historians (and who can), was a senator.

And don't seek a poetic style by inverting word order:

> Quiet was the night.
> The reason for her suicide, we shall never know.

Where it sounds natural, don't be afraid to begin a sentence with a conjuction or to end it with a proposition. (And suddenly I realized where the money had come from.")

Abrupt Changes in Tone

Your tone is your personal voice, your way of saying things. This will vary with your audience and with your subject. You talk one way to an intimate friend and a different way to the local bishop. You would use formal diction when writing of the United Nations Charter, and you might use colloquial—and even coarse—language in describing life at your fraternity house. The important thing to remember is to keep your tone consistent. Don't jar your reader by describing a U.N. Charter provision as "a crap-headed experiment." And don't call your fraternity dining room "a haven of calculated insouciance."

If your tone is light enough to permit contractions (can't, wouldn't), use them right from the beginning of your essay. Don't begin to use them in the middle of a relatively formal paper.

Remember that any time your reader is more impressed by your writing than by your meaning, you have failed. No one can improve on the valuable advice Samuel Johnson gave in the eighteenth century: "Read over your composition, and where ever you meet with a passage which you think is particularly fine, strike it out."

EXERCISES

Correct weaknesses in these sentences.

1. Seaver was pitching beautifully until the seventh inning. And then the fireworks fell in.
2. When reading late at night, the book should be held under a strong light.
3. Pamela was pretty, energetic, and carried a file of history notes.
4. Secretary Vance was scheduled to attend the Geneva Conference, but he couldn't make the scene.
5. Professor Dendinger is giving a lecture tonight on student unrest in the faculty lounge.
6. We traveled for six days and the car broke down. We hitchhiked into Laredo, and I took a job gardening. I had the car towed into town, but nobody there could fix it.
7. I knew that Bill was home, that Tom was in the army, and Sam was at the University.
8. We saw the brawny black boxer bite the white fighter.
9. Cancer hit my family with full force this year, sending two of my aunts to the Mayo Clinic.
10. Mrs. L. M. Williamson earned her M.A. and Ph.D. at UCLA.
11. Who can say (certainly, not me) which is the best way—if there is just one best way—to pickle beets?
12. The teacher told him frequently to rewrite his essays.
13. Barton told the story of the half-restored store. But it was far too long for us to put up with.

RULE 8: AVOID MECHANICAL ERRORS

To write effectively, you need to know a number of elementary rules of usage. But there are a number you do *not* have to know. An important truth is expressed in this story:

A man went to his doctor and described his ailment. Clinching his right fist tightly, he said, "It hurts me when I go like that." The doctor prescribed the remedy: "Don't go like that."

The story tells you many things about writing: how to punctuate long and involved sentences, how to use apostrophes in unusual constructions, how to use quotation marks within quotation marks, and how to spell "evidentiary." The counsel: "Don't go like that."

The following rules on punctuation, abbreviation, number, and spelling should take you through most writing situations.

Punctuation

1. *Use Commas to Make Your Sentences Easier to Read.* Textbooks routinely tell you to put a comma before the conjunction in a compound sentence ("Pam is a good student, but she cannot learn economics"); after introductory clauses ("When I went home, I saw my brother's car"); and before the *and* in elements in a series ("I bought a suit, three ties, and a sweater").

The problem is that many professional writers do not punctuate like this. Hence you may be confused.

A good rule to follow is this: Always use commas in these constructions *when the sentences are long.*

Arthur had traveled fifty-seven miles through the desert to meet the Prince, and he knew that nothing in the world could make him turn back now.

When I saw that the young soldier was holding a gun on Martha and me, I became most obedient.

Suddenly Henry saw that the parable applied to him, that he must change his life, and that the time to start was now.

Similarly, you should always insert commas in these constructions *when there is a danger of misreading.*

The fox ate three chickens and the rooster ran away.

When we finished eating cigarettes were distributed to the soldiers.

They stopped looking for Irene became tired.

If you use normal word order and keep your sentences relatively short, you should have little difficulty with commas.

2. *Use a Semicolon to Show that Two Independent Clauses Are Closely Related.* Sometimes you want to indicate the particularly close relation-

ship between two statements. Here you merge the statements into one sentence and connect them with a semicolon.

> Her brother has been sick for years; now he is going to die.
> To know her is to love her; to love her is a mistake.

This construction often occurs when the second statement contains "however," "therefore," or "nevertheless."

> The 747 was two hours late; however, no one at O'Hare seemed particularly worried.
> Billy wanted to propose during final-exam week; he saw, however, that this would cause problems.

You can also use semicolons to separate on the halves of a compound sentence or the units in a series when the separated passages have commas within them.

> My boss, Harry Welch, was there; but before I could talk to him, he fell and broke his arm.
> Among those present were Dr. Williams, an English professor; Mr. Rainey, head of the Presbyterian meeting; and Mrs. Milliken, president of the P.T.A.

If you have problems punctuating such long sentences, don't write them.

3. *Use a Colon to Introduce a Unit.* You use a colon to introduce something: an announcement, a clarification, or a formal series.

> In May, the professor made his decision: he would leave the university.
> The difference between fathers and sons used to be a simple one: fathers earned the money and sons spent it.
> Molly excelled in active sports: tennis, swimming, badminton, and gymnastics.

When a complicated sentence follows a colon, the first word may be capitalized—especially if the sentence is long. ("In May, the professor made his decision: <u>H</u>e would leave the university, move to Washington, and take a position with the Tobacco Institute.")

In general, you will never use a colon except after a complete statement. Don't write, "Her favorites were: Andy Williams, Tim Conway, and Charles Matlock." Write,

> These were her favorites: Andy Williams, Tim Conway, and Charles Matlock.
>
> or (better)
>
> Her favorites were Andy Williams, Tim Conway, and Charles Matlock.

It is permissible to use a colon after "the following." ("He did it for the following reasons: . . .") But when you can avoid it, don't write "the following" at all. (Write, "He did it for these reasons: . . .")

4. *Use an Exclamation Mark to Show Emphasis.* Because adding an exclamation mark is an easy way to show emphasis, you may be tempted to overuse it. Try to reserve it for "Wow!" or "Fire!" or some comparable outcry.

Never use two or more exclamation marks to seek additional emphasis. Never!

5. *Use a Question Mark After a Direct Question.* You will, of course, put a question mark after a question. But be sure it is a direct question.

Have you had your Wheaties today?
He asked, "Did you see my son there?"

Don't use a question mark after an indirect question or after a question form that is really a polite command.

She asked if I knew the way to school.
Will you please hand in your bluebooks now.

Try not to use question marks to express uncertainty or irony.

John Wilcox was born in 1657(?) and died in 1760.
Those amateurs(?) made a very good living playing tennis.

These are weak constructions. Say instead that Wilcox was born "about 1657"; criticize "those so-called amateurs."

6. *Use Hyphens to Form Compound Adjectives and to Divide Words at the End of a Line.* Use a hyphen to join a compound adjective when it *precedes* a noun. You can say that "the theory was out date," or you can call it "an out-of-date theory." In examples like these, the hyphens make your meaning clearer:

a Monday-morning quarterback
a dog-in-the-manger attitude
a long-term investment

Use a hyphen to divide a word at the end of a line. But remember that you must divide the word between syllables ("when-ever," "in-tern," "pho-bia"). You should not divide a word so that only one letter appears on a line ("a-bout." "phobi-a"); and you should never divide a one-syllable word ("doubt," "called," "proved").

If you don't know where to divide a word, consult your dictionary.

If you don't have a dictionary at hand, don't divide the word; write it all on the next line.

7. *Use a Dash Where You Need It.* Like commas and parentheses, dashes can be used to set off an element. If you want to set off an idea that is closely related to your sentence, use commas. ("My father, who always loved fruit, died eating an orange.") To set off a unit that is less closely related, use dashes (or parentheses). ("My father—he would have been thirty-nine next month—died eating an orange.")

Indeed, a dash—used in moderation—is acceptable punctuation in many circumstances.

> Don't bet on Red Devil—he's a loser.
> He thought about the situation for weeks—never able to get it all together.
> It became clear that only one man could be the murderer—Dr. Dorrill.

The dash is a handy mark of punctuation. Just don't overuse it.

EXERCISES

Punctuate these sentences. Insert commas, semicolons, colons, exclamation marks, hyphens, and dashes where needed.

1. When the outfielder caught the second hand baseball he saw that the hide was torn
2. Charles Lackey the famous actor died on stage last week
3. He never complained he knew it would do no good
4. The nun asked me if I knew the way to Elm Street
5. During the summer I spent $11000 on eighteenth century furniture
6. Phillip said there were three TV shows he would never miss *Mash Kojak* and *Police Woman*
7. The price and I can't tell you how pleased I am to say this is only $4800
8. After six weeks of trying my brother finally learned to play hearts
9. Do you have something for a headache
10. I think *The Iceman Cometh* is the best American play written in the century and I absolutely refuse to teach it to this know nothing class.
11. Would you kindly play this bill by the first of the month
12. The wife got the stereo the television and the Thunderbird but the husband insisted on keeping the dog
13. They insisted on waiting for John had never been there before

The last punctuation rules concern apostrophes, quotation marks, italics, and capital letters. These can cause problems.

8. *Use Apostrophes to Show Possession, to Indicate an Omission, and to Form Unusual Plurals.* As a general rule, you show possession by adding *'s* to any singular or plural noun that does not end in *s*.

the dog's collar	Jim's football
the woman's hand	the men's boots

For nouns ending in *s*, you add either an *'s* or simply a final apostrophe. Punctuate it the way you say it; add the *'s* where you pronounce the extra syllable.

the girls' room	James's reign
the Clardys' house	the Harris's car

(Notice in reading of the Hiss-Chambers case that most writers speak of *Chambers'* accusations and of *Hiss's* response.)

In more complicated cases it is often better to avoid the issue. Don't speculate on how to punctuate "Charles and Bobs television," "Jesus parables," or "the last three months pay." Write "the television Charles and Bob bought last June," "the parables of Jesus," and "pay for the last three months."

You also use apostrophes to replace omitted letters or numbers in contractions ("I've," "it's," "couldn't," "the class of '45") and to form unusual plurals.

A good essay is not full of *and*'s.
Today Ph.D.'s can't get a job.
I got one A and four C's.

If you wonder whether you should use an apostrophe with particular proper nouns ("Diners Club," "Veterans Administration," etc.), there is no rule to help you. You must check your telephone directory to see how these organizations spell their names. (Neither "Diners Club" nor "Veterans Administration" has an apostrophe.)

9. *Use Quotation Marks to Enclose the Exact Words of a Source, Titles of Short Works, a Word Used as a Word, and (Sometimes) Words Used in an Odd or Ironic Sense.* Use quotation marks to enclose material taken directly from a book or person.

In 1855, Charles Freeman wrote that the failure of democracy would derive from the "continuing derision of the mob."
Reynolds said, "There is no reason to suspect murder."

But don't use quotation marks for a paraphrased statement.

Reynolds said that there was no reason to suspect murder.

Put quotation marks around titles of shorter works: magazine articles, short stories, poems, artworks, and songs.

"A Rose for Emily"
Frost's "Mending Wall"
Oldenburg's "Toaster"
"Hey Jude"

Titles of longer works are put in italics.

Use quotation marks to indicate that you are using a word as a word rather than as a meaning.

I can never spell "surgeon."
"Cellar door" has a pleasant sound.

The usage here varies. Many writers use italics in such instances.

Finally, use quotation marks to show the odd or ironic use of a word.

The Prime Minister lifted the first volume of the *Encyclopaedia Britannica* from his desk and "clobbered" his secretary.
These "teachers" are a disgrace.

Try not to use quotation marks to indicate such usage. When you can, just write the words.

Where do you put punctuation marks when you are quoting? The rules are uncomplicated. At the end of quoted material, put periods and commas *inside* quotation marks. Put semicolons and colons *outside*. And put question marks and exclamation marks inside if they are part of the quotation; otherwise, put them outside. These examples show the pattern:

"When you come," Nick said, "bring your boat."
Molly had said, "I'll never forget you"; but she forgot me in two weeks.
Becky asked, "How long has this been going on?"
Who wrote "the uncertain glory of an April day"?
All I can say is "Wow!"
I did too say "Monday"!

To show a quotation within a quotation, use single quotes.

Jack complained, "I can never remember who wrote 'to be or not to be.' "

A better suggestion: Reconstruct your sentence so you don't have to put quotes within quotes.

Jack said that he could never remember who wrote "to be or not to be."

10. *Use Italics for Titles of Longer Works, for Foreign Words, and (If You Have to) for Emphasis.* You indicate *italic type* by underlining.

Use italics to mark titles of longer works: books, magazines, newspapers, movies, plays, television shows, operas, and long poems, as well as names of ships and airplanes.

> Walker Percy's *Love in the Ruins*
> *Psychology Today*
> the *Washington Post*
> *King Kong*
> *Barnaby Jones*
> *Carmen*
> *Paradise Lost*
> the *Titanic*

Do not use italics or quotation marks for the Bible—or books of the Bible—or for famous documents like the Declaration of Independence or the Magna Carta.

A useful rule: Whenever you are in doubt whether to use quotation marks or italics to indicate a title, use italics.

Use italics for foreign words. But remember that many foreign words have now become part of the English language and do not need italics.

> He was permitted to graduate *in absentia.*
> Do not use clichés.
> Kathy has a certain *élan,* but she acts like a prima donna.

What should you do about foreign words that have almost become English ("a priori," "coup d'état," "non sequitur")? When in doubt, do not italicize them.

Finally, you can use italics to give a word some special emphasis.

> That's *precisely* the reason I am here.
> Virgilia did not merely act like a princess; she *was* a princess.

It is best not to use italics for emphasis, but there are occasions where you will want to.

11. *Use Capital Letters with the Names of Specific Persons or Things.*
Knowing when to use a capital letter is not always easy, but the main rules are clear enough.

Capitalize the names of *people,* as well as their titles and words derived from their names; *places,* including countries (and national groups), states, counties, cities, and defined areas; *time units* like days of the week, months, and holidays; *religious entities; organizations,* their abbreviations and brand names; *historical* events and documents; *titles* of books, magazines, plays, poems, stories, movies, television programs, musical compositions, and art objects; and *structures* like buildings, monuments, airplanes, and ships. These examples show the common usage.

Woody Allen	General Motors
Captain Kirk	G.M.
Addison's Disease	Ovaltine
Shakespearean sonnet	the Battle of Hastings
Holland	the Gettysburg Address
the Dutch	the Magna Carta
Europeans	*The Heart of the Matter*
the Riviera	Chapter One
Wisconsin	Epilogue
Jackson County	*Newsweek*
Black River Falls	*The Importance of Being Earnest*
Tuesday	"The Killers"
February	"Mending Wall"
Memorial Day	*Kojak*
God	"Hey Jude"
Methodist	Beethoven's Seventh
the Pope	the Empire State Building
the Archbishop of	the Washington Monument
Canterbury	the *Spirit of St. Louis*
Genesis	the *Titanic*

You should have little problem with such examples.

Some words are capitalized in one context and not in another. They are capitalized when they name or relate to a specific entity. These instances show the distinction:

I knew *Major* Jones.	He rose to the rank of *major*.
I saw *Mother* there.	I see my *mother* there.
I support the *Democratic* candidate.	I believe in the *democratic* system.
I attend Spring Hill Baptist *Church*.	We drove by a *church*.
I love the *South*.	We flew *south*.
This is the Sewanee *River*.	We swam in the *river*.
Turn to *Chapter* One.	Read the next *chapter*.

Any word is capitalized, of course, when it begins a sentence or when it begins a line of poetry.

Do not capitalize words like "spring" or "freshman."

Finally there are the words that present problems. With these, the usage of educated writers varies, and you may have to make your own decision. Here are some guidelines:

"A.M." or "a.m." Either form is correct. Just be consistent.

"Coke" or "coke" When a product is vastly popular, its trade name may become the name of the product itself and thus lose its capital letter. This has happened to "ping-pong" and "thermos bottle" and is now happening to "Xerox."

Right now it is probably best to write "Coke" when you specifically mean Coca-Cola, and "coke" when you mean any soft drink.

"The Pill" or "the pill" In general usage, the birth-control pill is distinguished from every other kind of pill. Write "the Pill" or "the pill."

President or president When referring to the President of the United States, capitalize "president" routinely. Write, "Eisenhower served two terms as President"; "There have been four Presidents since Kennedy"; or "Many men have sought the Presidency." Don't capitalize "presidential."

To denote the president of a corporation or a fraternity, capitalize the word only when it appears with a proper name.

"Roman numerals" or "roman numerals" Sometimes a national reference becomes part of a common word and no longer conveys a sense of nationality; it may then lose its capital letter. (You would not capitalize "*french* fries" or "*turkish* towel.")

Some words are still changing. At present, you can write either "Roman numeral" or "roman numeral." But be consistent.

"Psychology" or "psychology" You should always use the capital letter with specific courses ("Psychology 201") and lower case with the area in general ("I used psychology to persuade my mother"). However, capital letters are sometimes used to discuss psychology courses in a general way. You could write, "The University has strong programs in Psychology and Sociology, but it is weak in Languages."

"Black" or "black" This can be a sensitive area, and there is no firm, consistent convention for you to rely on. A decade ago the word was routinely capitalized. Thereafter, most people capitalized it when it referred specifically to race ("the Black heritage") but not when it was merely descriptive ("the black boxer"). Currently, following the usage of noted black leaders, many writers no longer capitalize "black" (or "white").

Judge the likely response of your reader before you decide to capitalize (or not capitalize) "black." No usage is correct if it offends someone you didn't want to offend.

"Truth" or "truth"   From time to time, you will be tempted to capitalize a word to show emphasis ("Tom and Laura used to be Close Friends") or to show irony ("Earl thinks of himself as a Very Important Person"). You may want to praise a poet or philosopher by stressing his "continuing pursuit of Truth." Try to avoid using capital letters in this way.

Despite the complexity of some of these examples, most uses of capital letters follow a simple rule: You capitalize proper names—the names of specific persons, places, things, and events.

EXERCISES

Punctuate these sentences. Add apostrophes, quotation marks, italics, and capital letters where they are needed. Remove them where they are not needed.

1. The lawyer asked if I read Georges mail. I said Never in a million years!
2. My Mother loved to read the *Bible,* especially the story of Moses's flight from Egypt.
3. I told him that my favorite show was all in the family.
4. It became an idée fix: he was sure he could find a word to rhyme with jeffersonian.
5. They worked hard on it, but the boys buick was still a wreck.
6. I prefer Yeats poem which celebrates Ulysses courage.
7. Every president takes an oath to uphold the constitution.
8. His first poem winter dreams was published in the Atlantic Monthly.
9. The Professor asked In what year did Coleridge write Christobel?
10. No wonder he gets straight Cs in mathematics. His 7s all look like 1s
11. The details of the coup d'état were published in last sundays New York Times.

Abbreviations

Since your writing should be an extension of the way you talk, you would do well not to use abbreviations at all. You say words, not abbreviations. Clearly, you would sound unusual talking like this:

> We'll be there the second week in Feb.
> In Madison, Wis., I worked for the Rodgers Express Co.
> This is the St., but I don't know the No.

However, many abbreviations *are* words. You would sound odd saying this:

> I have to hurry to my Reserve Officers Training Corps class.
> At two post meridian, she drove her car into the Young Women's Christian Association parking lot.

The rule is to follow your own voice. Write the word where you say the word and the abbreviation where you say the abbreviation. Thus you can write either "television" or "TV," either "CIA" or "Central Intelligence Agency." Probably you would never write "Blvd.," "MSS.," "e.g.," "anno domine," or "University of California at Los Angeles."

There are a few exceptions to this rule. Standard usage dictates that "Dr.," "Mrs.," "Rev.," and comparable abbreviations can be used before proper names. Similarly, it permits you to write "etc." instead of "et cetera." In general, however, you should not use abbreviations that are not also words. (And use "etc." sparingly.)

You use periods after most abbreviations ("B.C.," "p.m.," "M.D.," etc.). But some abbreviations are so much a part of the language that they become words themselves. You do not need to punctuate these acronyms:

UNESCO	CORE
YMCA	NBC-TV
UCLA	IBM

If you have a doubt in such cases, probably you should not use the periods.

Numbers

The question is whether to write out a number in words ("three hundred and sixty") or to use numerals ("360"). The usage varies here.

A good general rule is to write out numbers when they are small (say, under 100) and when there are only a few of them in your essay.

> There were seventy-two people in the plane, but only two of them were injured.

On every other occasion, use numerals.

You should always use numerals in dates, addresses, percentages, units of measurement, page numbers, and hours followed by "a.m." or "p.m." Use these forms.

December 15, 1976	4.2 minutes
15 December 1976	page 37
639 Azalea Road	8:20 A.M.
16 percent	14,987 students

When writing large numbers remember that numerals look larger than words. If you want to defend America's national debt, say it is sixty billion dollars. If you want to protest it, say it is $60,000,000,000.00. (A neat objective practice is to round off figures and write *$60 billion.*)

If you have more than several numbers to express, use numerals throughout your essay. But don't begin a sentence with a numeral.

Spelling

The one best way to improve your spelling is to read extensively.

The best short-term way is to keep a dictionary at hand and look up words you are in doubt about. You should have doubts when you face plainly difficult words, commonly misspelled words, and words you have had trouble with before.

You should never misspell "rhododendron," "bourgeoise," "alumnae," and "hieroglyphic." You know these are difficult words; you should consult your dictionary and spell them right. (If you don't have a dictionary, consider using a different word.)

You would do well to survey this list of commonly misspelled words. If any of them looks unusual to you, circle it; then try to memorize this correct spelling.

absence	calendar	exaggerate
accept	capital	excellence
accommodate	capitol	existence
achievement	category	fascinate
acquainted	cemetery	February
addressed	changeable	forehead
advice	choose	fourth
advise	colonel	government
affect	committee	grammar
aggravate	comparative	handkerchief
all right	compliment	humorous
allusion	conceive	immediately
a lot	conscience	influence
amateur	contemptible	initiate
analyze	cooperate	intellectual
angle	courteous	irrelevant
apology	deceive	its—it's
apparent	desert	let's
appreciate	dessert	library
Arctic	dictionary	maintenance
athletic	difference	mathematics
attendance	dormitories	misspelled
believe	eighth	occasion
benefited	embarrass	occurrence
Britain	environment	omitted
bureau	especially	pamphlet

parallel	receive	subtle
perform	recommend	syllable
permanence	Renaissance	temperament
personnel	resemblance	tendency
persuade	reservoir	than—then
playwright	restaurant	their—there
politician	rhythm	until
preferred	seize	usually
prejudice	sense	villain
principal—	separate	Wednesday
principle	sophomore	were—where
pronunciation	stationary	whether
psychology	stationery	writing

Finally, make a list. Keep track of words you have misspelled on your papers or on the rough drafts of your papers. Learn these words. There is no excuse for misspelling "separate" twice.

EXERCISES

Correct any errors in abbreviations, numbers, and spelling that you may find in these sentences.

1. Mrs. T. J. Wilkins, representative of the U.S. Chamber of Commerce, will arrive on the ninth of Febuary.
2. The suspect lived at 901 West Blvd. for 6 months. When he was familiar with the area, he burglerized a jewelry store, taking stones valued at ten thousand three hundred and fifty dollars. He was never indited for the crime.
3. Nearly fifteen percent of the students at M.I.T. do not want to work in the U.S. Most want to get their doctor of philosophy degree, emigrate to Canada, and make thirty-five thousand a year working for the aircraft industry.
4. I can't give you any more. Your education already has cost me thirty-six hundred dollars. By the time you get you're M.A. in math, I'll be bankrup.
5. Citizens of Washington, District of Columbia, love Pres. Carter. 10,000 people attended his speech praising the C.I.A.
6. We watched TV from eleven ante meridiem until after midnight. However no more than 10% of the shows were worth watching.

Final Counsel

It's not creative unless it sells.
                              —Al Hampel, Benton & Bowles, Inc.

The eight rules should help to make you an effective writer. You may be
further helped by four areas of general counsel.

CREDIT YOUR SOURCES

In general writing, you do not need formal scholarly documentation. But
commonly, you will want to specify your sources. Don't use footnotes for
this; few people read them. Put information about your sources in your
text. Any of these forms is acceptable.

> According to Genie Hamner (*Bald Windows*, 1975), man had en-
> dured. . . .
> In *Bald Windows* (1975), Genie Hamner argues. . . .
> In her article "Decision Making in Washington Transportation Sys-
> tems" (*Fortune*, June 1977), Kathleen Kelly describes. . . .
> According to *Time* (February 15, 1977), President Carter enjoys. . . .

This kind of informal documentation need not be elaborate. But it is
good to give your reader enough information to be able to refer to the
sources you used.

USE YOUR SPEAKING VOICE

Try to get your speaking voice in your writing. You would never say, "This radio needed repair from the date of purchase"; you would say, "This radio hasn't worked since I bought it." In talking you tend to use short sentences, plain words, active voice, and specific details. You don't worry about beginning a sentence with "and" or "but." You don't use words like "shall" or "secondly" or "apocalyptical." You would never say, "My reasons were the following" or, "Quiet was the night."

Trust your ear. What sounds like good spoken language—at a level suited to your subject and your audience—will be good writing. In this book, you have been advised to keep the same grammatical subject through a paragraph, to tuck words like "however" and "therefore" in the middle of sentences, and to avoid "there is" and "there are" forms. Whenever you think this advice would make your writing sound awkward, don't follow it.

GET HELP FROM FRIENDS

In all likelihood, you will never be asked to write an essay or letter or report that someone else will read and judge immediately. Impromptu themes may be assigned in college classes, but in the outer world you will always have time for reflection and revision. As part of your revision, have a friend or spouse or teacher or secretary or colleague read through your essay for clarity and correctness.

Correctness in matters of punctuation, italics, number, idiom, and spelling is important. A misspelled "their" or "it's" can make a well-informed paper seem illiterate. An omitted comma can make an important sentence almost unreadable. A "not" that is typed "now" can cause big trouble.

Of course you should resort to a dictionary or an English handbook when you have difficulties. But serious errors may exist where you don't recognize a problem. If a particular piece of writing is important to you, invite a knowledgeable friend to look it over.

REMEMBER YOUR AUDIENCE

Keep in mind the kind of audience you are waiting for. It makes a difference.

There is a danger in assuming that your reader knows what you know. This can lead you to commit what Edgar Dale calls the "COIK fallacy" and to write casually about Ken Maynard or Riverside Drive or real time because these terms are clear and meaningful to you. They are *Clear Only If Known.*

Addressing an educated audience, you can use words like "arcane" and "protean." Writing to a specialized audience (scholars or athletes or priests), you can refer to romantic poetry, a trap play, or John 3:16. But do not use such terms with a general audience; they will not understand it. Don't say, "They can look it up"; they won't.

A problem arises when you are forced to use an obscure term. Here, along with the word, you should include an explanation of what it means. But you don't want to sound preachy or condescending. ("I suppose I have to explain to you that a shard is a piece of pottery.") In such instances, you want to give the explanation in an indirect way. See how the necessary clarification is included in these sentences:

> Only a new premier like *Léon Blum* could have handled the situation.
>
> The *trap play* worked perfectly: the linebacker charged through the space we left open and was blocked out of the play.
>
> No one ever understood what motivated Lizzy Borden. She remains an *enigma.*
>
> As spokesmen for the Jewish establishment, the *Scribes and Pharisees* were immediately hostile to the message of Jesus.

Remember that the burden is on you to make your meaning clear to your particular audience.

REMEMBER YOUR PURPOSE

The motto of one New York advertising agency is, "It's not creative unless it sells." There is a good deal of truth in that. Keep in mind the purpose of your writing. (Remember what you're trying to "sell.")

The eight rules just given are based on the assumption that you want to communicate information in a clear and emphatic manner. But this is not always the case.

There are situations where you will want to express yourself indirectly. You might want to spare the sensibilities of your reader ("By the time he was twenty, Earl had demonstrated a range of sexual abnormalities"). You might want to quietly discredit an enemy ("The initial response to his book seems to be favorable") or to veil a threat ("If you pay this bill promptly, your credit rating will remain excellent"). Such situations are not uncommon.

Suppose, for example, you are obliged—in a school or business situation—to write on a subject you know little about. Now your purpose is to conceal your deficiency. You want to fill up a page, to sound fairly learned, and to avoid any specific assertion that could reveal your ignorance. So you reverse many of the rules in this book. You will add "which" clauses and sprinkle modifiers (like "truly," "more or less," and "on the other hand") to insure that no sentence has fewer than twenty-five words. You will write of *quintessential* issues and suggest that *procrustean* tactics are the *ne plus ultra* of folly. (This will obfuscate your message.) You can avoid proper names by using the passive voice ("a decision was made that" or "word was received that"). You will write of vague entities like "business leaders," "the former," and "fair play." These can be described as "adequate" or "unfortunate"; but if you want to avoid even this minimal level of judgment, you can call them "impressive," "notable," "meaningful," or "significant." (These words don't mean good or bad or much of anything.) The resulting paragraphs will be fairly meaningless. But in particular situations—where you can't or don't want to communicate directly—this may be exactly the kind of writing you want.

Most of the time, however, you write to say something specific. You want to show someone you are overworked. You want to persuade your audience that marijuana should be legalized, that gas rationing is essential, or that Sacco and Vanzetti were guilty. You want to describe your new boat. You want someone else to give you a job, to buy mutual funds, or to settle that insurance claim in your favor. In such cases, the eight rules will help you produce effective writing.

Anything that thwarts the purpose of your writing (misspelling, wordiness, errors of fact, or even direct and meaningful statements) should be avoided. And anything that furthers your cause with a particular reader (even such features as expensive paper, threats, folksy language, neat typing, and footnotes) should probably be used.

Good writing may not always win you the final effect you want—that job, that insurance adjustment, that sale. But it will do all that language can do to achieve that end.

Subjects for Argumentative Essays

Abortion
Absurd drama
Alcohol
Amnesty
Astrology
Atlantis
Bible
Biorhythms
Birth control
Black power
Brainwashing
Capital punishment
Censorship
Chiropractors
Cloning
Communism
Cryonics
Cults
Day-care centers
Daylight-savings time
Death
Disarmament
Divorce
Drugs
Ecology
Ecumenicism

Electoral College
Endangered species
Energy crisis
ESP
Evolution
Exorcism
Faith healing
The family
Federal aid to cities
Fluoridation
Football
Foreign aid
Gambling (legalized)
Glossolalia
God
Guaranteed annual wage
Gun control laws
Heredity
Heterosexuality
Homosexuality
Hydrogen bomb
Income taxes
Instinct
IQ tests
Iran
Jesus Christ

Jews
Jogging
Kennedy assassination(s)
Labor unions
Libel Laws
Life in space
Literature classes
Loch Ness monster
Love
Man as animal
Marijuana legalization
Marriage
Medicine
Military-industrial complex
Miracles
Modern art
Modernism in the churches
NATO
Natural law
New morality
Nuclear power
Panama Canal
Patriotism
Patty Hearst
Playboy philosophy
Poetry
Pollution
Population explosion
Pornography
Price controls
Private schools
Prostitution as a crime
Public smoking laws
Pyramid power
Racial superiority
Religion

Rhodesia and South Africa
Rights of the accused
Right-to-work laws
Rock music
Roman Catholicism
The Rosenberg trial
Royal jelly
Sacco-Vanzetti
Schools
Sex education
Shock treatments
Smoking and health
Space program
Standard English
Stonehenge
Student rights
Supreme Court decisions
Talking animals
Tax relief
Television
Third parties
Tranquilizers
UFO's
Unions
University curricula
Viet Nam
Vitamin E
Vivisection
Vote fraud
Watergate
Weapons (development)
Welfare
Wilderness (preservation)
Women's liberation
Yoga

Appendix

The following essay demonstrates the effect of varying kinds of persuasive argument. It is also interesting as a human document.

In many quarters, the Alger Hiss case is still in dispute. Hiss was convicted in 1950 and spent almost four years in jail. Books and articles appeared over the years contesting the issues. And the case returned to prominence in 1976 when John Chabot Smith published *Alger Hiss: The True Story* which argued Hiss's innocence. In 1978, Allen Weinstein produced a large volume *Perjury: The Hiss-Chambers Case,* which declared his guilt. Both books provoked a number of critical articles, some of them quite bitter.

From this essay and the books and articles available in your library, you should be able to write brief themes on a number of specific topics.

A list of possible topics is given at the end of the essay, along with a selected bibliography.

Irving Younger

WAS ALGER HISS GUILTY?

It is time to think again about Alger Hiss. The cold war is over, and its casualties petition for rehabilitation. While committees publish advertisements demanding posthumous justice for the Rosenbergs, Alger Hiss acts for himself. He asks the Supreme Judicial Court of Massachusetts to reinstate him to the Bar of the Commonwealth on the ground that he is presently of good moral character, and in New York he announces to the press that he will soon move to reopen his case and demonstrate his innocence. "In 1948," he says, "a man named Whittaker Chambers swore that he had been a Communist spy, and that I, a State Department official, had given him government papers in 1938. I never gave him secret papers. But largely because a young Congressman named Nixon said he believed Chambers, I was convicted of perjury when I denied the charges and went to jail for 44 months." Nixon ended his career in fraud, Hiss seems to suggest, and he began it with fraud. The prosecution was

Reprinted from *Commentary*, August 1975, pp. 23–37, by permission; copyright © 1975 yet another Nixon connivance, a deception whose purpose was to destroy Hiss and convict an entire generation of American liberals.*

Before making up our minds, we had better find out what happened in the case. There are 3,307 printed pages of testimony, another thousand pages of exhibits, 595 pages of lawyers' briefs and affidavits, and three judicial opinions. Out of this welter of materials, let me try to winnow answers to the two questions which are the subject of this article. What was the evidence? Does the evidence justify the verdict of guilt?

I have relied almost entirely upon the transcripts, the exhibits, and the briefs, telling the story largely in the words of the witnesses and the lawyers. I have no new information to offer and hence no revelations to make. I am personally acquainted with none of the participants except the prosecutor, Thomas F. Murphy, who in 1951 became a federal judge and before whom I tried several criminal cases in the early 1960's, first as an Assistant United States Attorney and then as defense counsel. If I have any special claim to competence in the matter, it is this: I am a trial lawyer, and, so far as I know, no one with the skills and experience of a trial lawyer (apart from those who prosecuted and defended Alger Hiss) has ever publicly examined the evidence.†

On September 3, 1939, two days after the Hitler-Stalin Pact, Whittaker Chambers went to see A. A. Berle, the Assistant Secretary of State. Berle made notes of the conversation, listing the names of various people in government who, according to Chambers, were Communists. Of Alger Hiss, the notes say:

> Ass't. to Sayre—CP—1937
> Member of the Underground Com—Active Baltimore boys—
> Wife—Priscilla Hiss—Socialist—Early days of New Deal.

Nothing happened until March 20, 1945, when Raymond Murphy, a security officer for the State Department, interviewed Chambers. Murphy's memorandum of the interview reads in part:

> It seems that in 1934, with the establishment of the Agricultural Adjustment Administration and the introduction of much reform legislation in Washington, the Communist party decided its influence could be felt more strongly by enlisting the active support of underground workers not openly identified with the party and never previously affiliated with the party, but whose background and training would make them possible prospects as affiliates under the guise of advancing reform legislation. The

* I have adapted the phrase from Alistair Cooke's book about the case, *A Generation on Trial.*
† I do not except Earl Jowitt, a distinguished English lawyer, who says several times in his *The Strange Case of Alger Hiss* that much about the way the case was tried is foreign to him.

Hungarian, party name J. Peters, was selected by the Central Committee to supervise the work from New York. His Washington representative and contact man was the informant [Chambers], and he personally met and discussed many times various problems with the persons listed below except those specifically named as coming under another person's jurisdiction. The persons listed below are said to have disclosed much confidential matter and to have arranged among themselves a program committing this government to a policy in keeping with the desire of the Communist party.

The opportunity presented itself for the formation of an underground group with the appointment to a leading position in the Agricultural Adjustment Administration in 1934 of one Harold Ware. Ware had worked for years in agricultural collectivization projects in Russia. He was a son of Ella Reeves Bloor, veteran American Communist, by one of her numerous marriages. On being assigned to this agency, Ware found a group of very promising, ambitious young men with advanced social and political ideas. Among them were Lee Pressman, Alger Hiss, Henry Collins, and Charles Kramer (Krivitzky). They all joined the Communist party and became leaders of cells. No cell had over ten members. This was the nucleus of the Communist underground organization in Washington. The purpose was for each member to advance as high as possible in the government to shape legislation favorable to the program of the Communist party. The top leaders of the underground were:

1. Harold Ware
2. Lee Pressman
3. Alger Hiss

In the order of their importance.

Murphy spoke with Chambers again on August 28, 1946. His memorandum reads in its entirety as follows:

The Communist underground in Washington is believed to have been set up some time in 1933 after the inauguration of President Roosevelt. My informant [Chambers] does not know how or when it was set up, but he believes that Harold Ware had a prominent part in creating the underground and in enlisting key members. Ware, of course, would have acted pursuant to orders from the Central Commitee of the Communist party of the United States.

My informant entered into the Washington picture in the summer of 1935 and left it and the party at the end of December 1937. The group was already in being and functioning actively. His superior was the Hungarian known as J. Peters, the national head of the Communist underground movement. My informant acted as a courier between Washington and New York. He participated in oral discussions in Washington with the group which Peters himself conducted. They met only the top layer—in other words, leaders of cells of the Communist underground in government circles.

My informant did not know the Coe who taught at McGill University, but he understood that he was a Communist. The other Coe he definitely knew to be a Communist. Harry White was reported to be a member of one of the cells, not a leader, and his brother-in-law, a dentist in New York, is said to be a fanatical Communist. Alger Hiss was never to make converts. His job was to mess up policy. The Post of the State Department was a cell member. He thought he was of Nat Perlow's group. Post was formerly on the WPA, where he measured skulls. He was definitely of minor importance in the movement compared with Hiss.

The heads of the various underground groups in Washington who met with Peters were the Hisses, Kramer (Krivitzky), Henry Collins, who was either secretary or treasurer of the group, John Abt, Lee Pressman, Nat Perlow, and Nat Witt. These men met regularly at special meetings. With the exception of Donald Hiss, who did not have an organization, they headed parallel organizations. But they did not know the personnel of the different organizations.

Hal Ware was the top man of these organizations. Upon his death in 1936 a fight broke out for leadership, but Nat Witt won out. Some time after 1937 Witt is said to have been succeeded by Abt.

(There were other underground Communist groups operating in Washington, but this was the elite policy-making, top-level group.) This group did not exchange secret documents from the government departments, but did give sealed reports on the membership of the groups and on policy. It was not a spy ring, but one far more important and cunning because its members helped to shape policy in their departments. Henry Collins, as secretary or treasurer, delivered most of the sealed reports to my informant. At that time Henry Collins was believed to be working in the Forestry Division of Agriculture.

Peters was in the agricultural department of Hungary under Bela Kun. He was in the Austrian army in World War I. He is a little dark fellow, small feet and wavy black hair.

At the meetings in Washington with this group Peters would give pep talks on Communist theory. He would then talk to each leader separately. Peters often discussed the morale with my informant. He praised the Hiss boys to my informant very highly, but was doubtful of Pressman. He had a high opinion of Witt, a slightly less high opinion of Abt, thought Kramer was a nice boy but shallow, and had very little use for Perlow. He liked Henry Collins.

My informant asked Alger Hiss personally to break with the party in early 1938, but Hiss refused with tears in his eyes and said he would remain loyal to the party.

After his break with the party, Grace Hutchins telephoned the mother of my informant on Long Island one night and said that if he did not return to the party by the following Thursday it was a question of his death.

Who was the man telling this lurid tale?*

---

* What follows is the recitation, moderately edited, of Chambers' life contained in a question asked by Hiss's lawyer of Dr. Binger, a witness at the second trial. For more nuanced pictures of Chambers, see Chambers's autobiography, *Witness*, and Lionel Trilling's recreation of Chambers as Gifford Maxim in *The Middle of the Journey*, written before Trilling had heard anything about the Hiss case.

Whittaker Chambers was born in 1901 in Philadelphia and spent his boyhood years on Long Island. He attended the Rockville Centre High School, where he wrote the class prophecy. The school authorities read it and told him not to deliver it. Chambers wrote a second prophecy, but, at the graduation ceremony read the first. The consequence was that he did not receive his diploma with the rest of his class.

When he was eighteen, Chambers ran away from home. He did day labor on street railways in Washington and in New Orleans under a false name. He returned home and worked for about six months in an advertising agency under another false name. Then he enrolled at Williams College, leaving after two days. A few later, he wrote his former roommate at Williams asking him to pick up a letter at the post office addressed to someone other than Chambers and forward it to Chambers. The roommate picked up the letter, opened it, and recognized it to have been written by Chambers.

In 1920, Chambers enrolled at Columbia College. He edited a student magazine called *Morningside*, which published a play by Chambers entitled, *A Play for Puppets*. The play represents Jesus dressed in a gray kimono with long red hair, obstinate and proud, distrustful of women. This caused trouble at Columbia, and Chambers withdrew from the college in January 1923. He reapplied for admission in September 1924. That month, Chambers wrote to Professor Mark Van Doren that he had "quite simply lied" at his readmission interview by saying that he wanted to return to school in order to teach history, whereas the truth was that he had acquired an "unconventional partner" who wanted him to complete his education. He was readmitted, but left again after one semester.

On February 17, 1925, Chambers joined the Communist party. He was working at the time in the New York Public Library. In April 1927, his employers accused him of theft. They went to his locker and discovered eight library books and some Communist leaflets. Chambers took the officials to his home, where 56 books from the Columbia library were found. He was fired.

Chambers had a brother, Richard, born in 1904 (the year of Hiss's birth). In September 1926, Richard committed suicide by putting his head in an oven. Before this, Richard had asked Whittaker to enter into a suicide pact with him. Richard's death had a paralyzing effect on Whittaker. He remained in bed immobile for two or three months.

Attributing the suicide to Richard's inability to cope with an irrational world, Chambers now became a fanatical Communist. In 1929, because of an intramural dispute, he left the party, but returned in 1932. His job was writing for the *Daily Worker*. Throughout these years, Chambers used false names and gave false information on applications for a passport, government positions, and the like. He broke with the Communist party in 1937 or 1938.

Having professed atheism until then, in 1940 Chambers was baptized an Episcopalian. About a year later, he and his wife and children became Quakers.

In April 1939, Chambers went to work for *Time* magazine as a book reviewer. He wrote foreign news, art, and cinema, finally becoming a senior editor. A physical breakdown required that he rest at home for some eight months, after which he returned to the magazine as a writer of cover stories on such people as Pope Pius XII, Arnold Toynbee, Marian Anderson, Reinhold Niebuhr, and Albert Einstein, earning $30,-000 a year. He resigned on December 10, 1948.

And who was Alger Hiss, the man Chambers said was a member of the Communist underground?*

He was born in 1904. After graduation from Johns Hopkins (and election to Phi Beta Kappa), he went to the Harvard Law School, where he was an editor of the Law Review. His first job, in 1929, was that of law clerk to Justice Holmes. In October 1930, Hiss became associated with the firm of Choate, Hall, and Stewart in Boston, which he left to work for the firm of Cotton, Franklin, Wright, and Gordon in New York. In 1933, he entered government service as assistant general counsel of the Agricultural Adjustment Administration. Two years later, he became legal assistant to the Special Committee of the United States Senate Investigating the Munitions Industry (the Nye Committee). After a year, he entered the Justice Department, where he served as a special attorney in the office of the Solicitor General. In 1936, he transferred to the State Department as assistant to Francis Sayre, the Assistant Secretary of State. When Sayre left to become High Commissioner to the Philippines, Hiss joined the staff of Stanley Hornbeck, Adviser on Political Affairs. From that position, he went to the newly created Office of Special Political Affairs. In 1944, he was secretary to the American delegation to the Dumbarton Oaks Conference. Early in 1945, he was appointed director of the Office of Special Political Affairs and accompanied President Roosevelt to Yalta. He was secretary-general of the San Francisco Conference where the Charter of the United Nations was signed, and it was he who carried the executed copy of the Charter to President Truman in Washington. At the end of 1945, with the title of principal adviser, he accompanied the United States delegation to the first meeting of the United Nations General Assembly in London. In February 1947, Hiss left government service to become president of the Carnegie Endowment for International Peace, of which John Foster Dulles was chairman of the board.

* This is Hiss's *curriculum vitae* as narrated by him from the witness stand.

Given each man's record and asked to choose between the two, I think that any fair-minded person would have taken the word of Alger Hiss. Until August 3, 1948, however, no one needed to make the choice, for Chambers' allegations were unknown to Hiss.* Things soon changed.

On August 3, 1948, J. Parnell Thomas† of New Jersey was chairman of the House Un-American Activities Committee, Richard M. Nixon of California was a member, and Rober E. Stripling was the Committee's chief investigator. In the spring of 1948, Stripling had sent two investigators to New York to speak with Chambers. Chambers said that he had been a Communist, that he had broken with the party, and that he did not want to appear before the Committee. Stripling paid no further attention to him until July (immediately after Elizabeth Bentley named several government employees for whom she had been a Communist courier). A subpoena was served on Chambers, and he appeared in executive session on the morning of August 3. At 11:00, the Committee heard him in public. Chambers testified that he had worked for the Communist underground in Washington, attached to a group which included Alger Hiss.

The next morning, the Committee announced that it had received a telegram from Hiss:

> My attention has been called by representatives of the press to statements made about me before your Commiteee this morning by one Whittaker Chambers. I do not know Mr. Chambers and insofar as I am aware have never laid eyes on him. There is no basis for the statements made about me to your Committee. I would appreciate it if you would make this telegram a part of your Committee's record, and I would further appreciate the opportunity to appear before your committee to make these statements formally and under oath.

Hiss testified in public session the following day. This was his prepared statement:

> I was born in Baltimore, Maryland, on November 11, 1904. I am here at my own request to deny unqualifiedly various statements about me which were made before this Committee by one Whittaker Chambers the day before yesterday. I appreciate the Committee's having promptly granted my request. I welcome the opportunity to answer to the best of my ability any inquiries the members of this Committee may wish to ask me.
>
> I am not and never have been a member of the Communist party. I do not and never have adhered to the tenets of the Communist party. I am not and never have been a member of any Communist-front organization.

* Sometime in 1947, Hiss had been asked by the FBI whether he knew various people, Chambers among them. Hiss said that he did not know Chambers. Perhaps this explains the curious bit of testimony by Donald Hiss, Alger's brother, that in June of 1947, Alger had told him that he (Alger) might need a lawyer.

† Later convicted and sent to jail for padding his Congressional payroll.

I have never followed the Communist party line, directly or indirectly. To the best of my knowledge, none of my friends is a Communist.

As a State Department official, I have had contacts with representatives of foreign governments, some of whom have undoubtedly been members of the Communist party, as, for example, representatives of the Soviet government. My contacts with any foreign representative who could possibly have been a Communist have been strictly official.

To the best of my knowlege, I never heard of Whittaker Chambers until 1947, when two representatives of the Federal Bureau of Investigation asked me if I knew him and various other people, some of whom I knew and some of whom I did not know. I said I did not know Chambers. So far as I know, I have never laid eyes on him, and I should like to have the opportunity to do so. [Here, Hiss says that Collins, Pressman, Witt, Abt., Kramer, and Perlow, all named by Chambers as members of the Communist group, were nothing more than professional acquaintances of Hiss.]

Except as I have indicated, the statements made about me by Mr. Chambers are complete fabrications. I think my record in the government service speaks for itself.

Stripling showed Hiss an Associated Press photograph of Chambers taken three days before. Hiss said that he could not swear he had "ever seen that man. I would like to see him. Then I think I would be better able to tell whether I had ever seen him." After some additonal testimony, Hiss was excused with the Committee's thanks for his cooperation and candor.

On August 7, the Committee examined Chambers in executive session. He confirmed that the Alger Hiss shown in newspaper photographs was the Alger Hiss he had known as a Communist, and went on to describe various personal facts about Hiss and his family. Hiss was interested in ornithology, for example, and had once seen a prothonotary warbler.

On August 16, the Committee examined Hiss in executive session. Shown two different pictures of Chambers taken in the 1930's, Hiss said that he could not "recall any person with distinctness and definiteness whose picture this is, but it is not completely unfamiliar." He wanted to see the man face to face. After being asked several questions about his children and his wife, Hiss complained "that details of my personal life, which I give honestly, can be used to my disadvantage by Chambers if he knows them." After further discussion along these lines, the following occurred:

MR. HISS: May I say something for the record?

MR. NIXON: Certainly.

MR. HISS: I have written a name on this pad in front of me of a person whom I knew in 1933 and 1934, who not only spent some time in my house but sublet my apartment. . . . If I had not seen the morning papers with an account of statements that he knew the inside of my house, I don't think I would even have thought of this name. I want to see Chambers face to face and see if he can be this individual.

I do not want and I don't think I ought to be asked to testify now that man's name. I have written that name on a piece of paper. I gave that name to two friends of mine before they came to this hearing. Perhaps I am being overanxious about the possibility of unauthorized disclosure of this testimony. But I don't think, in my present frame of mind, it is fair that I be asked to put on record personal facts which, if they came to the ears of someone who, for no reason I can understand, had a desire to injure me, would assist him in that endeavor.

MR. NIXON: Is this man who spent the time with you in 1933 and 1934 a man with whom you are still acquainted?

MR. HISS: He is not. He was not named Carl and not Whittaker Chambers. . . . The name of the man I brought in—and he may have no relation to this whole nightmare—is a man named George Crosley. I met him when I was working for the Nye Committee. He was a writer. He hoped to sell articles to magazines about the munitions industry.

There was more testimony about Hiss's personal life, including ornithology and the prothonotary warbler, ending with arrangements for a confrontation between Hiss and Chambers.

The confrontation took place on the afternoon of August 17, in Suite 1400 of the Hotel Commodore in New York City. Chambers was in the bedroom when Hiss arrived. After Hiss read a statement complaining about news leaks of supposedly secret testimony, Chambers entered.

MR. NIXON: Sit over here, Mr. Chambers. Mr. Chambers, will you please stand? And will you please stand, Mr. Hiss? Mr. Hiss, the man standing here is Mr. Whittaker Chambers. I ask you now if you have ever known that man before.

MR. HISS: May I ask him to speak? Will you ask him to say something?

MR. NIXON: Yes. Mr. Chambers, will you tell us your name and your business?

MR. CHAMBERS: My name is Whittaker Chambers.

MR. HISS: Would you mind opening your mouth wider?

MR. CHAMBERS: My name is Whittaker Chambers.

MR. HISS: I said, would you open your mouth? You know what I am referring to, Mr. Nixon. Will you go on talking?

MR. CHAMBERS: I am senior editor of *Time* magazine.

MR. HISS: May I ask whether his voice, when he testified before, was comparable to this?

MR. NIXON: His voice?

MR. HISS: Or did he talk a little more in a lower key?

MR. MCDOWELL: I would say it is about the same now as we have heard.

MR. HISS: Would you ask him to talk a little more?

MR. NIXON: Read something, Mr. Chambers. I will let you read from—

MR. HISS: I think he is George Crosley, but I would like to hear him talk a little longer.

MR. MCDOWELL: Mr. Chambers, if you would be more comfortable, you may sit down.

MR. HISS: Are you George Crosley?

MR. CHAMBERS: Not to my knowledge. You are Alger Hiss, I believe.

MR. HISS: I certainly am.

MR. CHAMBERS: That was my recollection. (*Reading*): "Since June"—

MR. NIXON (interposing): Just one moment. Since some repartee goes on between these two people, I think Mr. Chambers should be sworn.

MR. HISS: That is a good idea.

MR. MCDOWELL: You do solemnly swear, sir, that the testimony you shall give this Committee will be the truth, the whole truth, and nothing but the truth, so help you God?

MR. CHAMBERS: I do.

MR. NIXON: Mr. Hiss, may I say something? I suggested that he be sworn, and when I say something like that I want no interruptions from you.

MR. HISS: Mr. Nixon, in view of what happened yesterday, I think there is no occasion for you to use that tone of voice in speaking to me, and I hope the record will show what I have just said.

MR. NIXON: The record shows everything that is being said here today.

MR. STRIPLING: You were going to read.

MR. CHAMBERS (reading from *Newsweek* magazine): "Tobin for Labor. Since June, Harry S. Truman had been peddling the labor secretary-ship left vacant by Lewis B. Schwellenbach's death in hope of gaining the maximum political advantage from the appointment."

MR. HISS: May I interrupt?

MR. MCDOWELL: Yes.

MR. HISS: The voice sounds a little less resonant than the voice that I recall of the man I knew as George Crosley. The teeth look to me as though either they have been improved upon or that there has been considerable dental work done since I knew George Crosley, which was some years ago. I believe I am not prepared without further checking to take an absolute oath that he must be George Crosley.

MR. NIXON: May I ask a question of Mr. Chambers?

MR. HISS: I would like to ask Mr. Chambers, if I may.

MR. NIXON: I will ask the questions at this time. Mr. Chambers, have you had any dental work since 1934 of a substantial nature?

MR. CHAMBERS: Yes; I have.

MR. NIXON: What type of dental work?

MR. CHAMBERS: I have had some extractions and a plate.

MR. NIXON: Have you had any dental work in the front of your mouth?

MR. CHAMBERS: Yes.

MR. NIXON: What is the nature of that work?

MR. CHAMBERS: That is a plate in place of some of the upper dentures.

MR. NIXON: I see.

MR. HISS: Could you ask him the name of the dentist that performed these things? Is that appropriate?

MR. NIXON: Yes. What is the name?

MR. CHAMBERS: Dr. Hitchcock, Westminster, Maryland.

MR. HISS: That testimony of Mr. Chambers, if it can be believed, would tend to substantiate my feeling that he represented himself to me in 1934 or 1935 or thereabout as George Crosley, a free-lance writer of articles for magazines. I would like to find out from Dr. Hitchcock if what he has just said is true, because I am relying partly, one of my main recollections of Crosley, was the poor condition of his teeth.

MR. NIXON: Can you describe the condition of your teeth in 1934?

MR. CHAMBERS: Yes. They were in very bad shape.

MR. NIXON: The front teeth were?

MR. CHAMBERS: Yes; I think so.

MR. HISS: Mr. Chairman.

MR. NIXON: Excuse me. Before we leave the teeth. Mr. Hiss, do you feel that you would have to have the dentist tell you what he did to the teeth before you could tell anything about this man?

MR. HISS: I would like a few more questions asked. I didn't intend to say anything about this, because I feel very strongly that he is Crosley, but he looks very different in girth and in other appearances—hair, forehead, and so on, particularly the jowls.

MR. HISS: Did you ever go under the name of George Crosley?

MR. CHAMBERS: Not to my knowledge.

MR. HISS: Did you ever sublet an apartment on Twenty-ninth Street [he meant Twenty-eighth Street] from me?

MR. CHAMBERS: No; I did not.

MR. HISS: You did not?

MR. CHAMBERS: No.

MR. HISS: Did you ever spend any time with your wife and child in an apartment on Twnety-ninth Street in Washington when I was not there because I and my family were living on P Street?

MR. CHAMBERS: I most certainly did.

MR. HISS: You did or did not?

MR. CHAMBERS: I did.

MR. HISS: Would you tell me how you reconcile your negative answers with this affirmative answer?

MR. CHAMBERS: Very easily, Alger. I was a Communist and you were a Communist.

MR. HISS: Would you be responsive and continue with your answer?

MR. CHAMBERS: I do not think it is needed.

MR. HISS: That is the answer.

MR. NIXON: I will help you with the answer, Mr. Hiss. The question, Mr. Chambers, is, as I understand it, that Mr. Hiss cannot understand how you would deny that you were George Crosley and yet admit that you spent time in his apartment. Now would you explain the circumstances? I don't want to put that until Mr. Hiss agrees that is one of his questions.

MR. HISS: You have the privilege of asking any questions you want. I think that is an accurate phrasing.

MR. NIXON: Go ahead.

MR. CHAMBERS: As I have testified before, I came to Washington as a Communist functionary, a functionary of the American Communist Party. I was connected with the underground group of which Mr. Hiss was a member. Mr. Hiss and I became friends. To the best of my knowledge, Mr. Hiss himself suggested that I go there, and I accepted gratefully.

MR. HISS: Mr. Chairman.

MR. NIXON: Just a moment. How long did you stay there?

MR. CHAMBERS: My recollection was about 3 weeks. It may have been longer. I brought no furniture, I might add.

MR. HISS: Mr. Chairman, I don't need to ask Mr. Whittaker Chambers any more questions. I am now perfectly prepared to identify this man as George Crosley.

MR. NIXON: Would you spell that name.

MR. HISS: C-r-o-s-l-e-y.

MR. NIXON: You are sure of one "s"?

MR. HISS: That is my recollection. I have a rather good visual memory, and my recollection of his spelling of his name is C-r-o-s-l-e-y. I don't think that would change as much as his appearance.

MR. STRIPLING: You will identify him positively now?

MR. HISS: I will on the basis of what he has just said positively identify him without further questioning as George Crosley.

On August 25, Hiss and Chambers testified in public. Hiss identified Chambers as George Crosley, the writer he had met in 1933 or 1934. Chambers identified Hiss as a member of the Communist underground in Washington. And that would have been that—one of the two obviously a liar, no corroboration of either, and thus no possible conviction for perjury*—when, on August 27, Chambers appeared on a radio program, *Meet the Press*. The first question was, "Are you willing to say now [when

---

* A perjury conviction may not be obtained in a case of one man's testimony against another's. Corroborating evidence is required.

your statements are not privileged] that Alger Hiss is or ever was a Communist?" Chambers replied, "Alger Hiss was a Communist and may be now." One month later, Hiss sued Chambers for libel.

As is customary in civil actions, Hiss's attorney in the libel suit took Chambers' deposition. He asked Chambers, at a session on November 5, 1948, whether Chambers had ever obtained documents from Hiss for transmittal to the Communist party.* Chambers had not. The examination was then adjourned to November 16. On that day, Chambers' attorney told Hiss's attorney that Chambers was unavailable, and Mrs. Chambers was questioned in his place. On the afternoon of November 17, Chambers appeared. At the trial, Chambers described his activities over the preceding three days as follows:

> I went to New York—or I went to Brooklyn to see Nathan Levine, my wife's nephew, to get an envelope in which, as I recalled it, were some handwritten specimens from Mr. Hiss. I remembered giving [Nathan Levine] the envelope; I remembered that there were some typewritten notes. I believe it was in May or June of 1938. I went first [on November 14, 1948] to Mr. Levine's apartment, which is on Sterling Place, and then walked over to his mother's house—no, I am mistaken about that—we drove over to his mother's house. That is the house at 260 Rochester Avenue. We went upstairs, and Mr. Levine stood on the bathtub and reached into an old dumbwaiter shaft, and brought out an envelope which was very dusty, and handed it to me. I took the envelope into the kitchen which was at the end of the little hall from which the bathroom was, and opened it. Mr. Levine came into the kitchen for a moment to get a broom and a dustpan, or something, to clean up the mess he had made in the bathroom. He came back into the kitchen . . . in five or more minutes, I am not quite sure. In the envelope I found . . . three or four handwritten notes, in Mr. Hiss's handwriting, and some 45 pages of typed documents which Mrs. Hiss typed . . . and three cans of film, I believe, and a small cylinder of strip, developed film, two short strips of developed film. I did not appear the following day to continue my deposition. I told Mr. Cleveland, my lawyer, that I would like a day to consider the question of introducing these documents into the pre-trial examination. Mr. Cleveland

---

* One might speculate why Hiss had the temerity to sue and to allow his lawyer to ask this question, if he really had given papers to Chambers. As to the suit, Hiss's need to save his reputation, the likelihood that any judge or jury would prefer him to Chambers, and the failure of Chambers to produce any corroborating evidence at the HUAC hearings, would have led Hiss, I think, to risk everything on the outcome of a libel action. Oscar Wilde had done the same. As to the question, one of the purposes of a deposition is to "pin the witness down." The lawyer asking the question already knows what the answer will be; he asks it to insure that the witness will not later testify to something else. Since HUAC had asked nothing about espionage, Hiss could be confident that Chambers had made no such accusation. That being so, it was good practice to pin Chambers down to a denial that Hiss had ever given him documents.

therefore arranged with Mr. Marbury [Hiss's lawyer] for my wife to de-
pose on the day when I would otherwise have deposed. On November 17,
I continued my deposition and gave my lawyer [the notes in Hiss's handwriting and the documents typed by Mrs. Hiss].

These papers were produced at the deposition on the 17th. They
were copies or summaries of State Department documents dated in the
early months of 1938. Chambers stated that he had received them from
Hiss for transmittal to Colonel Bykov, a Soviet agent in the United
States.

Chambers' testimony at the trial continued as follows:

The film [photographs of State Department documents] I kept in my
house for a few days. I was called to Washington to testify before a loyalty
Board in the State Department, and that morning, as I was about to leave
the house—I already had my overcoat on—the telephone rang, and Mr.
Stripling of the House Un-American Activities Committee asked me to
meet him in Washington that day. When I stepped into Mr. Stripling's
office, about two o'clock in the afternoon, he served me with a subpoena
duces tecum to bring with me or turn over to the Committee all materials
in my possession relative to a list of people who were specified in the subpoena. When I finished in the State Department, I was accompanied
home by Mr. Wheeler and Mr. Appell, two investigaors of the Committee. At the farm [Chambers' home in Westminster, Maryland] I took them
into the kitchen and went out into the yard to get the documents, and get
the film. Before I went to Washington that day, I had put the film inside a
pumpkin. The investigators for Mr. Hiss had been in and out of my farm
and the neighborhood for some time . . . and so I put these documents in a
hollow pumpkin. I took these men from the Committee out into the yard.
I picked up the pumpkin and took out the documents and handed them
over to them. This pumpkin which contained the documents grew naturally at the edge, the far edge of this little patch, and I was able to find it
by its position on the edge but by no Euclidean direction. I handed the
documents over to the investigators and they left directly thereafter.

When I handed the handwritten and typewritten documents to Mr.
Marbury at the deposition, I told him that I had had a twofold purpose in
testifying up until that time: one part of the purpose was to destroy or
paralyze the Communist conspiracy within the country and the government; the other part of my purpose was to do as little injury as possible to
the human beings involved in that conspiracy.

I pointed out that in my own case a kind of grace had been given me to
find the strength to break and time had been given me in which to work
out a new life.

I pointed out that in breaking with the Communist party that time is a
most essential factor. Therefore I had wanted to give these people some of
the same opportunity which had been given me. But I had now been
forced into a position where I had no choice but to introduce those docu-

ments into evidence. I had previously testified both in the House Committee and the grand jury that I had no evidence of espionage, and what I have just said is the reason why I so testified. After the introduction of the documents [at Baltimore on November 17], I went before the grand jury and told about these espionage activities. I added in the grand jury that in disclosing the conspiracy, some damage was inevitably done to the people involved, people mentioned by me, but that there was a distinction, at least in my mind, between disclosing the ultimate perfidy, by which I mean espionage, and merely disclosing the fact that these people were Communists.

I further said to the grand jury that, I think in general, there are two kinds of men; the one kind that believes God is a God of justice and the other kind believes that God is a God of mercy, and I am so constituted that I will always range myself on the side of mercy.

Hiss's response to Chambers' assertions is contained in a statement he gave to the FBI on December 4, 1948. It reads in part as follows:

On the afternoon of November 17, 1948, in the course of the pre-trial examination, Mr. Chambers introduced 56 letter-sized pages of typewritten material and four small sheets of paper bearing handwritten material. For simplification, hereafter in this statement the 65 pages will be referred to as the large documents and the four smaller pages as the small documents.

With reference to the large documents, I would say from a cursory examination of them that they appear to be authentic copies of United States State Department documents or summaries of such documents. From the date standpoint, these documents appear to be restricted to a period extending from about January to March 1938. At that time I was assistant to the Assistant Secretary of State, the Honorable Francis B. Sayre. Documents similar to these normally passed over my desk for perusal prior to being referred to Mr. Sayre. I do not have any independent recollection of having seen any of these documents or the documents summarized while I was in the employ of the State Department. By and large, these do not appear to be documents of a very highly confidential nature, and would not have been treated in the State Department with any special precautions at that time, according to security regulations in effect then.

With reference to the smaller documents, three of the four pages appear to be in my handwriting. The fourth page, consisting of five handwritten lines, may or may not be in my handwriting, but it does not look to me as if it were.

I have learned from talking with Mr. Marbury and from reading the above-mentioned deposition that Mr. Chambers claimed these documents and others like them were obtained by me from the State Department, and that I took them to my home, where typewritten copies of the larger documents were made on a typewriter in my home by either my wife or me. Chambers claimed that I then returned the documents to the State Department files. The agents have told me that Mr. Chambers claims that on some occasions I turned over the actual State Department documents to him, upon which he would have photographic copies made in a manner unknown to me, and then would return the original documents to me for replacement in the files of the State Department.

I deny that any of the above claims of Mr. Chambers is true. I also deny that I ever gave the originals of the small documents to Mr. Chambers at any time for any purpose whatsoever.

From Mr. Marbury and the deposition, I have also learned that Chambers claims he introduced me to a Russian named Peter, who he claims later to have discovered was Colonel Bykov. Chambers claims that this meeting took place on the mezzanine floor of a movie theater in Brooklyn, New York. Chambers claims that after the meeting, the three of us took a long walk and that during the conversation while walking, Colonel Bykov asked me if I could obtain documents for him from the files of the State Department. Chambers claims that I agreed to cooperate in this regard with this Colonel Bykov and that as a result of this oral agreement I later produced the documents mentioned above. I deny that any of these claims of Chambers is true. I have never met and had never heard of any Russian named Peter or Colonel Bykov until I was told of the testimony given by Mr. Chambers.

On December 15, 1948, Hiss was called before a grand jury sitting in the United States Court House, Foley Square, Manhattan. Asked whether he had ever given government documents to Chambers, he said no. Asked whether he had ever seen Chambers after the winter of 1936, he said no. That afternoon, the grand jury handed up an indictment charging Hiss with two counts of perjury.* Each of his denials, the grand jury alleged, was false.

The case of Alger Hiss went to trial on May 31, 1949, in the United States District Court for the Southern District of New York before Judge Samuel H. Kaufman and a jury. Thomas F. Murphy represented the government, Lloyd Paul Stryker† the defendant. The trial lasted until July 8, 1949, when the jury reported itself deadlocked and was discharged. The final vote had been eight to four in favor of conviction.

The retrial began on November 17, 1949, before Judge Henry W. Goddard and a jury. Murphy again represented the government; Claude Cross of Boston now represented Hiss. Because both sides wanted to appear to the jury to be holding nothing back, to present every person they could find whose life had touched Chambers' or Hiss's, no matter how tangentially, the witnesses numbered one hundred and twelve.

---

* The statute of limitations had run out on espionage.

† Stryker was one of the celebrated courtroom performers of his generation. It is rumored among lawyers that, before the trial began, Judge Jerome Frank of the Court of Appeals (who had been the general counsel of the AAA for which Hiss worked when he first went to Washington) urged Stryker to waive a jury and let Judge Kaufman decide the case. "I can't," Stryker replied. "It would be like a ball player going to bat with one hand tied behind his back."

The case may well have been overtried. The story was essentially simple, be it the government's or the defendant's, and the verdict turned on only one thing—the jury's assessment of the credibility of the two protagonists, Chambers and Hiss. As we shall see, most of the "corroborating" witnesses on both sides in fact corroborated nothing. The documentation, however, was a different matter entirely.

This was the substance of Chambers' testimony:

In 1934, while in Washington as a member of the Communist underground, Chambers was introduced to Alger Hiss at a downtown restaurant by Harold Ware (organizer of a Communist apparatus in Washington) and J. Peters ("head of the whole underground of the American Communist party"). Peters stated that Hiss "was to be disconnected from [Ware's] apparatus" and "was to become a member of a parallel organization" under Chambers.

At the time, Hiss was counsel to the Nye Committee, and his first assignment in the new organization was to obtain official documents dealing with the munitions traffic. He did so.

In 1936, Hiss entered the State Department. In January 1937, Chambers arranged a clandestine meeting among himself, Hiss, and Colonel Bykov, Chambers' superior in the underground. At this meeting, Bykov stated that Russia was endangered by the Fascist powers and that Hiss "could greatly help if he would procure documents from the State Department." Hiss said that he would. He began to bring documents home every week or ten days. Chambers would pick them up, take them to Baltimore for photographing, and return the originals the same night. This proved unsatisfactory, in that "just the documents of a single day" were obtained. In the middle of 1937, Chambers instructed Hiss to change the practice—"to have the papers brought out every night, or approximately every night and some of them typed as nearly verbatim as possible and some of them paraphrased." This was done. The typist was Mrs. Hiss.

In addition to the typed copies, Hiss would turn over to Chambers the originals of those documents which came to hand on the day of a visit from Chambers, as well as handwritten notes "about documents which had passed under his eyes quickly and which, for some reason, he was unable to bring out." Everything was photographed. Chambers then returned the original documents to Hiss, burned the typed copies and handwritten notes, and delivered the photographs to Bykov.

On April 15, 1938, Chambers broke with the Communist party and ceased his espionage activities. He retained some of the papers and exposed film which Hiss had given him earlier in the year. Sealed in an envelope, he delivered them to Nathan Levine for safekeeping.

Apart from the covert relationship between them, Chambers and

Hiss and their families saw each other frequently and intimately. They stayed in each other's homes and took out-of-town trips together.

This was the substance of Hiss's testimony:

In December 1934, or January 1935, Hiss was counsel to the Nye Committee. Chambers came to see him, introducing himself as George Crosley, a free-lance writer of articles on the munitions investigation. At one of several subsequent luncheon meetings, Chambers (as Crosley) told Hiss that he was planning to come to Washington for a few months to complete his articles, and was looking for a place to live with his wife and child. The Hisses had recently moved from an apartment at 2831 28th Street, Washington, to a house at 2905 P Street, and Hiss had the balance of the apartment lease at his disposal. Accordingly, he sublet the apartment to Chambers.

When the time came for him to move in, Chambers said that the furniture van had been delayed. Hiss thereupon allowed the Chamberses to live for a few days with the Hisses in the P Street house. Chambers later moved into the apartment. He never paid the rent, however, and he and Hiss met only a few more times. The last meeting was in the spring of 1936, when Hiss refused Chambers' request for the latest in a series of small loans.

The Hisses never visited the Chamberses. The Chamberses never visited the Hisses except for the brief time the two families spent together in the P Street house. There were no trips together except for one occasion when Hiss gave Chambers a ride from Washington to New York City.

Hiss had never been a Communist. He had never given State Department documents to Chambers. His loyalty and devotion to the interests of the United States were known to a large number of persons of unquestionable integrity.

In studying the evidence at the second trial, it has struck me that a reasonable juror trying to determine where the truth lay would consider ten points.

First, Chambers' familiarity with Hiss's personal life. This has figured large in later writing about the case. How could Chambers know that Hiss once saw a prothonotary warbler, for instance, unless his story were true? The answer, I think, is that Chambers' knowledge of Hiss's personal life is irrelevant. Chambers' ability to recount the homely details of daily existence in the Hiss household does nothing to prove the grand jury's charge, which, one must keep in mind, was perjury: that Hiss had lied about delivering official documents to Chambers. Since by Hiss's own testimony he and Chambers had been acquainted, with the Chambers family once spending a few days as house guests of the Hisses, Chambers' knowledge of personal details was understandable and perfectly consistent with Hiss's innocence.

Second, the testimony of the "corroborating" witnesses. As stated earlier, both sides seem to have called every possible witness who might have buttressed or contradicted one story or the other. This evidence amounts to very little. Three examples:

Chambers said that, in 1934 or 1935, while lunching with Hiss at a Georgetown restaurant, Hiss had introduced him to a woman named Plum Fountain. Hiss said that it never happened. Mrs. Olivia Fountain Tesone testified that her nickname was "Plum" and that she knew Hiss but had no recollection of ever meeting or seeing Chambers. So what? If Chambers were telling the truth, it is hardly remarkable that Mrs. Tesone would fail to remember a passing introduction some fourteen years after it occurred. And if Chambers were lying, he might have heard Hiss once mention his friend, Plum Fountain, and simply retained the name for future use.

Chambers said that, on August 10, 1937, he and the Hisses took an automobile trip to Peterboro, New Hampshire, where they saw a production of *She Stoops to Conquer* and stayed overnight at an inn called Bleak House. The Hisses denied it all. The prosecution proved that *She Stoops to Conquer* was performed by a local company in Peterboro on August 10 and that Hiss's employment records showed him on annual leave from August 2 to August 14. The defense proved that the Bleak House guest book contained no registration for Chambers or the Hisses under their own or any other name. The evidence is equal, then. It corroborates each man in part and positively proves the truthfulness of neither.

Hiss said that the Hisses never visited the Chamberses. In 1936, the Chamberses were living in an apartment on Eutaw Place, Baltimore, under the name "Cantwell." Mrs. Edith Murray was their maid. She was called as a government witness and testified on direct examinatiin that Mrs. Hiss was a frequent visitor to the Cantwell home, on one occasion accompanied by Mr. Hiss. On another occasion, Mrs. Hiss stayed the night to care for the Chamberses' child while Mrs. Chambers went to New York for a doctor's appointment. This seems powerful, especially since the Hisses denied any such events. But on cross-examination, Mrs. Murray testified that, before coming to the courthouse and identifying Mr. and Mrs. Hiss, she had been shown photographs of them by the FBI. To Mrs. Hiss's picture, her first response was, "It looked like—I thought maybe it was an actress or something . . . I said to myself maybe it was in the movies." To Alger Hiss's picture, Mrs. Murray's first response was, "It looked like I had seen him, but I told [the FBI] I wasn't sure . . . I told [the FBI] I did not know." Further, it developed that Mrs. Murray had suffered a nervous breakdown in 1942 and that, before testifying, the FBI had taken her to Chambers' farm for a three-hour conversation with

him. I do not know where Mrs Murray's testimony was false*: I doubt
that any juror would be persuaded by it.

Third, Chambers' testimony about other persons. Chambers names
several persons other than Hiss as part of the Communist underground in
Washington—Julian Waleigh, Donald Hiss, Lee Pressman, Nathan Witt,
John Abt, etc. One, Wadleigh, admitted it. He testified at the trial that
he had given government documents to Chambers but knew nothing
about Hiss's activities. Another, Donald Hiss, denied it. The others
wouldn't say. They were called before HUAC in 1948 and declined to
testify on the ground of self-incrimination. In 1950, after the trial, Pressman told a HUAC hearing that he had been a member of Harold Ware's
Communist group in Washington and that Hiss was not a member. The
jury as the second trial had only Wadleigh's admission and Donald Hiss's
denial. They cancel each other, and since in any event neither of them
was able to shed any light on the relations between Chambers and Alger
Hiss, I think the entire matter of little relevance. The question, really, is
not whether Chambers told the truth about Wadleigh, *et al.* It is whether
he told the truth about Hiss.

Fourth, Hiss's character. Nineteen persons of great eminence testified to Hiss's reputation for loyalty, honesty, and veracity. In his summation, Cross urged:

> Mr. Hiss had been in government service; he has been with the Carnegie
> Foundation; and everyone who has taken that stand as a character witness
> has told you of the high respect in which he is held. . . . Something may be
> said by Mr. Murphy about character witnesses, that anyone can get char-
> acter witnesses. Maybe they could before the facts are out, but after all
> the newspaper publicity since August of 1948, since the first trial, you can
> rely upon the fact that every witness in that chair who testified to the
> character of Alger Hiss believed in his innocence or he would not have
> been in that chair.

Mr. Murphy in summation did say something about character witnesses:

> What else is extraordinary? The defendant has called nineteen character
> witnesses, more than one-third the number of his total witnesses, and they
> have testified to his reputation for integrity, loyalty and honesty, veracity.
> They have told you what the gossip is that they have heard, the accumu-
> lation of gossip over the years that they have known him and what that is.
> Most of them said his reputation was good. . . .
> I ask you ladies and gentlemen what kind of a reputation did a good spy
> have? Of course it must be good. The fox barks not when he goes to steal
> the lamb. It has to be good. But we are here on a search for truth. We are
> not concerned with reputations. Poppycock.

* In his 1952 motion for a new trial, Hiss presented the affidavit of a man who attested
that the Cantwells (Chamberses) employed no maid at Eutaw Place.

Just think how many people could call good reputation witnesses. Just think. Benedict Arnold, a major general in our army—a major general—and he sold out West Point to the enemy. Before they caught Major André right up here in Tarrytown don't you believe that Major General Benedict Arnold could call George Washington? Couldn't he call all of the members of the General Staff, one of their men?

And Brutus: before he stabbed Caesar don't you think he could have stood in front of the Roman Senate and called upon the great Augustus and said, "Tell him what a man I am."

And Judge Manton, he had character witnesses. You might recall one of the character witnesses who testified in this trial was one of his.

And lastly the devil himself. You remember that story that Mr. Chambers wrote. The devil was a fallen angel and before he was thrown out of Heaven he was in the sight of God. He could have called upon the Almighty himself for his reputation.

Ladies and gentlemen, character witnesses belong to another era. This is the age of reason. This is the age of common people. And what we want are facts. We are here, you are here, Judge Goddard is here to ascertain the facts. We don't want gossip.

There is no answer to this. The evidence of Hiss's reputation comes to nothing one way or the other.*

Fifth, Chambers' mental state. The defense proposed to call a psychiatrist to give his professional opinion of Chambers' mental state. Murphy objects:

This is the first time in the history of Anglo-Saxon jurisprudence that the testimony of a psychiatrist is being admitted to impeach the credibility of a mere witness, when there has not been one scintilla of proof indicating that the witness, Mr. Whittaker Chambers, has had any institutional confinement or treatment by a doctor other than for his teeth and heart. . . .

Cross argued that the outcome of the trial depended upon the jury's determination of Chambers' credibility and that the psychiatrist's opinion might well help the jury come to a conclusion on the matter. Judge Goddard agreed: he would allow the testimony.†

Dr. Carl Binger took the stand. An alumnus of Harvard College and of the Harvard Medical School, he had studied psychiatry at Heidelberg and Zurich and presently was associate professor of clinical psychiatry at the Cornell Medical School. He had never met Chambers, but he had observed his testimony, he had read many of his writings, and he had been told the facts of Chambers' life, upon the basis of all of which he had "an opinion within the bounds of reasonable certainty as to the mental condition of Whittaker Chambers."

* In his charge, Judge Goddard told the jury that "evidence of good character may, in itself, create a reasonable doubt where, without such evidence, no reasonable doubt would exist."

† In the first trial, Judge Kaufman had excluded it.

What was it? "I think Mr. Chambers is suffering from a condition know as psychopathic personality, which is a disorder of character, of which the outstanding features are behavior of what we call an amoral or an asocial and delinquent nature." Among the symptoms of the condition are "chronic, persistent, and repetitive lying . . . . and a tendency to make false accusations."

Murphy's cross-examination of Dr. Binger is famous among trial lawyers. It runs some 190 pages, of which this is one:

Q. Doctor, when you testified the other day on direct examination you made these statements—I am reading from page 3686—the question was in relation to what you had observed at the last trial of Mr. Chambers as a witness when you were here those five or six days, and the question was:
> Q. What did you observe about Mr. Chambers when you saw him in court at the first trial and here?
> A. May I say that I would not attempt to make a diagnosis of psychopathic personality purely on the observation of a person. . . . [But] there are certain confirmatory things that I did see.
> Q. Will you tell us what they were?
> A. Well, he sat in this chair or in a similar one, and he apparently had very little relationship with the inquirer. He frequently looked up at the ceiling as if trying to recall something that he had previously said.
Now, Doctor, we made a count this morning of the number of times that you looked at the ceiling, and during the first ten minutes you looked at the ceiling 19 times; the next 15 minutes 20 times; and the next 15 minutes 10 times; and the following 10 minutes 10 times, making a total in 50 minutes of 59 times, and I was wondering, Doctor, whether that had any symptoms of a psychopathic personality?
A. Not alone.
Q. Not alone?
A. No.

It was good sport, and when the jury retired to deliberate, I doubt that Dr. Binger's testimony played any part at all.

Sixth, the time of Chambers' break with the Communist party. In his conversation with Raymond Murphy of the State Department on August 28, 1946, and again in his testimony before HUAC, Chambers fixed the time of his break as the end of 1937. At the trial, he said it was April 15, 1938. The difference is crucial. Most of the government documents which Chambers produced at the Baltimore deposition or turned over to HUAC are dated in 1938 (none later than April 1). If Chambers had left the party in 1937, he could not have obtained the documents from Hiss in the manner he described. If he had left the party on April 15, 1938, he could have.

The only explanation offered by Chambers was that his earlier statements had been mistaken and that, when he came to testify at the trial, his memory was more accurate. Considering that his break with Communism was perhaps the most important event of his life, I find Chambers' fuzziness of recollection somewhat difficult to accept (and so, I think, might the jury). Were there nothing else to support his testimony, the verdict would have to be for Hiss. The government must prove the charge, remember, beyond a reasonable doubt. But there is a great deal else to support Chambers' testimony.

Seventh, the rug. Chambers testified that, a short time before the clandestine meeting among himself, Hiss, and Bykov, he had been given money by Bykov for the purchase of four Oriental rugs, one of which was to be presented to Hiss as "a gift from the Soviet people in recognition of the work of the American Communists." Chambers sent the money to a friend from his days at Columbia, Professor Meyer Schapiro, asking Schapiro to buy the rugs and send them to a George Silverman in Washington. In January 1937, behind a restaurant on the Washington-Baltimore road, Chambers carried one of the rugs from Silverman's car to Hiss's, and Hiss drove away with it.

Hiss, on the other hand, testified that, in the winter or spring of 1936, Chambers came to Hiss with a rug which he said a wealthy patron had given him. Hiss took the rug as part-payment of Chambers' rent on the 38th Street apartment.

Professor Schapiro testified that, on December 23, 1936, with money given him by Chambers and at Chambers' request, he bought four Oriental rugs from the Massachusetts Importing Company for $876.71. The government put into evidence a Massachusetts Importing Company shipping order. It shows that the company delivered the rugs to Schapiro's home on December 29, 1936. A few days later, Schapiro testified, he sent the rugs to a man named Silverman in Washington. Cross had no cross-examination.

Chambers' account of how he acquired the rugs is patently true. Professor Schapiro's word was not questioned; and where would Chambers have obtained $876.71 in 1936 if not from Bykov? Equally clear is Hiss's receipt of a rug from Chambers. They disagree only on circumstances. I think it would take a very gullible jury to accept Hiss's version.

Eighth, Chambers' purchase of a car. On November 23, 1937, Chambers bought a Ford four door sedan from the Schmidt Motor Company in Randallstown, Maryland, trading in his old car, a 1934 Ford sedan, and paying $486.75. How did Chambers get the cash? According to Chambers, he talked with the Hisses:

> I said that I wished to buy a car; that Colonel Bykov was opposed to my using a car, but that a car was very necessary in the work I was doing; and either Mr. Hiss or Mrs. Hiss then offered me [$400].

If this is true, if Hiss did give Chambers $400 in November 1937, then Hiss's assertion that he last saw Chambers in the spring of 1936 is false, and a jury might rationally go on to conclude that the rest of Hiss's testimony is also false.

Mr. and Mrs. Hiss had a joint savings account at the Riggs National Bank in Washington. The bank's records show a withdrawal of $400 on November 19, 1937, four days before Chambers bought the car.

The Hisses shrugged it off as a coincidence. They had withdrawn the $400 to buy furniture for their new house. But the government proved that the lease on the new house was not signed until December 2 at the earliest and that the Hisses had charge accounts at various department stores as well as a checking account, thereby making cash purchases unnecessary.

If the $400 withdrawal was a coincidence, it goes beyond any I would ever expect a jury to believe.

Ninth, Hiss's transfer of a car. In 1935 and part of 1936, Hiss owned a 1929 Ford. According to Chambers, Hiss gave him the use of it. "I used it to drive around Washington and I once drove from Smithtown . . . to Washington in it." Chambers knew what had happened to the car. Hiss "proposed to turn the car over to the open Communist party [as distinguished from the underground apparatus] for the use of some poor organizer." Chambers talked with J. Peters about Hiss's plan, and told Hiss "that Peters had agreed, although reluctantly, to have it turned over to the open party." Later, Chambers said, Hiss reported "that he had turned the car over according to an arrangement made between him and Peters."

Before HUAC, Hiss testified that he "sold" the car to Chambers. At the trial, Hiss said that he threw it in with the 28th Street apartment he had sublet to Chambers. Sometime in the early spring of 1936, Chambers took the car "for good," and Hiss never saw it again.

Here is what the documents show. The car's certificate of title bears an assignment of title filled out in Hiss's handwriting. The assignee is Cherner Motor Company (a large Ford agency in Washington), and Hiss's signature is verified by W. Marvin Smith, a notary public, on July 23, 1936. Smith was a lawyer in the Justice Department with Hiss.

The dealer's reassignment form on the certificate of title was executed on July 23, 1936, by Cherner Motor Company. William Rosen is the assignee. Rosen's signature appears on the purchaser's application for a new certificate of title.

Cherner's invoices for July 22, 23, and 24, 1936, run consecutively with none missing. There is no invoice for the Hiss-to-Cherner-to-Rosen transaction.

I don't see how a jury, presented with these documents, could disbelieve Chambers. As Chambers had said, Hiss arranged to give the car to a Communist party worker; and someone helpful to the Communists at the Cherner Motor Company handled the transfer without entering it on the company's books.

William Rosen was called as a government witness. Asked whether he had been a member of the Communist party in 1936 and whether he had any connection with Hiss's car, he declined to answer on the ground of self-incrimination.

Tenth, the papers—photographs Chambers had concealed in the pumpkin and pencil memoranda and typewritten copies disclosed at the Baltimore deposition.

The photographs were in two rolls of developed microfilm containing a total of 58 frames and constituting eight documents, five memoranda about negotiations for a trade agreement with Germany, and three incoming cables. Almost all show on their face that they were received in Sayre's office, and Hiss's initials appear on the cables. The latest is dated January 13, 1938. The government proved that the 58 frames had been exposed at the same time with a camera owned by Felix Inslerman, Chambers' chief photographer, on film manufactured by Kodak in 1937. Chambers said the source of the documents was Hiss; Hiss denied it; and no independent evidence pointed either way. But it was at least possible that Chambers had a source other than Hiss, for Wadleigh admitted turning over government papers to Chambers, and Chambers "without mentioning names ... made it abundantly clear" to Wadleigh that Chambers "had other sources inside of the State Department," and thus the jury might well have found itself unable to conclude beyond a reasonable doubt that Hiss rather than Wadleigh or someone else was the source of the microfilmed documents.

There were four pencil memoranda summarizing State Department cables, each in Hiss's handwriting.* The earliest is dated January 28, 1938, and the latest March 11, 1938. Two of them are on "Office of the Assistant Secretary of State" letterheads with the printed legend torn off. The other two are on common scratch paper. None is crumpled. Chambers testified that these memoranda were made by Hiss when he was unable to take documents out of the office. Hiss testified that they were made for his own use in briefing Sayre and then either thrown away or filed with the cables they summarized. Again, there is no independent evidence to show that Hiss gave the memoranda to Chambers. Perhaps Chambers found them in a wastepaper basket. Perhaps someone stole them and gave them to Chambers. Perhaps Hiss prepared them for use in briefing Sayre, as he said, but then passed them on to Chambers, as Chambers said; and one wonders why, if they were thrown away, they are neatly folded rather than crumpled. On balance, though, I think a

---

* The envelope Chambers retrieved from Nathan Levine also contained a memorandum in the handwriting of Harry Dexter White.

jury would decide that Chambers' story had not been proved beyond a reasonable doubt.

Finally, the 43 typewritten papers, each a copy or a summary of a State Department document dated between January 5, 1938, and April 1, 1938. Chambers testified that they had been typed by the Hisses and given to him for transmittal to Bykov. The Hisses denied it. And so we have the question at the heart of the case: were these papers typed on the Hiss typewriter?

The FBI interviewed Hiss on December 4, 1948, a few days after Chambers produced the papers in Baltimore. This was Hiss's statement about the typewriter:

> During the period from about June 1, 1936, to about January 1938, I re-sided with my family at 1245 30th Street, N.W., and subsequent thereto, until sometime in 1943, at 3415 Volta Place, N.W., both Washington, D.C. During the period from 1936 to sometime after 1938, we had a type-writer in our home in Washington. This was an old-fashiioned machine, possibly an Underwood, but I am not at all certain regarding the make. Mrs. Hiss, who is not a typist, used this machine somewhat as an amateur typist, but I never recall having used it. Possibly samples of Mrs. Hiss's typing on this machine are in existence, but I have not located any to date, but will endeavor to do so. Mrs. Hiss disposed of this typewriter to either a secondhand typewriter concern or a secondhand dealer in Wash-ington, D.C., sometime subsequent to 1938, exact date or place unknown. The whereabouts of this typewriter is presently unknown to me. Prior to this typewriter coming into the possession of my immediate family, it was the property of Mr. Thomas Fansler, Mrs. Hiss's father, who was in the insurance business in Philadelphia. Mr. Fansler lived the later years of his life on Walnut Street in Philadelphia, but is now deceased, having died in the early 1940's.

Hiss was mistaken about the typewriter's make. It was a Woodstock, not an Underwood.

Mrs. Hiss testified before the grand jury that she had given the type-writer to a junkman. She had not. She had given it to her maid, Mrs. Catlett, for use by the Catlett sons. If the Hisses had kept it through 1938, as Hiss said at first, it was in their possession in the early months of 1938, when according to Chambers, the documents were typed. The Hisses later corrected their testimony and said they gave the typewriter to Mrs. Catlett in December 1937.

In any event, the FBI had not found the Woodstock as of the time of the first trial. Even so, the government was able to prove that it was the machine on which the documents had been typed.

Every typewriter's type is, like a fingerprint, unique. Given a known sample and a questioned sample, an expert compares the two. If they are identical, the questioned sample was typed on the machine which typed the known sample. If they are different, the samples were typed on separate machines. The FBI found a 1937 report to the Bryn Mawr alumnae association concededly typed by Mrs. Hiss on the Woodstock. It was compared with the State Department documents, and they were identical. The FBI expert said so. Cross told the jury that the defense experts said so too.

Where was the Woodstock? It had passed from the Catletts to several other people. In early 1949, one of Hiss's lawyers, Edward C. McLean, tracked it down.* He produced it at the first trial and offered it as a defense exhibit. It has become notorious, but we see that it played almost no part in the proof. Nothing would have changed had the Woodstock never been found. It was by comparison with Mrs. Hiss's concededly authentic alumnae report, not by comparison with the machine McLean brought to court, that the authenticity of the State Department documents was established.

Chambers said that the documents were typed by the Hisses, and the experts agreed that they were typed on the Hisses' Woodstock. Hiss had no reason other than espionage to prepare them. Chambers could have had them from no hand but Hiss's. Evidence doesn't come any clearer than that, and this, from Cross's summation, was the defense explanation:

> I say, well, how did Chambers know about that? How did he get it? Anybody? He did not do it himself, you can bet your life on that. He gets through confederates, anybody who can get through confederates and steal top-secret documents from the State Department would not have much trouble locating a big office typewriter. Now I can suggest there might be several ways. I can suggest a way that he could have easily found out. Suppose someone had called up, or come over, when he knew the Hisses weren't there, and asked [the maid] saying that they were a typewriter repair man and had come to repair the Woodstock typewriter. What would she have said? "Why, they have given it to my boys." He wouldn't have much difficulty locating [the maid's] place, and with that open house, with the cellar there, I mean the closet; with all the people coming and going, all the people living there, and their friends, and the dances and all. How easy. Am I talking through my hat?

Murphy answers in his summation as follows:

> Now, let us get back to the theory No. 103 as to who did it. This is No. 103. And how was it proved? Well, you start off with the fact that the Catletts had the typewriter, and here is a picture of their hall. You see how these two things follow. The Catletts had it. Here is the hall where they used to keep it. Here is the picture of the back entrance. You see all

---

* McLean, like Murphy, became a federal judge in the Southern District of New York. They completed their careers as colleagues.

the space back there, people come in and out there all the time. Then there is the den, then there are the dancers.

Now, what probably happened, Mr. Cross testified, is that somebody, not Chambers—he is too smart, but one of his conspirators, one of his confederates—those are good names, "conspirators," "confederates"—he went up to the Volta Place house and asked innocent Clidi Catlett, "I am the repair man. Where is the machine?"

I can just see it now. It's terrfic. You can have this guy coming with a Woodstock hat on, "Woodstock Repair," with a jumper, "Woodstock," ringing the bell—no, it isn't a bell, you have to pull that one, I think—and saying to Mrs. Catlett, "I am the repair man to fix the typewriter."

Then Clidi says, "Well, which one do you want? The Remington, the Royal, the L.C. Smith? Which one?"

"No. We want the Woodstock."

"Oh, that's over in my boy's house, over at P Street."

And then the next scene, it is the middle of one of these dances. And you see Chambers sneaking in at night, mingling with the dancers, and then typing, typing the stuff, holding the State Department document in one hand—

Oh, Mr. Cross, you've got to do better than that.

Before he was sentenced, Hiss said to Judge Goddard, "In the future, the full facts of how Whittaker Chambers was able to carry out forgery by typewriter will be disclosed." This disclosure was attempted in 1952. Hiss made a motion for a new trial on the ground of newly discovered evidence. The main item of newly discovered evidence was "that the typewriter found and produced by the defense in the belief that it was the original Hiss machine was in fact a carefully constructed substitute, which could only have been fabricated for the deliberate purpose of falsely incriminating Alger Hiss [by forgery of the typewritten documents]."

It took a technician employed by the defense one year to build a duplicate Woodstock, and the result was imperfect at that. Obviously, Chambers could not have built one himself. Defense counsel's single thought as to who might have done it was that Chambers knew "people who were skilled in doing the kind of thing the Communist party does." I don't think he meant that the Communists had framed Hiss, although Judge Goddard and Murphy took the remark to mean just that. I think he meant the federal government, and specifically the FBI, which surely is "skilled in doing the kind of thing the Communist party does." If I am correct, Hiss was claiming that the FBI had framed him. Apart from the question of motive, there are two powerful reasons not to believe it.

First, assume that the FBI made a counterfeit Woodstock. Then it was the very machine discovered by McLean and produced by the defense at the trial; that is to say, the FBI planted it for Hiss to find after using it to forge the documents which prove Hiss's guilt. Why? Not to show that Chambers' papers were typed on it: that was done by comparison with Mrs. Hiss's alumnae report. To leave the counterfeit Woodstock lying about for the defense to pick up and examine would serve only to expose the whole scheme to the risk of discovery—and for no reason. An FBI bright enough to forge typewritten documents is bright enough to destroy the instrument of forgery as soon as it has done its work.

Second, no FBI agent would fabricate a typewriter and forge documents without the approval of some higher-up. In the 1940's and 1950's, the FBI had only one higher-up, J. Edgar Hoover. Assuming that Hoover was disposed to give his consent, he would not have shouldered the responsibility himself. Consummate bureaucrat that he was, Hoover needed someone still higher to whom to pass the buck should the imposture come to light. In view of Hoover's position and the enormity of the fraud, that could only be one person—President Truman. If Truman had authorized the forgery, his public position on the prosecution would have been either silence or approval. Yet from the beginning, Truman called the HUAC hearings "a red herring." At his first press conference after the disclosure of Chambers' possession of State Department documents and the indictment of Hiss, Truman was asked whether he still thought the case a red herring. He did.

The conviction was returned on January 21, 1950. Judge Goddard sentenced Hiss to five years' imprisonment. The Court of Appeals for the Second Circuit affirmed, and the Supreme Court declined to review the case. In March 1951, Hiss went to jail. A year later, Judge Goddard denied Hiss's motion for a new trial on the ground of newly discovered evidence. The Court of Appeals affirmed, and the Supreme Court denied certiorari.

This was no mere contest of oaths. Three things—the evidence of the rug, of Hiss's $400 loan to Chambers, and of the transfer of Hiss's car to William Rosen—prove beyond any reasonable doubt that Chambers' account of their relationship, not Hiss's, was true. One thing—the evidence of the typed State Department papers—proves beyond any reasonable doubt that, when Hiss denied to the grand jury that he had ever given official documents to Chambers, he was lying. Twenty out of twenty-four jurors have been sure of his guilt, and they were right.

POSSIBLE TOPICS FOR SHORT ESSAYS

1. Being a Communist in 1937–38 versus being a Communist in 1948
2. Chambers' early life
3. Hiss's early life
4. Chambers' break with the Communist Party
5. Hiss' public statements at the time of the initial accusations

6. The confrontation scene at the Hotel Commodore
7. One incident recalled in contradictory ways—who is lying, if anybody?
8. Cross-examination of particular witnesses in court
9. Implicating personal details that Chambers knew about Hiss's life
10. Crucial and disputed dates in testimony on both sides
11. The Oriental rug
12. The $400 loan Chambers claimed Hiss made to him
13. The strange disposal of the 1929 Ford
14. The handwritten documents
15. The typed documents
16. "Forgery by typewriter"
17. Effect of psychiatric testimony
18. Effect of character witnesses
19. The other "Communists" whom Chambers accused along with Hiss (Wadleigh, Donald Hiss, Pressman, Witt, Abt, etc.)
20. Richard Nixon's role in the investigation
21. President Truman's attitude toward the case
22. Reasons either man would have to lie about the other
23. Mr. Murphy's summation attacking Hiss
24. Mr. Cross's summation defending Hiss
25. Hiss's statements made in recent years
26. An analysis of any published article that is strongly for or against Alger Hiss

SELECTED BIBLIOGRAPHY

Andrews, Bert, and Peter Andrews. *A Tragedy of History.* Washington: Robert B. Luce, 1962.

Blum, Richard H. *Surveillance and Espionage in a Free Society.* New York: Praeger, 1972.

Buckley, William F. (and the editors of the *National Review*). *The Committee and Its Critics: A Calm Review of the House Committee on Un-American Activities.* New York: Putnam, 1962.

Chambers, Whittaker. *Odyssey of a Friend* (William F. Buckley, ed.). New York: Putnam, 1969.

Chambers, Whittaker. *Witness.* New York: Random House, 1952.

Cook, Fred J. *The Unfinished Story of Alger Hiss.* New York: Morrow, 1958.

Cooke. Alistair. *A Generation on Trial.* Baltimore: Penguin, 1952.

Hiss, Alger. *In the Court of Public Opinion.* New York: Knopf, 1957.

Hiss, Tony. *Laughing Last.* Boston: Houghton Mifflin, 1977.

Jowitt, William Allen, 1st Earl. *The Strange Case of Alger Hiss.* Garden City, N.Y.: Doubleday, 1953.

Mazo, Earl. *Richard Nixon.* New York: Harper, 1959.

Morris, Richard B. *Fair Trial.* New York: Knopf, 1953.

Nixon, Richard M. *Six Crises.* New York: Pocket Books, 1962.

Reuben, William A. *The Honorable Mr. Nixon and the Alger Hiss Case.* New York: Action Books, 1956, rev. ed., 1958.

Smith, John Chabot, *Alger Hiss: The True Story.* New York: Holt, Rinehart and

Appendix

Winston, 1976. The paperback Penguin edition (1977) contains a new "Afterword."

Weinstein, Allen. *Perjury: The Hiss-Chambers Case.* New York: Knopf, 1978.
Zelig, Meyer A. *Friendship and Fratricide.* New York: Viking, 1967.

The file of articles on the Hiss-Chambers case from 1948 to the present is voluminous, filling many pages of the *Reader's Guide to Periodical Literature.* Some of the more important articles appeared as critical reviews of the books listed.

81 82 9 8 7 6 5